Mus

by

Siân Pritchard-Jones & Bob Gibbons

© **Siân Pritchard-Jones & Bob Gibbons, Expedition World and Map House, 2025**

All rights reserved. No part of this publication may be reproduced or transmitted in any form or by any means without the prior written permission of the copyright holders.

ISBN: 9798304857314
First edition 2025

Important note
Since 01 April 2023 all foreign visitors heading into the Nepal Himalaya have been required to have a licensed guide booked through a registered local agency; ask to see the guide's licence. They must pay Rs2000 for the TIMS card; E-TIMS are apparently due to be introduced soon. Guides and permits are required for all National Parks, except perhaps the Khumbu; this is still under negotiation. Permits will be checked at posts across the 14 different trekking areas; trekkers who fail to have a guide will be fined Rs12,000 and made to leave the park. It remains to be seen how the new rules will be implemented and for how long.

Due to the present uncertainty, if you wish to visit independently ie without a guide, please check the relevant websites to see if the rules have changed since this book went to press. There are very few checkposts in reality, if any!

Text:	Siân Pritchard-Jones and Bob Gibbons
Photos:	Siân Pritchard-Jones and Bob Gibbons except where credited
Concept:	Pawan Shakya (www.maphouse.org)
Design:	Bob & Siân
Maps:	Map House (www.maphouse.org)

Front cover: Mardzong Bon outcrop
Back cover: Tange chortens
Bon deity at Naurikot
Title page: Crossing the Samdzong La road pass

Mustang

by road

Siân Pritchard-Jones & Bob Gibbons

Highlights

Fabulous mountain scenery – Samdzong Valley outcrops

Routes – approaching Chodzong by pony

Culture – Lo Manthang harvest time

People – life in Lo Manthang

Mansail from the trail to Samdzong La Pass

Samdzong Valley outcrops

Typical scenery in Upper Mustang – Konchok Ling

Rinchenling Cave

Drakmar Cave trek route

Scenic grandeur

Annapurna I from Kalopani

Dhaulagiri and the Ice Fall

Sakar Danda east of Lo Manthang

Drakmar cliffs

Yara cliffs and caves

Konchok Ling ridge trail

Trail to Konchok Ling

Chosar chortens

On the road to Konchok Ling (photo: Sanjib)

Damodar Himal from above Syangmochen

Khumjungar Peak

Tilicho Peak

Cultural highlights

Kagbeni male Kheni image

Geling village & monastery

Ghami village & stupa

Tsarang chortens and palace in 1992

Lo Manthang first views

Lo Manthang gates (1992)

Thinggar village

Ancient fortresses north of Lo Manthang

Samdzong village

Rinchenling Cave complex

Yara village

Luri Caves

Luri monastery

Luri Cave image

Mardzong Bon caves

Ghar Gompa (Lo Gekar) monastery

Chodzong Gompa outcrop

Chodzong monastery and outcrop

Meeting the people

Curious child

Guardian at Tetang citadel

Off season carpet-making

Cooking at Ghar Gompa (Lo Gekar)

Child & baby in Tsarang

Preparing butter tea

Modern fuels carried in traditional way

Preparing for the hard winter to come

Keeping the potatoes fresh underground

Catching the sun on a cold winter's day

The man with the key to Rinchenling

Ponyman Tashi approaching Chodzong Valley

Sweet dreams

Siân and Tashi, the artist & guide in Lo Manthang

'Ancient' cave dweller

Another ancient cave dweller at Rinchenling

On the road

Kali Gandaki valley before Chele

Road carved into the cliff between Chele and Samar

New black-top tarmac road to Muktinath

Drakmar cliffs & village

Lo Manthang East Gate Chortens

En route to Samdzong

Samdzong village

Sijha Jhong Caves (above)   Chodzong Gompa (below)

Swapping horse power for 'horsepower'

Horse Power Workshop in Lo Manthang

Typical lodge dining area

Panoramic views high above Tetang

> The greater danger for most of us is not that our aim is too high and we miss it, but that it is too low and we reach it.
> **Michelangelo**

Advice to readers
We have done our best to ensure the accuracy of this guidebook at the time of publication. However, changes can and will occur during its lifetime. We advise you to check information about such things as transport, accommodation and food locally. Landslides and local politics may also change routes over time.

Exciting but exposed roads and trails

Warning

Please remember that travelling in remote, high mountain areas is potentially dangerous. The publisher and authors have taken every care in producing this guide, but readers must take ultimate responsibility for themselves. Road, trail and weather conditions can change suddenly and readers must understand these natural risks. Tracks in the Himalaya are sometimes exposed and narrow, and unsuitable for anyone who does not have a good head for heights. Those who are unsure or inexperienced should relish the additional safety of employing a fully trained and experienced Nepalese trekking guide.

Neither Map House, Books Himalaya, Karma Press, Expedition World nor the authors can accept liability for damage of any nature (including damage to property, personal injury or death) arising from the information in this book, directly or indirectly.

Although there are now some local mobile phone networks throughout most (but definitely not all) of the trekking routes, foreign mobile phones may not work. Local people may be able to help and call a helicopter if necessary, but this will be expensive.

There are more health posts in the popular regions than across most of Nepal, but that does not mean many. Apart from the marijuana growing freely alongside some of the trails, drugs are not available everywhere on most routes. Take a supply of all the medicines you are likely to use, as well as those you do not expect to need! Beware of yaks and mules on the crowded trails. Always be prepared to help yourself in any eventuality. It may be the only way.

Additional warning

Due to the nature of most of Upper Mustang, a special warning is given here. Some roads/trails are particularly prone to landslides and are narrow, soft, slippery and exposed. Some trails are stony, unforgiving and ankle-twisting. Some routes follow riverbeds that are OK in late autumn and winter. Crossing rivers in the deeper gorges and canyons is not uncommon between more isolated settlements or on wild routes/trails with no habitation. Beware of using any river canyon route in the afternoon, when the water level can rise significantly from its benign trickle of early morning.

Much of Mustang is remote, a desert with few or no waterholes. That lot should put off most people, even if the permit costs don't!

Seriously, forewarned is forearmed. Visiting Mustang is exhilarating, mind-blowing and gives immense satisfaction; this region is, after all, the 'Abode of the Compassionate Buddhist Icons'.

Rockfall near Yara

It's a dangerous business, Frodo, going out your door. You step on to the road, and if you don't keep your feet, there's no knowing where you might be swept off to.
***The Lord of the Rings*, J R R Tolkien**

New road construction is affecting trails

Earthquakes in Nepal: 2015

In April and May 2015 two powerful earthquakes struck Nepal, causing massive disruption to the country. Although many older houses and some historic temples were left in ruins across Kathmandu, the majority of buildings and infrastructure remained intact. Sadly the rural areas adjacent to the two quakes suffered more serious damage, including Sindhupalchowk.

Most work has been completed rebuilding the historic heart of Kathmandu. It is to be hoped that the historic world heritage monuments, the amazing architectural wonders of the Kathmandu Valley, will once again be fully regenerated.

The country certainly needs the tourism sector to blossom again as soon as possible. Your trek will help this to happen more quickly.

Earthquake Diaries: Nepal 2015

We were in Kathmandu during the month of May. Having become instant aid workers (buying up rice, tarpaulins, tin sheets and warm, locally made clothing using generous donations), we witnessed a remarkable few week in the country. After the first days of shock thousands of local people, young and old, engaged in the relief and rebuilding process with amazing energy. The resilient people of Nepal were back on their feet well ahead of expectations.

Anyone wishing to know how 'amateur' aid works can read our *Earthquake Diaries: Nepal 2015*, published by Expedition World and available on Amazon websites worldwide, in colour and Kindle.

Acknowledgements

Thanks to Pawan Shakya, Roman Shakya and all the teams at Map House, Books Himalaya and Karma Press. Thanks to Rajendra Lama, Sanjib Gurung, Amber Tamang, Surendra Rana, Amrit Bhadgaonle and Devendra Basnyat for their support. Thanks to Rajendra Suwal for his natural history section.

Special thanks as ever to Sanjib Gurung, Trip Himalaya and our great driver, Tanka Ghale. Thanks to Tashi and his horses, who made our Chodzong trip possible. Thanks to John Millen for reaching the parts we could not reach! Thanks to Tashi Gurung in Lo Manthang yet again, and to Candy for her photos of Tiji 2024. Much appreciation to Rajendra Lama of Friends Adventure Trekking, who helped us arrange the trek in 2015, and our excellent guide Venn and porter/cook Ben who accompanied every step. Thanks to Binay Lama, along with Barry and Jenni Pizer, for their updates.

Thanks to the Hotel Elegant in Pokhara, Kalopani Guest House in Kalopani and the Hotel Grand Shambala in Muktinath for their warm hospitality. And to Paulo Grobel and Sonia Baillif, plus Christine Miqueu-Baz from France.

Huge thanks to Sunil, Uttam and Hari plus all the staff at the Hotel Moonlight, our winter home. Thanks to all at the Kathmandu Guest House for many years of happy stays. Also to Ganesh Shrestha and Sohan Shrestha at the Hotel Acme Inn.

Thanks to Dr Kailash Sah for his friendship and support, David Durkan for his contribution, and to Niraj Shrestha. Thanks to Ram Tamang at the Tamang Trekking Shop behind the KGH, Sitaram Bhandari, Mingmar Sherpa, Ian Wall, Bill Crozier, Candace Kolb, Kim Bannister, Paulo Grobel, and the Northfield Café for their scrumptious enchiladas and chocolate brownies.

Over the years, thanks to Rajendra Lama, Sanjib Gurung, Pasang Dawa, Ravi Chandra, Mr Dhir, Jitendra Jhakri Tarali Magar, Jag Budha Magar, Kul Bahadur Gurung, Purna Thapa Magar, Chhewang Lama, Binay Lama, Akshaya K. Dulal, and their guides and porters. Every one of them has been a vital part of the trekking experience.

In Chamonix, thanks to Dr Yann Hurry and Dr Michel Cadot for their magic knee potions. In the UK, thanks to Kev Reynolds, Dr Martin Ridley and Mike Berry.

And finally, thanks to the reader, who can help to keep this book updated.

Please send your suggestions and updates to sianpj@hotmail.com, www.expeditionworld.com

Contents

Acknowledgements	41
Preface	49
Introduction	50

BEFORE THE TRIP — 55

Country background — 53
Geography	55
Climate	56
Natural history	56
Brief history	63
Religion and festivals	72
Cultural aspects	83
Helping the people	86

Practicalities — 89
Getting to Nepal	89
Visa information	92
Money matters	93

Trip planning — 95
Permits and TIMS	95
Maps	99
Budgeting	100
Style of trip	101
Independent trips	102
Fully supported group trips	102
Accommodation	104
Food	105
What to take	106

Staying healthy — 107
Altitude sickness & precautions	111
Mountain safety	113
Weather	113
Security	114

Kathmandu – gateway to the Himalaya — 114
Pokhara – after the trek — 119
Other places of interest — 120
Using this guide	123
Pre-trek checklist	124

THE ROUTES 125
Mustang Explorer 125
Lo Manthang 152
Chosar, Nyphu & Garphu 161
North of Lo Manthang 165
Konchok Ling 167
Samdzong 173
Mardzong 177
Rinchenling 183
Chodzong 189
Drakmar 201
Other Classic Routes in Mustang 207
Monastery Cave Circuit Trek 221
Lower Mustang 227
The Kali Gandaki Route 239
Road summary: Jomsom – Pokhara – Kathmandu 246
The last word 248

APPENDICES 249
Appendix 1: Trip summaries and suggestions 249
Appendix 2: Bibliography 251
Appendix 3: Glossary 253
Appendix 4: Nepali language hints 257
Appendix 5: Useful contacts 259

Maps 261
About the authors 267
Other books by the authors 270

Welcome to Nepal!

Hotel Moonlight
www.hotelmoonlight.com
hotelmoonlight@gmail.com
+977-1-4380636

"Your Home in Kathmandu probably the best accommodation in Kathmandu"

"A great value garden hotel in the heart of Thamel"

HOTEL ACME INN
www.hotelacmeinn.com
+977-1-4700236, 4701049

Trip Himalaya Treks & Expedition (P) Ltd

www.triphimalaya.com   www.himalayabike.com

Post Box No.21097, KapurDhara, Kathmandu, Nepal.
Ph: +977-1-4386652
E-mail: info@triphimalaya.com

Climbing Himalaya

"Let Climbing Himalaya take you to the summit of your dreams"

www.climbinghimalaya.com
+977-9841190881 (Sanjib Gurung)

Operated by: Professional Trekking Guides

"Specialists in the Mustang region"

For Trekking, Mountaineering, Canyoning & Tours in
Nepal
Tibet
Bhutan
Ladakh

Recommended by tripadvisor

Friends Adventure Team P. Ltd.
P.O.Box: 21276
Samakhushi, Kathmandu, Nepal
Tel: +977-1-4364838 Mob: +977-9851027397
E-mail: lamateam@wlink.com.np
www.nepalcanyoning.com

www.friendsadventure.com

Heritage Hotel, Suites & Spa
Celebrating Mountains, Lakes & Legends !

www.heritagehotelpokhara.com

Hotel Elegant
Rooms with a view in Pokhara

hotelelegantnepal.com
hotelelegantnepal@gmail.com
+977 061-465423

Preface

> The Alps are the playground of Europe, the Himalayas the playground of the gods.
> ***The Kanchenjunga Adventure,* Frank S. Smythe**

Of all the areas of Nepal, there is no doubt that Mustang stands apart. Wild and secretive, remote for the most part and sublime in its many facets, the dreamlike apparitions of Mustang are unworldly. The sweeping landscapes, panoramic mountain vistas and unimaginably intoxicating geological contortions can only be described as a stunning tapestry of nature's hand – still an exotic lost horizon, the veritable location of Shangri-La.

Standing serene in the sky, the great Himalayan range of Annapurna hides this majestic frontier. Upper Mustang hosts a myriad of trails and trekking routes as well as climbing peaks. The region lies well beyond the forests of most of Nepal. Here are peaceful upland meadows brushed with sweet-smelling juniper and windswept yak pastures. High above, sweeping snowy faces, artistically fluted ice walls and breathtaking glaciers loom large.

Many of these great giants are considered by local people to be the pristine haunts of gods and goddesses, and as such their summits remain undefiled by human presence.

To delve into the heart and soul of this arid high plateau region, where stupendous spires and fairytale turrets stand like ghostly apparitions and sublime spirits, requires much physical effort and determination.

Yet these obstacles merely draw in those adventurous spirits – trekkers, mountain bikers, motorcyclists, jeep passengers and other curious visitors, – and maybe even a few lurking djinns too!

The aim of this adventure guide to Mustang is to introduce not only the routes, but also the amazing, almost unique, culture. Each of the monasteries and hidden cave shrines of Mustang holds a spellbinding allure. In one or two of the caves, even stranger and very dark secrets from the ancient past have been unearthed.

The once pristine valley of the Kali Gandaki has been a trade route since ancient times. Today new trade links forge ahead, changing the daily and seasonal patterns of life along the main artery of Mustang. Some of the most secretive jewels of the Mustang Himalaya are rarely seen. They shine only for those with the physical and mental strength to travel far away from the Kali Gandaki into the high and wild country beyond the reach of most visitors. Such expeditions need to be very well equipped and fully self-sufficient.

Preface

With the development of the road from Jomsom to Lo Manthang and beyond, Mustang is indeed changing, but no earthly mortal can tear apart the phenomenal sights of nature here – only nature herself and those fiery, hot-headed demons that are suppressed by the stronger forces of the cosmos.

Siân Pritchard-Jones and Bob Gibbons
Kathmandu 2025

View from Sijha Jhong Caves

Introduction

> It is impossible for any thinking man to look down from a hill on to a crowded plain and not ponder over the relative importance of things.
> ***The Mountain Top*, Frank S Smythe**

The Himalaya of Nepal extend for over 800km from the Indian borders of Sikkim in the east to the Indian Garhwal in the west. They divide the frequently hot, sultry plains of India from the far horizons of the windswept Tibetan plateau. The highest peaks – Kanchenjunga, Makalu, Everest, Lhotse, Manaslu, Annapurna and Dhaulagiri – are located along the northern borders of Nepal. All exceed 8000m in height.

The country of Nepal was isolated for centuries, a forbidden land, seemingly a garden of paradise. Hidden below the Himalaya behind rugged foothills and impenetrable ridges was a lush and plentiful kingdom, locked in a time warp until 1950. The rhythms of life remained intact; the daily rituals, the bonds of religious beliefs and the pace of life rolled on with an imperceptible motion.

Today villages still echo to the sounds and chants of a Hindu Brahmin priest or Buddhist monastic chorus; festivals dictate the never-ending rhythms of rural life. Farmers plough their small terraced fields while women keep a watchful eye on inquisitive children, intent on new daily discoveries. At higher altitudes the people eke out a hardy living in harsh conditions, where even the vegetation struggles to survive. The people of Nepal are one of its greatest assets – endearing, brimming with humour, boisterous, versatile, vibrant and hungry for change, just like most people across the planet.

The architectural wonders of the Kathmandu Valley provide the opening scene of the magnificent unfolding drama that is any trek in Nepal. The mystical religious life of the country will baffle and intrigue even the most non-spiritual soul.

Visitors to the main trekking regions of Nepal can enjoy an amazing variety of geographical landscapes and cultural differences. On the southern slopes of the great Himalaya, the countryside is lush, fertile and alive with life. The high-altitude crags of the Himalayan giants hide a different secret: holy lakes that offer inspiration and renewal to a jaded spirit. The heavenly high valleys sing only to the tunes of soaring predatory vultures.

From the sublime viewpoints along the routes, some of the most magical mountains in the world are on show, including Annapurna, Dhaulagiri, Tukuche Peak, the Nilgiri summits, and even further from civilisation, the Damodar Himal peaks.

Introduction

For some, the advent of the new roads has blighted the once pristine nature of Upper Mustang, but change is happening across the world and this region is no exception. On the positive side, it means that many more people can get to the region, who would otherwise be unable to contemplate the hard trekking required before.

The roads are for the most part very quiet, especially away from the main route between Pokhara and Jomsom. The scenery is as beguiling as ever, whether on foot or on wheels. A mix of driving and some short trekking will get visitors to many once-inaccessible places, where history, culture and wild grandeur are on offer.

Mustang Explorer

The Mustang Explorer encapsulates everything that defines the Mustang region. As short as 10–12 days, the route climbs steadily from the northern ramparts of the Annapurnas near Jomsom to the high and wild windswept hills of Lo Manthang. En route a variety of settlements host lively people, quaint monasteries and spellbinding scenery, dotted with atmospheric chortens.

The climax of the trip is the first tantalising panoramic view of the fabled walled city of Lo Manthang, as picture-postcard today as it was to the first explorers. Most visitors linger a few days to soak up the charms of the city and take day trips to some of the nearby cave monastery retreats.

A relatively short trip, it does not reach any too-dizzying altitudes, allowing those older or less able to trek at high altitude to enjoy its charms. The return route can be varied; new dirt roads on both sides of the Mustang Khola (Kali Gandaki) valley enable many options to be contemplated and explored.

The scenery and geological grandeur on the eastern side of the Mustang Khola is about as unimaginable as anyone can – well – imagine! Even on the approach to Lo Manthang along the western side of Upper Mustang, there are some little-known treasures to discover: places like Chungsi Ranchung Cave and the panoramic viewpoint above Syangmochen. Drakmar and Ghar Gompa (Lo Gekar) are not new destinations, but that doesn't mean they aren't special places of immense interest and spectacular scenic beauty.

North of Lo Manthang, don't miss the isolated and astonishing cave retreats of Sijha Jhong (Chosar), Rinchenling and Konchok Ling. East of Lo Manthang are the Samdzong Valley plus the astonishing Chodzong Valley and monastery outcrop. Heading south from Lo Manthang, the trail is sensational, with cultural interest everywhere in places like Dhi, Yara, Luri, Tange and Tetang. The mind-blowing and wind-blown scenery will remain etched in the memory just as deeply as nature's hand has left its astonishing marks on the physical landscape.

Monastery Cave Circuit Trek

Still not on most visitors' radar, the harder-to-reach monasteries and canyons east of Lo Manthang are steadily being discovered as the main trails see the increasing motorisation of the once-pristine slopes. Places like Samdzong, Chodzong and Sakau Danda were generally ignored by the first trekkers, who had only limited time for the major sights. Not a specific route as such, the Monastery Cave Circuit Trek describes the areas of Upper Mustang that can be contemplated by those willing to spend a few days longer in the region. As with any off-beat destination, only campers and trekkers can truly get under the skin of these remote attractions.

Remote Mustang

For more remote options that involve multi-day trekking, see our Trekker's Guide to Upper and Lower Mustang. Such destinations include the **Mustang High & Wild Expedition**, which explores the eastern region of Upper Mustang, and the **Damodar Kund / Saribung Expedition** linking the wilds of Eastern Upper Mustang and the stupendous mountains that dominate the hidden valleys of Phu and Nar. The even wilder **Teri La Pass Expedition** heads into virtually unknown territory and is not always successfully crossed. It links Tange in Upper Mustang with the lower valley of Nar below Phu. Camping is the only way to trek here, and the rhythms of caravan life soon dispel notions of modernity.

The area of Lower Mustang is generally considered to be the region along the Kali Gandaki delineated by Tukuche in the south and Kagbeni in the north. Looking eastwards, Muktinath and the Thorong La pass mark the borderline. To the west the region is normally delineated by the Jungben La pass that leads to Chharka in Dolpo. The routes and trekking trails here are well known, being mostly part of the famous Annapurna Circuit Trek. One highlight not to be missed is the Bon community in the village of Lubra. It is located next to the river east of the main trail between Kagbeni and Jomsom; it can also be accessed from Muktinath en route to Jomsom.

Mustang Trail Race

For those who enjoying trail running, what could be more of a challenge and a pleasure than a race through this fantastic scenery and culture? This is beyond the scope of this guidebook, so please see www.mustangtrailrace.com for more information.

****

Of course any venture into untamed and wild places presents some risks and dangers. A trek to the Himalayan regions needs careful preparation and informed planning by any prospective visitor. Part of this guide is devoted to those aspects.

Introduction

That 'once-in-a-lifetime' visit to Nepal is likely to be life-changing and habit-forming! The aim of this guide is to inspire the readers to go beyond the familiar, to discover the treasures of Nepal – its mountains, its people and its culture.

> I remember looking over the Himalaya and not feeling that I had closed the door on exploration, but rather just the opposite. I remember thinking, 'God, the possibilities are endless – this range will never be fully explored.' It looks like I was right.
> **Sir Edmund Hillary**

Amazing geology above Tange & near Rinchenling

BEFORE THE TRIP

Country background

Geography

It is believed that a sea existed about 100 million years ago in the region of Nepal. According to the theory of plate tectonics, India and Tibet began to collide at least 50 million years ago. These plates within the earth's crust create mountains where they collide. Approximately 40–45 million years ago, the northbound Indian plate began to force up the Tibetan plateau. The Himalayan chain was formed some 20 million years ago and continues to rise to this day.

From the Hindu Kush ranges of Afghanistan and Pakistan in the west to the Indian states of Arunachal Pradesh in the east, the Himalaya form an unbroken chain of over 2500km that divides the plains of India from the Tibetan plateau. The country of Nepal is approximately 800km long and 250km in width, with some variations from east to west. Kanchenjunga, Makalu, Everest, Lhotse, Manaslu, Annapurna and Dhaulagiri, all exceeding 8000m in height, are the country's highest peaks.

Rising abruptly from the plains of India are the steep but fragile Siwalik Hills. The forested Mahabharat Hills, towering to over 3000m, mark the southern edge of the middle hills of Nepal, where most of the rural population live. The rolling hills are characterised by impressive terraces and dotted with quaint farmhouses. The valleys of Kathmandu and Pokhara are in this area. Further north are the rocky buttresses and sheer-sided canyons that form the immediate foundations of the great ice peaks. The main Himalayan range is not a watershed but is cut by raging, fast-flowing rivers that allow access to the higher valleys. The watershed is north of the Nepal Himalaya in Tibet.

The altitude range varies from 600m–8848m, the summit of Everest, although most trekkers will reach a maximum height of 5550m. Trails are rarely undulating or flat, so all visitors need to be relatively fit for a trek here in Nepal.

> A terrible wind whistled in my ears, in my eyes, spitting sand as it whipped across this parched landscape, howling in the canyons and buffeting the hills... I found myself exclaiming: This is Mustang! I must be mad! I will find nothing here but desolation.
> ***Mustang: A Lost Tibetan Kingdom***, **Michel Peissel near Samar**

Climate

The climate of Nepal is influenced heavily by the Himalaya, a natural barrier that divides the main weather systems of Asia. The Indian plains to the south are generally hot and dry, while north India has cooler, high pressure-dominated winters. During the northern summer, the humid monsoon brings life-sustaining rains to India.

North of the Himalaya, the mountains create a rain-shadow, making the climate in Tibet sunny, but harsh, cold and windy. As a general rule, throughout autumn and spring, the temperatures on the southern slopes of the Himalaya range from 10°C–30°C. North of the great mountain barrier, the temperature will range from 15°C down to -10°C and colder at night. The spring season after early April will have generally higher temperatures and more wind. During the monsoon, temperatures rarely dip below freezing, except in the highest meadows. Annual precipitation is normally less than 500mm.

Natural history

Plants

> He told them tales of bees and flowers, the ways of trees, and the strange creatures of the Forest, about the evil things and the good things, things friendly and things unfriendly, cruel things and kind things, and secrets hidden under brambles.
> **The Lord of the Rings**, **J R R Tolkien**

With so many climatic zones, Nepal is a paradise for botanists – no one can be surprised by the great variety of plants, recently estimated to exceed 6500 different types of grasses, plants, flowers, and trees. In the 19th century the noted botanist, Joseph Hooker, visited the Himalaya of Sikkim and eastern Nepal, and discovered many of the plants now familiar to gardeners the world over. The plants found in Nepal are naturally similar to those of neighbouring Sikkim.

The lowland slopes and steamy jungles of the Siwalik hills bordering the Indian plains are home to sal trees, simal, sissoo, khair and mahogany. Behind these rapidly eroding sandy foothills are the sheer and abruptly rising Mahabharat ranges. Here are the ubiquitous pipal and banyan trees that shade the frequent porter rest-stops (*chautara*). Chestnut, chilaune and bamboo are found here, while in the succulent cloud forests are an amazing variety of weepy lichens, ferns, rattans and dripping lianas. Prolific orchids, magnolia, broadleaf temperate oak and rhododendron (locally called *Laliguras*) drape the higher hillsides.

Further up the hillsides are spruce, chir pine, fir, hemlock, blue pine, larch, cedar and sweet-smelling juniper. Poplar and willow are found

Natural history

along streams in the higher reaches of the arid zones and in the highest pastures are hardy berberis and stunted juniper.

Amazing rhododendrons

Orchids

Even higher are caragana, cotton trees, cotoneaster and, fleetingly, honeysuckle. Hardy flowers and plants, such as colourful gentians, survive in even the most windswept or icy meadows. Surprisingly, some shrubs like rhododendron survive better on the north-facing slopes, because of the insulation offered by the snow.

Natural history

Animals

> The spell of silence on this place is warning that no man belongs here.
> ***The Snow Leopard,*** **Peter Matthiessen**

Snow Leopard near Jomsom (photo: Rajendra Suwal)

Nepal is home to an incredibly diverse population of mammals, reptiles and birds. The Terai is home to the endangered Asian one-horned rhino, a tough and rugged beast that hides in the tall grasses of the plains and sal forests. Elephants are rarely wild but are used for forest work and to ferry tourists around the national parks in search of the elusive Bengal Tiger, as well as the sloth bear, from a safe vantage point. Spotted deer and sambar deer scurry about in small herds to avoid their predators.

Crocodiles, alligators, the smaller related gharals and marsh mugger lurk in the murky waters of the marshes and rivers that drain further south into the Ganges River. These jungles, once dense, impenetrable and infested by malarial mosquitoes, still host an amazing number of semi-tropical birds. Beyond the lowlands in the middle hills, almost all the hillsides are either covered by undisturbed, dense, spooky forests or are highly developed and extensively cultivated. Yet a great number of animals call these areas home, especially the ones most easily observed, such as the monkeys and langurs that abound in the forests.

At higher elevations the observant trekker will see marmots, pika (a small mouse-like animal, related to the rabbit), mouse hare, Himalayan golden weasel, ermine, dwarf hamster, Tibetan hare, Himalayan hare, Himalayan Tahr (a species of mountain goat) and more often – blue sheep. Tibetan sheep, wolf, wild dog, brown bear and the famed musk deer (a prized trading item, used in perfume and ayurvedic medicine) are rarely seen. Other animals are the kiang (a wild ass), red fox and Tibetan fox. The endangered red panda inhabits the higher reaches too.

Increasingly fewer wild yaks still roam in isolated, remote valleys; most yaks are now domesticated. They can live for 15–20 years and are mature by 4–5 years. Yak (nak) milk is used by herders to produce cheese and yoghurt (some sun-dried). The dzo – a cross between a yak and a cow – is commonly used as a pack animal, along with ponies and mules. Herders also keep sheep and goats.

Yaks are used for carrying loads

Even herders virtually never see the snow leopard. Hunting blue sheep in the dawn or twilight hours, they are extremely wary animals. Big budget television crews have waited years to get any pictures of these beautiful creatures. Let us know if you see a yeti!

Trekkers are almost never likely to encounter dangerous animals in Nepal, although domestic guard dogs can be a menace and quarrelsome yaks should be avoided.

Birds of the Nepalese Himalaya
by Rajendra Suwal, ecologist

The Trans-Himalayan region of Mustang in Nepal is a magnificent delight for birdwatchers and those keen on sighting the rare and elusive snow leopard. This region embodies an almost untouched Tibetan plateau with fascinating culture and wide biodiversity. This is probably one of the driest parts of Nepal and also very gusty too along the stretch of the river between Marpha and Chele. It is a wind passageway during the warmer months from the southern Terai plains, and during the winter there is a cold draught from the vast Tibetan plateau. The area encompasses the Palaearctic in the north and borders the Indo-Malayan realm in the south. It represents bioclimatic zones such as Temperate, Subalpine, Alpine and Nival.

The Tibetan plateau was once the bed of the ancient Tethys Sea. Mustang is drained by the Kali Gandaki and multiple tributaries. The Kali Gandaki River bowdlerised the rising Himalaya and created what is said to be the deepest gorge in the world between Mt. Annapurna and Dhaulagiri, both scaling over 8000m. This river also helped to surface the ammonites that moulded into fossils deep under the Tethys Sea. It is considered as an ecological delineation for the Eastern and Western Himalayan flora and fauna.

Within the Mustang region there are many types of ecosystems; a variety of vegetation is found. Lower down, rare forest types include mountain oak, blue pine, spruce, cedar, cypress and birch. Other represented types of vegetation are caragana bushes and steppe grassland, as well as dry and moist Alpine scrub.

Birds move mostly in flocks, hunting insects at different levels of altitude and vegetation. During the first few hours in the morning you might spot up to a dozen different species, depending on the season. There are diurnal, crepuscular, nocturnal, and seasonal and altitudinal migrants; birds such as the cuckoo, redstarts, thrushes, pipits, chats and wagtails visit during the spring for breeding. Midday is the best time to spot soaring vultures, eagles, buzzards and other birds of prey. Unique bird species include the Hume's Groundpecker, which feeds inside burrows.

The idyllic, quiet, often dreamy **riverbanks** and side streams are teeming with frisky birds. The streams are a favourite place for the fire-fronted serin. Fast-flowing streams at higher altitudes are feeding sites for white-breasted dipper. The banks along the stream towards Thinggar is a breeding site for the rare Ibisbill.

The **blue pine forest** of lower Mustang is a typical habitat of the very vocal spotted nutcracker, which prefers the upper canopies. More treasures are the tiny yellow-breasted greenfinch and European goldfinch, and Tibetan siskin, feeding under the canopy with territorial calls. Various species of rosefinches, finches and bullfinches, including the grosbeaks, may be seen feeding in the forest. Accentors, mostly brown and alpine, take shelter in the caragana bushes. Spot-winged grosbeaks favour the patches of forests surrounded by pastures and farms.

The **mountain** areas harbour a few rarely seen pheasant species; the Himalayan munal (known as danfe in Nepal, where it is the national bird), favours the tree line and more open pastures. The alpine area is the foraging ground of Himalayan snowcocks, Tibetan partridges and chukor partridges. Open patches of forest around Ghasa and Titi are favourite sites for Cheer and Koklas Pheasants.

Natural history

They are probably the most secretive among pheasants. They are probably the earliest risers, as they are very vocal long before the dawn breaks. Coveys of Chukor Partridges are common along the trails to Upper Mustang and Muktinath. Tibetan Partridges may be seen foraging along the pastures of Bhena.

The skies of the Kali Gandaki and Mustang are an important **flyway** for the spectacular migration of Demoiselle Crane, which have been the subject of various BBC documentaries. During the autumn migration, thousands of these cranes arrive from the Mongolian steppe. The high mountains and the strong wind are an obstacle for the cranes, exhausted after hundreds of miles of flight. As they take the help of thermals to gain height, golden eagles chase them in their hunt for prey. Sometimes bad weather compels them to land on the riverbanks or in the ripening buckwheat fields.

Occasionally a pair or two of black stork can be seen along their flight path. Eagles (Steppe and Imperial) and cinereous vulture, small birds of prey, pied and hen harriers and common buzzards may be seen flying past from the last week of September till the second week of November. Also **high in the sky** are the Himalayan and Eurasian Griffon and the majestic lammergeyer (with 3m wingspans). Vertical cliffs with ledges are breeding sites for vultures, lammergeyers and golden eagles, a formidable predator. They can bring down flying cranes and chukor partridges, and occasionally small mammals, including hares and blue sheep lambs.

At dawn the mountain slopes with **caragana** bushes become alive with white-browed tit babblers (a speciality of Mustang), different species of accentors, bush chats and rock buntings. Look for the Guldenstadt's and blue-fronted redstart, brambling and brown rufous-breasted and Altai accentor. Rock bunting inhabit areas between the upper forested zone and the drier regions. In the air you can observe the speedy insect-hunter white-rumped needletail, Nepal house martin, alpine swift and Himalayan swiftlets.

Snow pigeon and hill pigeon forage near trails, oblivious of caravans of yaks, mules, horses and humans on foot. Ravens are acrobatic birds seen in the alpine zones. Flocks of red and yellow-billed chough are very vocal and playful, foraging in the farms and villages.

The **mountainsides** of Mustang are home to blue sheep. These are the chief prey species of the snow leopard. Further north on the way to Kora La border is the habitat of the Tibetan Antelope. The alpine pastures and the rolling hills are also the habitat of hares and marmots. The freshly dug burrows are indicators of their presence. Pastures surrounding Damodar Kund are a melting pot of many rare mammals, including the elusive snow leopard, the 'Nayan', the great Tibetan sheep, and also a foraging sport for the mighty brown bear. Herds of Tibetan wild ass or 'Kyang' graze in the alpine pastures.

Natural history

Look along the **mountain skyline** at dusk and dawn for the silhouettes of stalking wolves and snow leopards. Snow leopards have been spotted south of Muktinath in the high mountain slopes as well as in remoter areas east and northwest of Lo Manthang.

Rajendra Narsingh Suwal

Rajendra holds a Master's degree in Zoology/Ecology and has over 40 years of experience in biodiversity conservation, ornithological research, wetland protection and eco-tourism. He began his career as a naturalist in Chitwan National Park in 1984. He later served as an ornithological consultant for the Department of National Parks and Wildlife Conservation in 1994 and the National Trust for Nature Conservation (NTNC) in 2000. He has contributed as scientific advisor to documentaries for the BBC and the Discovery Channel, including the renowned *Planet Earth* series. Rajendra has also worked as a consultant and evaluator for UNESCO World Heritage Sites and established the Lumbini Crane Sanctuary in association with the International Crane Foundation. He is a strong advocate for the conservation of the Sarus Crane and wetlands, focusing on the tallest flying bird, which was once saved by the Buddha. He is the founder of Nepal Nature Dot Com Travels, specialising in birdwatching tours and wildlife filming expeditions. Rajendra served as an Executive Member of Nepal's Environment Protection Council, chaired by the Prime Minister, and has been an Ashoka Fellow since 2002. His most cherished endeavour was guiding former US President Jimmy Carter on three birdwatching trips in Nepal. He currently leads Partnerships Development at WWF Nepal.

Bharal – Blue Sheep

Brief history

Nepal is one of the most diverse places on earth, its culture and people as varied as its scenic attractions. Kathmandu, with its long history of isolation, is the country's once-mystical capital. Its ancestry is an improbable cocktail of magical make-believe, exotic folklore, intriguing legend and historical fact.

The Kiranti people were probably the first recognisable inhabitants of the Kathmandu Valley. However, the first known historical facts in Nepal relate to the formation of the Buddhist religion. Around 550BC, in southern Nepal close to modern-day Lumbini, a prince, who would have an amazing impact across the Indian subcontinent and as far away as Japan, was born to a rich king. This prince, Siddhartha Gautama, who would become the earthly Buddha, lived a sheltered, indolent life in his comfortable palace. Tormented by his lifestyle, he left his wife and newborn son to search for the meaning of life. Seeking out sages, sadhus, priests and wise men, he found no answers until finally his meditations brought a ray of light. He discovered that the end to earthly suffering was achieved by adopting a middle path in all things and thus he found inner peace – nirvana.

Indian Emperor Ashoka, one of the first emissaries of Buddhism in India, travelled to Nepal in the third century BC, building the four-ancient grass-covered stupas of Patan and the pillar at Lumbini. After about 300AD the Licchavi dynasty flourished, but Buddhism declined in the face of the popular rise of the Hindu religion, a faith that had been born, but not nurtured, much earlier in India. Much later, as new trade routes and ideas developed between Tibet and India, Kathmandu became the most important Himalayan hub.

On the religious front, the decline of Buddhism in India and Nepal forced its diehard adepts to seek sanctuary across the Himalaya in Tibet. After hundreds of years, the version of Buddhism that came with those refugees adapted and absorbed Tibetan Buddhist themes and, ironically, slipped back once more into Nepal to mix with Hinduism, Shamanism and other animistic beliefs. The Tibetan version of Buddhism, now known as the Vajrayana path, provides an astonishingly colourful and exotic aspect to daily rituals and festivities in Nepal today.

In the 8th century a sage and Buddhist master, Padma Sambhava (Guru Rinpoche), travelled across the Himalayan region. His exploits in propagating the Tibetan Buddhist philosophy are recorded widely throughout the region as both myth and historical fact.

During the following period there are few records of life in Nepal. However, through the annals kept in Tibet, a great amount of historical fact can be found about the regeneration of the Buddhism found in Nepal. These facts centre on the ancient Tibetan region of the lost Guge Kingdom, located around Toling and Tsaparang. Many Indian masters came here to study and escape persecution from Hindu zealots in the 11th century.

Malla architecture, Bhaktapur Nyatapola temple

Records of Nepal's history come to life again in the 13th century, when the Malla kings assumed power. The Malla Period is often said to be the golden age of Nepal, and especially of the Kathmandu Valley, with its astonishing array of art and architecture. The Malla dynasties are admired for their vast concentration of elaborate and superbly executed multi-tiered palaces and pagodas.

Although the ordinary people lived in much less privileged conditions, their brick houses were also decorated with intricate wood designs.

One of the more powerful Mallas, Jayasthiti Malla, adopted the Hindu faith and consolidated his power in the Kathmandu Valley. He even declared himself to be a reincarnate of the Hindu god of preservation, Vishnu, a practice that was continued by the monarchs of Nepal until 2007. Jyoti Malla and Yaksha Malla were rather more benign dictators, who enhanced the valley with more spectacular temples and religious structures. Around 1482 the three towns of Kathmandu, Patan and Bhaktapur became independent cities, with each king competing to build the greatest Durbar Square, parts of which remain to this day.

Like all dictatorships, the Malla reign declined, as debauchery and corruption took hold. In 1769, from the hilltop fortress above the town of Gorkha (Gurkha), came Prithvi Narayan Shah and his forces, who rode in to capture the three cities of the Kathmandu Valley. In so doing he succeeded in unifying Nepal. In 1788 Nepalese armies moved on Tibet, but a vast army from China intervened to help the Tibetans repulse them.

In 1816 the Gurkhas, attempting to expand their domains into the colonial-ruled hills of northern India, were defeated by the British. Through the treaty of Segauli, Nepal ceded Sikkim to India and the current borders were delineated. The British established a resident office in Kathmandu. Soon after, Gurkha regiments were integrated into the British army.

In 1846, Jung Bahadur Kunwar Rana, a soldier of the court, hatched a devious plot. After a massacre in Kathmandu's Kot Square, the king was dethroned and the queen was sent into exile. Jung Bahadur Rana took power and became the first of the infamous Rana dynasty, who held power in Nepal for the next 100 years. They were despotic rulers, remembered for family intrigues, murder and deviousness. Calling themselves Maharajas, they built the sumptuous neo-colonial white colonnaded palaces seen around Kathmandu today. Until 1950 the country remained closed to all but a few invited guests, retaining its mediaeval traditions and corrupt governance.

When neighbouring India gained independence in 1947, a Congress Party was formed in Kathmandu. The powerless king became a symbol for freedom from the despotic Ranas. However, freeing the country from the shackles of the old guard meant great sacrifice. Many activists and freedom fighters were executed before King Tribhuvan finally ousted the Ranas in 1951.

After 1950, when Tibet fell under new masters, refugees and Khampa freedom fighters moved into the isolated valleys in the north of the Himalaya and established bases. Some refugees settled in the region of Rasuwa adjacent to the border. However, when Nepalese monarch King Birendra announced the 'Zone of Peace' initiative, most of the Khampas melted away.

A fledgling democratic coalition government was installed and the country was opened to foreign visitors. In May 1953 Mount Everest was finally conquered from the Nepalese side after so many failed expeditions from its northern faces in Tibet. King Tribhuvan died in 1955 and his son Mahendra assumed power. Becoming dissatisfied with political paralysis, King Mahendra ended the short experiment with democracy in 1960. He introduced a partyless governance, called the *panchayat* system, based on local councils of five (*panch*) elders, with a tiered system of representatives up to the central parliament. Following the death of Mahendra in 1972, King Birendra inherited the throne. His official coronation had to wait until an auspicious date in the spring of 1975.

The *panchayat* system was retained following the 1980 referendum. After 1985, rapid urban expansion changed the nature of the Kathmandu Valley. The traditional rural lifestyle began to disappear under a wave of construction as the population grew astronomically. In April 1990 full-scale rioting and demonstrations broke out, forcing the king to allow full democracy. Parliamentary democracy flourished with King Birendra as a ceremonial monarch and the country prospered. Unfortunately corruption and political ineptitude grew, and in the late nineties a grass-roots Maoist rebellion developed.

Many people had genuine sympathy with the need for greater social equality, but violent demands for a leftist dictatorship naturally met with resistance. In June 2001, after a tragic shooting spree, King Birendra and almost his entire family were wiped out by his son, Crown Prince Dipendra. Although not directly attributed to the Maoist uprising, the event changed the situation dramatically. King Birendra's brother Gyanendra became king, but in October 2002 he dissolved parliament and appointed his own government until elections could be held. The Maoist rebellion continued, with intimidation and coercion rife in the countryside. Following huge demonstrations on the streets of Kathmandu in 2006, King Gyanendra relinquished power.

The Maoist leaders entered mainstream politics after winning a majority in the subsequent election. However, almost ever since then, the governments have been paralysed, with a political stalemate derailing much development. A constitutional election was held in November 2013 with the Maoist vote significantly reduced. A new constitution was promulgated in September 2015 but it remains to be seen where the country's ruling elite will take it.

In 2018, after long discussions, the country was finally divided into seven regions, each divided into gaunpalikas (rural administrative districts), further sub-divided into 7–9 wards. The last general election was held in November 2022.

Political and economic instability have resulted in an increasing number of young Nepalese seeking work outside the country, particularly in the Arabian Gulf and Malaysia. Tourism also remains an important source of income and tourists are still given a warm welcome across the country.

Stony-faced politician!

History of Tibet and Guge

Although fairly peripheral to Western Tibet, much of the history of Mustang is inextricably linked to the Trans-Himalayan regions northwest of Lo Manthang. A brief outline of the history of Western Tibet and thus of the Guge Kingdom is relevant here. Some of the historical facts of Tibet have come from the annals of Dun Huang, recorded by the Chinese Tang Dynasty from 618–907AD.

The founding of the Guge Kingdom, centred on Toling, began under one of the Bon king Langdarma's heirs, O Sung (Namde Wosung). The great revival of Buddhism began in western Tibet in the 11th century under King Kord De, more commonly referred to as Lama Yeshe O. He was helped by his famous translator, Rinchen Zangpo (958–1055), whom he had sent to India to study. Rinchen Zangpo is credited with establishing one hundred and eight monasteries, some being across the border in India. Toling and Tsaparang in Tibet, as well as Alchi and Tabo in India, survive today, with their fabulous Kashmiri/Nepali-inspired paintings. Such art is also found in some caves across Mustang. An emissary of Rinchen Zangpo visited Mustang in the later years of the 11th century.

In order to further the cause of Buddhism, Yeshe O also invited another India master, Atisha (982–1054), to come to Tibet. Such was Yeshe O's devotion that, according to one legend, he gave up his life for the cause. Yeshe O was captured by raiders, but when his nephew had raised the ransom money for his release, he told him to use it instead to invite Atisha to Tibet. Atisha came from Nalanda University in India to Toling in 1042. He spent three years in Toling monastery and, through his great knowledge of Buddhism and his compassionate teachings, succeeded in reviving Buddhism. He founded the Kadam-pa sect during his time in Tibet.

Marpa, again from Nalanda, followed in Atisha's footsteps, and founded the Kagyu-pa sect, which placed more emphasis on physical and mental meditation methods. Milarepa (1040–1123) was his disciple; he became famous in Tibet and Nepal for his solitary meditation in numerous caves that are now revered in different parts of the plateau. The Kagyu-pa spread throughout the country and across the greater northern Himalayan region.

Tsaparang Citadel, Guge, Tibet

With little outside interference, Tibetan Buddhism diversified. In 1073, Konchok Gyalpo founded a monastery at Sakya, near modern-day Lhatse. Together with his son Kunga Nyingpo, he founded the Sakya-pa. The famous monasteries of Reting, Tsurphu and Drigung were built. The Sakya-pa sect emphasised the importance of systematic study of the Buddhist scriptures.

In the 13th century, the whole of China, Tibet and Mongolia was shaken by the conquering hordes of Genghis Khan. However, Tibet escaped most of the marauding armies' devastating expansion. One of the Mongol descendants, Godan Khan, effectively left Tibet alone, having been very impressed with the Buddhist ideals after a visit from

Sakya Pandita. Mongolia made the Sakya-pa the dominant ruling sect until 1326, although it did tolerate other sects. With the fall of the Mongol court, the region reverted to its former independent nations.

The Sakya-pa lasted around 100 years in Tibet. It is still found across much of Mustang.

By the mid-14th century there were effectively four major sects. These were the Nyingma-pa, Kagyu-pa, Sakya-pa and Kadam-pa. Tsong Khapa was born in 1357, and he studied the four branches, reforming the earlier Kadam-pa teachings of Atisha to create the Gelug-pa. This reform reintroduced some of the more austere practices, cleansing some of the more liberal ideas. The reforms were aimed, in particular, at removing some of the Tantric ideas which dwelt more on the self, suggesting that achieving enlightenment could be done through individual methods, including indulgence of the sensual pleasures.

Tsong Khapa established the great monastic institution of Ganden (New Kadam-pa), as well as Sera and Drepung. He drew in the Kagyu-pa by agreeing with their disciplined meditation, setting out a path which used their ideas to give greater insight. The Kadam-pa sect became the new Yellow Hat sect of the Gelug-pa, and they have remained the dominant branch in most of Tibet. The idea of reincarnation, a feature of the Karma-pa sect, was adopted by the Yellow Hats and hence began the long line of Dalai Lamas. The current one is the 14th in the line, although many never reached maturity, dying in suspicious circumstances.

History of Mustang

The history of Mustang is generally not very well documented and is patched together from manuscripts, texts and religious scriptures. Some scriptures called the Mollas seem to have been used to ascertain some of the more localised details. A lot of information referring to Mustang is found in the history of the greater Guge region of Western Tibet and the adjacent all-powerful region of Ladakh.

The region of Mustang was first chronicled in literature discovered in 652AD in the Silk Route caves at Dunhuang, now in the Chinese province of Gansu, north of Tibet. It was once part of the Yarlung dynasty that stretched from Tibet into Central Asia. This was at the time of Srongsten Gampo, who is credited as the founder of Tibet.

In the 10th century the original religious group of the Bon were in the ascendancy across Tibet. The demise of the Bon king Langdarma marked the rise of importance of Buddhism in Tibet and consequently in Mustang. Later a series of kings known as the Korsum dynasty of Ngari ruled. They came from Western Tibet, where the vast Guge empire was soon to become a regional player. The Guge kingdom was comprised of three regions: Ladakh (Maryul) including Spiti, Guge itself and Purang. Each was controlled by one of the three sons of Nyimagon. The Purang region extended as far east as Lo and Upper Mustang. The cultural, historic and religious connections between Guge and Lo are reinforced by the similarity of the art at Mentsi Lhakang (near Chuksang) and that found at Toling, Tabo (Spiti) and in Ladakh.

According to vague sources, a brief incursion hit the region in 1037. From southern Turkestan, located to the north of Ladakh, Muslim raiders known as the Quarakhanids appear to have made incursions across Western Tibet.

At the end of the 11th century, after the golden age of the Buddhist revival, there are references to the clans or tribes of the Menshang. They seem to have been the major local overlords of Mustang, although the region was still nominally under the hold of Guge. By the mid-12th century another clan called the Gungthang seem to have been in the ascendancy. Two other clans are also mentioned in some scriptures, the Nubri from lower Mustang and east towards Manaslu, and the more obscure tribe of the Mangyul, who probably lived in the Kyirong district.

Between the years 1230–40 a war broke out between the Gungthang clans and the Jumla kingdom of Western Nepal, known as Yartse to the Tibetans. By 1267, Dolpo, Lo (Mustang) and Gungthang had become one entity. The Menshang tribes appear to have reasserted their power briefly, as did the Jumla Malla kings. The Jumla kings held sway in the adjacent Dolpo region, where their power was more concentrated. During most of the 13th century the ebb and flow of power between the main protagonists – the Gungthang, the Jumla kings and the Menshang clans – oscillated until 1370.

King Amapal (1388–1447) is generally accepted as the founding father of Mustang (the land of the Lo people) that exists today. Some scholars believe that his father Chos Kyongbum, who overran Purang, was instrumental in gaining the favours of the Gungthang clans with his superior military prowess. Others believe it was Amapal who extended the rule of Lo as far as Purang and Guge. Under Amapal, Mustang prospered through the trade between lowland Nepal and Tibet. With the rise of the Sakya-pa order in Tibet, Mustang adopted the same sect. Amapal is said to have laid the foundations for Lo Manthang in 1441.

One of the most influential figures in Mustang was the Buddhist master, Ngorchen Kunga Zangpo (1382–1456), who was a master of the Sakya-pa sect. During the time of King Amapal, Ngorchen made his first visit to Mustang in 1427. After two subsequent visits the Ngor-Sakya-pa school gained more credence and remains evident in Mustang, where various cave and monastery images belong to the sect.

Lo Manthang in 1992

Agon Zangpo, the son of Amapal's second wife, extended the lands of Lo southwards after marrying a sister of the Guge king, Phuntshog. He appears to have ruled Lo from 1447 until around 1472, extending his influence into Purang. It is generally believed that Trashigon, the eldest son of Agon Zangpo, ruled until 1489. Purang was raided again by the Lo king Delegs Rgyamsho at the close of the 15th century. In 1505 a great earthquake hit the Himalayan region, but Mustang did not suffer as much as other regions. After this time the rulers of Ladakh appear to have been the chief protagonists in Guge, Purang and Lo.

The Guge Kingdom actually lasted over 600 years until 1630, when it was overthrown in strange circumstances. In August 1624 the Portuguese Jesuit missionary, Antonio de Andrade, entered Tsaparang from the Mana pass north of the Garhwal peaks in India. He left but later returned, and in April 1626 a church was built, with the support of the king. But in 1630 the Lamas of Tsaparang, fearing pollution from the new religion, connived with the neighbouring Ladakhis to overthrow the Guge monarch. The kingdom never recovered from this and went into decline.

Links with Ladakh influenced and enriched the cultural heritage of Guge and Mustang until 1768, when Prithvi Narayan Shah took control of the whole of Nepal. The Raja of Mustang joined the new state of Nepal, but continued to rule independently. The kingdom of Mustang was very isolated from the middle hills of Nepal, although the Kali Gandaki remained a major trade route between Tibet and India.

Legend of the Demon Black Monkey
Once upon a time there were two monks who were not allowed to practise their religion because of the demon black monkey, who resided in a fort in Mustang. One of the two monks eventually had a son, reputedly the incarnation of Chenresig, called Amapal. Amapal was given some land by the demon black monkey and he built a palace facing the demon monkey's fort in Mustang. The demon was angry because it faced his house. So Amapal had to pull the palace down, but he then built an even bigger, greater, circular fortress (Khacho Dzong). Later Amapal had three sons: Agon Tsangpo, Tsetin Trandul and Tsepe Sichun. Tsetin Trandul eventually killed the black monkey and took over many forts to the south of Lo Manthang. This story comes from the secret historic document, the Molla, which was discovered hidden in Tsarang. The spiritual director of Tsarang gompa showed it to Michel Peissel while he was there.

Traders' taxes transformed
Centuries ago the Kali Gandaki valley was the main trade route between India and Tibet, and all traders had to pass through the miniature kingdom of Lo. Every year they took salt and wool south to India, returning with tea, rice and other manufactured products. The rulers of Lo, ensconced in their powerful fortress, gained fabulous riches by imposing taxes on these traders. They then used these taxes to invest in cultural works, building the monasteries of Lo Manthang, Tsarang and Lo Gekar with the help of Newari artisans from Kathmandu and Buddhist masters from Tibet and India.

After 1950, when Tibet fell under new masters, Khampa freedom fighters used the isolated valleys as bases. However, when Nepalese monarch King Birendra announced the 'Zone of Peace' initiative, they left Mustang. The land reverted to its former status as a peaceful forbidden last frontier.

Sadly the turbulent years of the Maoist period and insurrections blighted the country and led to the resignation in 2008 of the last king of Mustang, Jigme Palbar Bistar.

Religion and festivals

> Holy places never had any beginning. They have been holy from the time they were discovered...
> ***The Land of Snows*, Giuseppe Tucci**

Life across Nepal is still significantly influenced by religious and traditional beliefs. Everywhere, from a hilltop monastery to the back-alleys of Kathmandu, people follow cultural traditions through daily rituals and frequent festivals.

Culture and heritage

Hinduism

Hinduism is the main faith of Nepal and until recently the country was a Hindu kingdom. Many Hindu ideals have come from the ancient Indian Sanskrit texts, the four Vedas. In essence, the ideas of Hinduism are based on the notion that everything in the universe is connected. This means that one's deeds in this life will have a bearing on the next. One's own bad actions might be the cause of misfortune. Natural disasters are seen as the vengeance of the gods. Although hundreds of Hindu gods exist, they are in essence one, being worshipped in many different aspects.

The three main Hindu gods are Brahma, the god of creation; Shiva, the god of destruction; and Vishnu, the god of preservation. They appear in many forms, both male and female. Brahma is rarely visible. Shiva has special powers of regeneration and many forms, such as Mahadev, or the dancing Nataraj. Shiva is Pashupati – the Lord of Beasts – and Bhairab in his most destructive form. Shiva's wife is Parvati; she also has many aspects, including Kali and Durga.

The trekkers' legend of Ganesh
Ganesh, the elephant-headed god, is the son of Shiva and Parvati. Hindu legends recount that Ganesh was born when Shiva was away trekking. When Shiva returned he saw the child and assumed that Parvati had been unfaithful. In a furious rage, he chopped off Ganesh's head and threw it away. Once Shiva had taken a bucket shower and fortified himself with a cup of rakshi, Parvati explained the matter. In great remorse, Shiva vowed to give Ganesh a new head from the first living being passing; it was an elephant.

Sleeping Vishnu on a bed of snakes, Budhanilkanta

The third god, Vishnu, worshipped in Nepal as Narayan, is the preserver of all life. Vishnu has ten avatars. The seventh avatar is Rama, a deity linked to Sita and the Ramayana texts. The eighth is the popular blue god Krishna, who plays a flute and chases after the cowgirls, while the ninth is Buddha. Other Hindu deities include Lakshmi, the goddess of wealth, and Hanuman, the monkey god. Machhendranath is the rain deity, the compassionate one with two forms, white (Seto) and red (Rato). Humorous Ganesh, popular with Buddhists as well as Hindus, is worshipped for good fortune.

Hindu festivals

Nepal has an extraordinary number of festivals. Any excuse is valid for a good celebration. In autumn, the Dasain and Tihar festivals are in full flow. The goddess Kali and Durga are feted during Dasain, and the terrifying white Bhairab is displayed in Kathmandu Durbar Square. Blood sacrifices are the most noticeable aspect of these celebrations. Tihar is a more light-hearted affair, with crows, dogs, cows and brothers showered with flowers and devotion before a night of fairy lights and candles.

During spring is Shiva Ratri, the night of Shiva, most fervently commemorated at the Pashupatinath temple in Kathmandu. Holi is another Hindu spring festival celebrated across the country. The main manifestation of this festival is the throwing of coloured dyes at passers-by; tourists and trekkers are not excluded! Normally in March the tall wooden chariot housing the white Seto Machhendranath idol – the rain god – is dragged with much merriment through old Kathmandu.

Sometimes the power lines are pulled down, adding to the electricity supply problems, and the top storeys of the old brick houses of Asan are almost obliterated. In May, during a similar festival, the red Rato Machhendranath is hauled around Patan and back out to Bungamati.

Buddhism

Buddhists are found in the Kathmandu Valley and in the northern regions of the country. Monasteries are encountered across the mountains. The Buddhist artistry and iconography is startling and is similar to that found in monasteries throughout the high Himalaya.

Buddhism could be considered as a philosophy for living, with adherents seeking to find peace of mind and a cessation of worldly suffering. Nirvana, perfect peace, is achieved through successive lives by good actions and thoughts. (For details of the Sakyamuni, earthly Buddha, see Brief history.) The earthly Buddha is also considered by Hindus to be an incarnation of their god Vishnu.

Buddhism has two main branches; Hinayana and Mahayana. The latter path is followed in Nepal and Tibet, where it has evolved into a more esoteric philosophy called the Vajrayana (Diamond) path. It blends ancient Tibetan Bon ideas with a phenomenon known as Tantra, meaning 'to open the mind'. Tantric themes suggest that all people can become a Buddha and find enlightenment from within.

Tantric Buddhism has many themes, but most involve meditation. Guru Rinpoche was one of Buddhism's greatest Tantric masters. Tantric Yoga is now widely known as one method of pursuing enlightenment. Recently interest has been aroused in ancient exercises, which involve sensual methods of reaching this goal. Curiously, it was the rejection of these liberal themes of Tantric Buddhism that led to the resurgence of Hinduism and the decline of Buddhism in India.

The numerous Buddhist images are not gods, but icons that can be used to direct the mind in meditations towards a true path of learning. The fearsome protectors are not true demons, but remind the follower of their darker side. Other deities can be invoked through meditation towards the search for its true nature. Buddhism has a vast collection of texts, teachings and many forms.

The following Buddhist sects are found across the country:

The **Nyingma-pa** is the oldest Red Hat sect; it was founded in the eighth century AD by Guru Rinpoche. Today adherents of the Nyingma-pa sect are found across the high Himalaya of Nepal, Tibet, Spiti and Ladakh.

The **Kadam-pa** school was developed by Atisha, a Buddhist scholar from northern India, following his studies at Toling gompa in the Guge region of Western Tibet. Followers are expected to find enlightenment after careful reflection and study of the texts.

The **Kagyu-pa** is attributed to the Indian mystic translator Marpa (1012–1097), a disciple of Atisha. Followers need to concentrate their meditations on spiritual matters and inner mental themes, and listen to the wisdom of their teachers. The Kagyu-pa sect split into a number of sub-groups, such as the Druk-pa, Taglung-pa, Karma-pa and Drigung-pa.

The **Sakya-pa** began under Konchok Gyalpo from the Sakya Gompa in Tibet in the 11th century. Its adherents study existing Buddhist scriptures. The Sakya-pa school initiated the creation of the Tangyur and Kangyur – the two great Tibetan Buddhist bibles.

The **Gelug-pa** is the Yellow Hat sect of the Dalai Lama, initiated by the 14th-century reformer, Tsong Khapa. He returned the Buddhist practices to a more purist format, removing the liberal themes of Tantra and putting more emphasis on morality and discipline. The Dalai Lama is regarded by most Buddhists as their spiritual leader.

Culture and heritage

Some Buddhist icons

There is a stunning array of Buddhist icons but the most prominent are Buddha in many forms including Maitreya, Guru Rinpoche, Chenresig and Milarepa. Other notable icons are Manjushri, Vajrapani and the White or Green Taras. The protecting deities of the monasteries are the four guardians seen outside the main chambers and those ferocious-looking, often multi-headed and armed images normally placed beside the doorways on the inside: icons like Yamantaka and Mahakala.

Guru Rinpoche

Guru Rinpoche (Padma Sambhava) is the most famous icon of Tibetan Buddhism. He was an Indian Tantric master who went to Tibet in the 8th century to help spread the message of the religion there. He established the Nyingma-pa, the oldest sect of the red hats. One of his consorts, Yeshe Tsogyal, wrote down his teachings in order that they could be revealed to future generations. According to legends, Guru Rinpoche visited many places across the Himalaya, meditating in cave retreats and teaching the faith.

Across Tibet, Ladakh and Mustang, one may encounter the eight emanations of Guru Rinpoche in monasteries. As the 'lake born', the Rinpoche is called Tsokye Dorje. Shakya Senge is the 'lion of Shakyas' and Nima Ozer represents the 'rays of the sun.' Guru Padma Sambhava (or Padma Jungne) is the 'lotus born' and this is the Sanskrit name of Guru Rinpoche. Loden Chokse is the 'wise seeker of the sublime' (like trekkers in Mustang) and Pema Gyalpo the 'lotus king'. In Senge Dradok, Guru Rinpoche is the 'lion subjugator of non-Buddhists'. Dorje Drollo is the 'wild and wrathful' version of the great master.

Guru Rinpoche & his consorts

Culture and heritage

Chenresig

Chenresig
Chenresig is the Tibetan name for the bodhisattva Avalokiteshvara, the compassionate one also known as Karunamaya. A disciple of the Buddha, he has chosen to remain on earth to help people reach enlightenment. In the Kathmandu valley Avalokiteshvara is linked to the rain god, the White Machhendranath, whose shrine is found in Asan, in old Kathmandu. Avalokiteshvara can appear with a thousand arms and eleven heads.

Milarepa, the poet/sage
Milarepa was born as Mila Thopaga in Kya Ngatse in the western Tibetan province of Gungthang. His name means 'joy to hear', hence his famed posture with one hand to his ear. However, tragedy struck when his father died. Mila was only seven years old. His uncle and his family then enslaved him and his sister, treating him so badly that their mother sent him away to a lama. That lama taught him black magic, and one day, so it is said, Mila put a curse on his uncle, causing his house to fall down and killing many people. Later Milarepa felt remorse for his actions and sought out a guru, turning to the great teacher Marpa.

Milarepa

Buddhist festivals

Losar Tibetan New Year festival (January/February). This festival is one of the major ones and is celebrated across the Buddhist areas of Nepal as well as lavishly in Boudha, Kathmandu. Celebrations involve Tibetan drama and colourful masked Cham dances that commemorate the victory of Buddhism over Bon.

Saka Lhuka Held in the first month of the Tibetan calendar; performed for an auspicious harvest later in the year.

Fagnyi Week-long festival of song and dance during the seventh Tibetan month.

Tiji This three-day-long lively masked dance celebration is held in Lo Manthang during the late spring. Various dancers in colourful costumes and masks seek to exorcise the demons. Different legends and folklore surround this festival, giving it varied interpretations.

Tiji festival

This is the most famous festival in Upper Mustang; it takes place every year in Lo Manthang. The festival has its origins in the Bon period, but is a celebration of Guru Rinpoche, who is portrayed on a massive thangka in the main square outside the palace. Guru Rinpoche was called to Tibet to appease and subjugate the local demons in the 8th century, in order to protect Buddhism and dispel misfortune, drought and famine. The choreography of the current three-day festival apparently dates from around 1450.

Dances are performed by monks wearing colourful and often fearsome-looking masks. The masks are not always worn; whether or not they are worn is determined by astrologers, who decide if it is auspicious. Some dances are only performed every three years. The colourful, exuberant dances are very spiritual; some are secretive in nature, with others representing, in a theatrical style, the monks' meditations to appease the demons.

Certain scholars have noted the similarities of these proceedings to some rituals in European cathedrals in the Middle Ages. The festival has very similar traits to those of Mani Rimdu in the Everest region, held at Tengboche, and to others held to celebrate Losar (the Tibetan New Year). The Bon also have similar celebrations for their New Year, celebrated at Triten Norbutse near Swayambhunath.

At sunset, the thangka of Guru Rinpoche is hauled up to the sound of drums and cymbals. In a blaze of colour and accompanied by evocative music, the first dance begins.

This celebrates the ten divinities of Vajrakilaya, the fearsome-looking protector who banishes the enemies of compassion. Prominent among the dancers is the Tsowo, a monk who has been in solitary retreat for three months before the festival to practice the necessary meditation rituals. It is said that the powers of Guru Rinpoche are transmitted to the Tsowo at the time of the festival.

For the duration of the festival, the Tsowo monk is the incarnation of Vajrakilaya (Dorje Jono in Mustang). The main demon to be vanquished is, surprisingly, the father of Dorje Jono. It will take 52 dances to banish the demon. One dance used to be performed by the oracles, who acted under spells in a trance-like state. This has been superseded by a dance where a masked dancer replaces the oracle (a sort of witch doctor/shaman). Oracles still perform in Ladakh at such festivals with similar dances. Humorous interludes and dances remind the throng that everything in this life is illusory and impermanent, so one should not take things too seriously.

The dances on the second day are more vigorous. A straw effigy is pierced by a dagger at the close of the day.

Culture and heritage

On the third day a dough effigy is also pierced with a dagger. This curious ritual is part of the 'chasing away' of the bad spirits, negative actions and bad karma of the town's citizens. The spirits of the people are hidden within, and represented by the strange straw effigy that normally sits above one of the streets. The effigy is chased out of the town and Dorje Jono shoots it with an arrow. Rocks are hurled at the image and finally a tiger skin is used to defeat the demon.

Previously the king used to preside over the festival, and that duty will fall to his heirs.

The Tiji Festival in full swing (photo: Candace Kolb)

Local lama in Tange monastery

Culture and heritage

In addition to the celebrations and drinking (to excess for a few!), there is a market bazaar held outside the walls, offering traditional products such as wool, turquoise, embroidery, Chinese goods and even horses and yaks.

Yartung Three-day celebration including horse races held in Lo Manthang, across Mustang (and around Manang). It takes place during the seventh–eighth month of the Tibetan year, usually around the autumn harvest period. People give thanks to Buddha for a good harvest after the summer. Horse races, dancing and archery are the prime activities of the festival.

Bon

Bon (Bonpo) religion was the earlier faith of Tibet, also seeking the eternal truth and reality of life. They worship natural phenomena like the heavens and mountain spirits, as well as the spirits of natural powers, such as thunder. Many facets and features of Tibetan Buddhism originated from the Bon. The only Bon monastery (and Sowa Rigpa Medical Centre) in the region is at Chhentung near Dhorpatan, where Tibetan refugees have lived for over 50 years.

There is evidence to suggest that the Bon came not from Tibet but from Olmolungring, a legendary place in Tazik, possibly once in the land of the Tajik people of Central Asia. Tazik is a name that appears in Bon literature. Southwest of Kailash lie the ruins of Khyunglung Ngulkhar – the silver castle of the Khyung bird. This place is believed to be the spiritual and ancestral home of the Bon and the centre of the realm of Shangshung. Not far away are Tirthapuri and the Gurugyam cave monastery, clinging to the side of a sheer cliff, thought to have originally belonged to the Bon.

The first known Bon monastery was founded in 1072 at Yeru Wensakha, which is situated close to the Tsangpo River, just east of Shigatse. It has since fallen into ruin, but other Bon monasteries exist today at Menri, Yungdrung Ling and Tradang. Closer to Nepal, near Mount Shishapangma, is Lake Pekhu Tso, where the Pelha Puk Bon monastery is located on the isolated east side of the lake. A Bon monastery is also located in the Tibetan Kyirong valley between Langtang and Ganesh Himal some 100km north of Kathmandu.

As well as Kailash, another major pilgrimage peak is Mount Bonri in southeastern Tibet, close to Mount Namche Barwa, where the Tsangpo River cuts through deep gorges before dropping into India as the Brahmaputra. Most Bon monasteries in Nepal are in Dolpo. In Kathmandu there is one near Swayambhunath – Triten Norbutse. Anyone interested should visit this monastic complex in Kathmandu, such is the rarity of any active Bon culture today.

The ancient Bon believed that all life started from an egg. Within Bon there are many animal-headed demons and deities – many are its protectors. In the Bon masked Cham dances, masks depicting the heads of animals and the protector Khyung-bird are used. The Khyung bird is very reminiscent of the Hindu god, Garuda.

The Bon's sacred symbol, the Yungdrung, is very similar to the Tantric Buddhists' dorje, the thunderbolt sceptre. The white yak is particularly revered. The Bon also use the swastika symbol, but theirs turns to the left. The use of prayer flags, the concept of the oracles (trance doctors), and many of their icons have been assimilated into Buddhism. In 1977 the Tibetan government-in-exile in Dharamsala recognised and accepted the Bon as a fifth Tibetan sect. The spiritual head of the Bon is known as Trizin.

The chief icon of the Bon is Tonpa Shenrap Miwoche, who according to legends descended from heaven to earth by way of Mount Kailash. Within the Bon religion there are the 'Four Transcendent Lords': Tonpa Shenrap Miwoche, Shenlha Wokar, Satrig Ersang and Sangpo Bumtri. The deities, both peaceful and wrathful, are used as focal points for adherents to meditate on different aspects in order to understand the whole and reach enlightenment. This idea is used extensively in Buddhism too.

Bon icons in Lubra

Other prominent deities of Bon include Kuntu Zangpo, who is similar to the Samantabhadra form of the primordial Adi Buddha of Buddhism. He is also a manifestation of Shenlha Wokar, being the 'enlightened one' who is unfettered by possessions. He is depicted in black, together with his white female consort. Kunzang Gyalwa Dupa (Gyatso) is a curious figure, being similar and perhaps a precursor to the thousand-armed Avalokiteshvara, the Tibetan

Chenresig deity, of whom the Dalai Lamas are considered incarnates. With nine heads, Welse Ngampa is a wrathful protector representing 'piercing ferocity'. He crushes the enemies of Bon.

Shamanism

With its roots in the mists of time, Shamanism is a difficult religious theme to observe. Much is only apparent through sightings of strange tokens such as bones, feathers and fetish-styled trinkets. Shamans have their own rituals and even medical treatments. These are often performed by *jhankris*/oracles, who communicate with the ancestors through trance-induced rituals. (In the west, *jhankris* are often called *dhami*). Shamans worship natural phenomena, much like the early Bon. Such practices seem very primitive to outsiders, but rely on ancient wisdom. Shaman traditions mixed with a brushing of the pre-Buddhist Bon culture, and sometimes Hinduism, are alive and observable in parts of Nepal. Many of their cultural activities and festive traditions utilise these ancient practices.

Shamans are believed to be able to channel the powers of the earthly gods, but not those of the heavens. In remote parts of the country, some of the shaman gods have been integrated into the local Buddhist faith. In communities where the absence of health posts, legal representation and education is the norm, shamans exercise considerable power. Through animistic means, shamans care for the health and well-being of the community, settle legal disputes and attempt to mitigate the effects of natural disasters.

Other religions in Nepal include Islam, Christianity and Sikhism.

Cultural aspects

Ethnic diversity

According to the latest estimate, the population of Nepal is around 33 million. (In 1974 there were just 8 million.) At least 26 major ethnic groups are encountered across the whole country. Most of the people in the southern zones can be broadly classified as Hindu, while those from the northern Himalayan valleys are Buddhist. However, there is no clear traditional divide in either the middle hills or the Kathmandu Valley, especially since the insurgency.

The **Newari** are the traditional inhabitants of the Kathmandu Valley; they are a mix of Hindu and Buddhist. Along the plains of the Terai are the **Tharu**, whose ancestry might be linked to Rajasthan in India. Other Terai people, also related to Indian Hindu clans, are collectively known as the Madhesi.

Throughout the central regions of Nepal, the people are mainly **Magar, Chhetri, Gurung** and **Brahmin**. The Brahmins are the higher caste priestly group, who traditionally paint their houses blue.

Chhetris are defined as a warrior caste. Gurungs are mostly found to the west, around Gorkha, along the Marsyangdi valley and towards Pokhara. Gurung men are particularly noted for their service to the Gurkhas. There is a large concentration of Magars and the smaller sub-clan of the Chantyal in the Myagdi district.

As you climb beyond the central middle hills, the people belong to the **Tibeto-Burmese** ethnic groups, with wide faces and Tibetan characteristics like the **Sherpas**. The **Tamang** people are almost pure Tibetan stock. They are located right across Nepal, mainly in the northern areas. They live in the country from Taplejung in the east through central, Rasuwa, Nuwakot, Dhading and Lamjung to the far west districts of Humla. Tamangs migrated from Tibet, perhaps as part of the unifying King Srongtsen Gampo's horsemen.

People of Mustang

Virtually all the people of Mustang are Buddhists, with a heritage linked to Tibet. Before the modern era there were four traditional castes across Mustang. These were the royal caste, the common folk, the blacksmiths and the butcher/milling caste. The common folk included the farmers, labourers, messengers and firewood gatherers who were all obliged to supply the rulers. These days the old caste system has virtually disintegrated and many people migrate to the lowlands for winter.

Cave dwellers

Some of the many caves seen along the trails of Mustang are thought to have been used as long ago as 4500 years, possibly by Indo-European clans that predated the Tibetan peoples. Tibetan migrants evidently used wool and leather and ate the meat of domesticated animals. Living along the artery of the Kali Gandaki, they were very likely traders, since the artefacts found suggest more wealth than the terrain could provide.

Some of the art in the caves discovered in 2007 proved that much of the painting was influenced by styles found across the Indian Buddhist regions like Kashmir, Ladakh and Spiti. Such art is also found in Western Tibet at Tsaparang and Toling. Some of the artwork found is attributed to the Bon faith that lost sway in Tibet in the 8th century.

More recent discoveries are starting to uncover yet more amazing facts or theories about the ancient cave dwellers. Human sacrifices might have been part of the story long before the religions of Bon and Buddhism took hold. Mustang is indeed an intriguing and beguiling place.

The staple diet of Mustang is tsampa, made from barley flour and mixed with butter tea. Other crops are buckwheat, wheat and mustard. With frequent water shortages in Mustang, farmers need to plan their crops carefully each season. Wheat is planted first, since it takes so long to ripen at these altitudes. Pears are also grown and take four months to bring to harvest. Buckwheat follows, and here and there mustard is cultivated. Trekkers will want to savour the abundant apples across Mustang; whether in pies or pancakes, they are a great supplement to the normal diet.

In common with much of the Nepalese high country, young people are leaving for the cities and overseas to the Gulf or Malaysia. There is now a labour crisis during the harvest in most of the hills of Nepal.

Basic customs

Despite contact with the outside world since 1950, Nepal remains a conservative country, especially in the remoter hilly districts. A few basic customs should be observed by visitors. In houses the cooking area, the hearth and fire should be treated with respect, so do not throw litter there. Never touch a Nepali on the head. Pointing the soles of your feet at your hosts, or stepping over their feet, should be avoided. Eat with your right hand if no utensils are supplied.

Non-believers are rarely allowed into the inner sanctuaries of Hindu temples anywhere in the country; remember that leather apparel, belts and shoes are not permitted inside.

When visiting Buddhist gompas, guests should remove trekking hats and boots before entry. Small donations are appreciated and trekkers should ask permission before taking photographs inside. On the trail, keep to the left of mani walls and chortens and circle them in a clockwise direction. The prolific array of mani walls, mani stones and prayer wheels display the mantra Om Mani Padme Hum – Hail to the Jewel in the Lotus. Bon mani walls and chortens should be circled anticlockwise.

Begging

The rest of the world often views Nepal as a permanent begging-bowl case. Perhaps it is this attitude that used to encourage the general malaise of development in the country. In fact, in recent years this aspect of the 'old Nepal' is rapidly becoming less obvious. Ordinarily no one will mind giving to those obviously in genuine need, but begging is not confined to the poverty-stricken lower classes; the other echelons often have the same attitude.

Inevitably Nepalese view all foreigners as rich, whether it's their governments or themselves. However, the 'make do and mend' culture shows a level of ingenuity that has almost disappeared in the throwaway societies of the developed world. Given the opportunity, Nepal will flourish and prosper.

Helping the people

The big donor organisations and charities are naturally attracted to Nepal, probably due to its welcoming people, many of whom are exceedingly industrious. Sadly the impact of these multi-national donations is rarely felt by the majority of the people. This means there is plenty of opportunity for guests to contribute to smaller initiatives. Often such projects like improving village water supplies or bringing local electrification can really make a difference. Some of these localised projects are listed below.

Asha Nepal is a human rights organisation working towards the social and economic empowerment of women and children affected by sex trafficking. Asha Nepal is fighting for women's social status to be raised, to help victims break free from this vicious, violent circle. 'Asha' is the Nepali for 'hope'. (www.asha-nepal.org)

Autism Care Nepal There was very little knowledge of this condition in Nepal when their son was diagnosed with autism, so two Nepali doctors founded this organisation to raise awareness and help others in the same situation. (www.autismnepal.org)

Beni Handicrafts *Giving Kathmandu's rubbish a new life* Beni's products are made by women forced to move from the hills to the city, providing them with training, employment and income for their families. They collect sweet wrappers, inner tubes and other waste from the streets of Kathmandu as well as mountain trails. The rubbish is then made into attractive and functional products; see the shop in the Northfield Café. Profits support the work of **Steps Foundation**.

Steps Foundation Nepal – Education, Hygiene and Health is a charity supported by profits from Beni Handicrafts. It works on the step-by-step principle that through education for all and increasing awareness of hygiene, the health and well-being of families will be improved. (www.stepsnepal.org)

Community Action Nepal co-founded by mountaineer Doug Scott, seeks to improve the infrastructure of villages in the hills by building schools, health posts, clean water projects and developing cottage industries. (www.canepal.org.uk)

Interburns is an international volunteer network of expert health professionals working to transform global burn care and prevention through education, training, research and capacity-building. Their work is guided by the philosophy that all burns patients can be provided with good quality care despite limited resources. (www.interburns.org)

International Porter Protection Group (IPPG) began in 1997 after a number of porters suffered unfortunate accidents. It seeks to raise awareness of the conditions and plight of frequently exploited porters. They focus on the shelter, medical care and provision of clothing for often-overlooked porters across Nepal. (www.ippg.net) and (www.portersprogress.org)

Kathmandu Environmental Education Project (KEEP) was established in 1992 to 'provide education on safe and ecologically sustainable trekking methods to preserve Nepal's fragile ecosystems'. They give important information to trekkers, help harness tourism for development, run environmental discussions and manage a porters' clothing bank. They also help to improve the skills of tourism professionals and run volunteer programmes as well as running wilderness first aid training. (www.keepnepal.org)

> **KEEP: Kathmandu Environmental Education Project**
> https://keepnepal.org

Light Education Development supplies solar lights, materials for schools and medical supplies. (www.lighteducationdevelopment.org)

Mountain People has the motto of 'Helping mountain people to help themselves'. It is a small, independent, non-profit, non-political, non-religious and cross-cultural organisation with a lot of energy and drive. They help with schools, porter welfare, women's projects and bridge building. (www.mountain-people.org)

So The Child May Live is a Liverpool-based charity working to improve paediatric care in Nepal, principally by supporting Kanti Children's Hospital in Kathmandu, the only dedicated children's hospital in Nepal. (www.sothechildmaylive.org.uk)

Destruction or development

There is no doubt that the fragile environment of the Himalaya needs the attention of local environmentalists and the good management of resources. However, much as we, as visitors, may wish to see the land untainted, we do not have to spend our lives shivering beside a smoky fire. Inevitably, if there is no viable reason for the youth to linger in the high Himalayan regions, the culture will be diluted.

Tourism is one obvious way in which the culture and livelihoods of the upland people can be sustained in the long term. The main trekking trails have already had almost sixty years of tourism and the effects have been generally positive. The difficulty is finding the right balance, by improving local living conditions without destroying that which every visitor wants to experience here.

It's not a unique problem, as anyone who has visited the popular Nepalese trails or anywhere else that attracts many visitors – even Chamonix or Machu Picchu – will have observed. Ultimately it is for the local people and the various tourism concerns to decide on the future of their region.

Tourism brings much-needed income

Lo Manthang backstreets

Rooftop view – a top attraction for tourists

Practicalities

Time and calendar

… eternity is not remote, it is here beside us.
The Snow Leopard, Peter Matthiessen

Nepal is 5hrs 45mins ahead of GMT. Nepal follows two calendars; the Gregorian calendar used by most of the world, and a lunar-solar Bikram Sambat (BS) calendar, which is approximately 56 years and 8 months ahead of the Gregorian dates. (i.e. 2025–26 corresponds to 2081–83 BS). The Bikram Sambat year begins in mid-April and was introduced by the Ranas in the mid-1800s. This calendar means that Nepal is ahead of the rest of the world, which it might be in terms of coping with adversity!

Getting to Nepal

Flights to Nepal

The following airlines serve Nepal from Europe, Southeast Asia, the Pacific, Australia and North America.

Air Arabia and **Fly Dubai** from The Gulf; **Batik Air** from Kuala Lumpur; **Air India** via Delhi, Kolkata (Calcutta) and Varanasi; **Bangladesh Biman** for travellers with time to kill via Dhaka; **Chinese airlines** link Kathmandu with Lhasa, Chengdu, Kunming and Guangzhou (Canton); **Dragon Air** from Hong Kong; **Druk Air** from Paro, Bhutan, to Kathmandu and on to Delhi; **Etihad Airways** via Abu Dhabi from Europe; **Korean Airlines** from the Far East; **Nepal Airlines** flies from Delhi, Bombay, Dubai and Hong Kong – for those with bags of time; **Himalayan Airlines** is another Nepali carrier; **Oman Airways** via Muscat; **Jazeera Airways** via Kuwait; **Silk Air** from Singapore; **SpiceJet** and **Indigo** are low-cost Indian carriers; **Thai Airways** via Bangkok; **Qatar Airways** via Doha; **Turkish Airlines** via Istanbul; plus **Virgin, BA, Vistara** and others to Delhi, then one of the Indian carriers to Kathmandu. This information is subject to change.

Overland routes to Nepal

Nepal has open land borders with India and Tibet/China. Land borders into Nepal from India are through Sonauli/Belahiya near Bhairahawa; Raxaul/Birgunj; Nepalganj; Mahendranagar; and Kakarvitta. The Sonauli/Belahiya border north of Gorakhpur is the most-used entry point from India. Buses connect Bhairahawa to Kathmandu and Pokhara. A long journey by local transport links Nepal to Delhi in the west, through Mahendranagar/Banbasa. Those travelling between Kathmandu and Darjeeling or Sikkim can cross the eastern border at Kakarvitta.

Kathmandu is also linked to Lhasa in Tibet by the new highway through the border at Rasuwa/Kyirong. The road is generally tarred to Lhasa but poor on the Nepalese side near Dhunche in the Langtang area. The 5–6 day journey to Lhasa will blow your mind. It climbs over a number of spectacular 5000m passes through Lhatse, Shigatse and Gyangtse to Tibet's once-forbidden capital, Lhasa. Unfortunately the original road via Barhabise, Zhangmu and Nyalam was badly affected by the 2015 earthquake and has not yet reopened; it remains to be seen if travel will restart on this route.

Travel within Nepal

Travel within Nepal is possible either by road or by air. Transport companies change frequently, with buses wearing out, and others buying newer models.

Bus and jeep

Road transport can be on a noisy, crowded public bus, a so-called 'tourist bus', or in a privately hired jeep or car. It's a compromise between comfort, safety, time taken and money spent.

Travelling between Kathmandu and Pokhara (200km) by bus is quite straightforward these days, since the road has been improved almost all the way (but roadworks are still ongoing!). The usual journey time is 6–8hrs, but traffic can get heavy in the afternoon if you are heading back to Kathmandu. Currently the most luxurious buses are operated by Swift, Greyhound and Jagadamba for around Rs1600. (From Pokhara the night buses depart from near Vintage Travels on Hallan Chowk (Camping Chowk) and day buses from the Tourist Bus Park.) Other slightly less deluxe (but generally reliable) tourist buses depart around 7am from various points for Rs1200.

More unreliable, and definitely not comfortable, are the 'local' buses, which are even cheaper and leave from the Gongabu bus depot, northwest of the city. These are only recommended for those wishing to rub shoulders intimately with the locals. Ironically the taxi fare to the bus station is normally more than the bus ticket, so there is little to recommend this option. The local buses often stop in Mugling, an infamous eating place which, in days gone by, served dishes of 'hepatitis and rice'. Micro buses are another speedy but scary choice. Road travel to places further afield can be long and tiring. Routes go via the Terai lowlands to the trekking areas of Kanchenjunga and Makalu to the east, and West Nepal and Dolpo to the west. Jeep dirt roads are pushing into previously remote areas with amazing speed. Don't expect a comfortable ride on often-dreadful tracks.

In Upper Mustang there are various jeep 'counters' selling tickets in Lo Manthang, Tsarang and Ghami. A whole jeep, known as 'reserve', costs from Rs27,000 from **Lo Manthang** to **Chuksang**. A seat for a foreigner costs more than for a local Nepali. Leaving around 8.00am every day, the ride takes around 4–5 hours to Jomsom. They have a selection of 9- and 12-seater jeeps, and everyone will have a seat. No chickens or goats inside and no one hanging on to the roof! Bad spirits are tucked away near the exhaust pipes with any spare tyres that might exist! It's best to book your seat the day before.

A new vision of the future – black-top tarmac road to Muktinath

Motorcycle trips

Usually the choice of the new breed of Nepalese domestic tourists, a reliable motorcycle offers a lot of flexibility. A few foreign visitors try this option with locally hired bikes – often using Royal Enfield models. Preparation for such a trip is beyond the scope of this guide. For more on planning for a motorcycle trip, see our Bradt Africa Overland guide, which has a detailed section of general motorcycle preparation for an overland-style trip.

Pony express

Ponies are a pleasant way to travel on excursions in Upper Mustang, or to get up a high pass more quickly. In Lo Manthang and Tetang, a pony will cost from Rs4000 per day plus pony man and tips. In Tange it may cost up to Rs4–5000+ for one day up to Pa and a little bit beyond, a very long, steep climb.

Internal flights

Operated by a few local airlines, the main routes are to Pokhara, Nepalganj and Biratnagar. The main mountain routes are to Lukla (for Everest) and Jomsom (for Mustang and the Annapurna Circuit). Other sectors with less frequent services are to Tumlingtar (for Makalu and the Arun Valley route to Everest) and Taplejung/Suketar (for Kanchenjunga).

Further away flights head to Juphal/Dunai (for Dolpo) and Simikot (for Rara Lake, Saipal and the Limi Valley). Flights are subject to delays caused by weather and occasionally by other 'Nepalese' factors. The price for foreigners is higher than for locals. Helicopters are becoming quite common for sightseeing charters as well as rescue missions. Across the popular areas, Everest and Annapurna groups are using helicopters to cut the length of the treks. With prices per day for trekking increasing, this is not as surprising as it seems.

Flying into a restricted area needs a permit for the flight, which could take up to five days to obtain, so forward planning is necessary. For a 5–6-seater helicopter, the weight limit is around 450kg of passengers, baggage and supplies. Prices range from OK (US$2000 per hour) to sky high!

Visa information

Nepalese visa

www.nepalimmigration.gov.np

All foreign nationals except Indians require a visa. Currently visas are available from embassies and land borders, as well as at Tribhuvan International Airport on arrival in Kathmandu (check for any changes before arrival). Entering or exiting the country at the remoter crossing points and from Tibet may be subject to change, so always check the latest requirements in all cases. Applying in your own country will cost more. Remember to apply well ahead of travel, in case there are any holidays at the embassy due to festival periods in Nepal.

Obtaining a visa on arrival is normally the easiest option, but check in case of any new restrictions. To save time at the airport, fill in the preliminary form online at home and print a copy. The maximum length of stay in Nepal is five months in one calendar year; the fifth month is not always possible. Tourist visas are available for 15, 30 or 90 days, at a fee of $30, $50 and $125 (payment in cash) respectively.

Extensions in Kathmandu are obtained at the Immigration Department at a cost of $US45 (the minimum fee, for 15 days) or for a daily charge of $US3 per day. Anyone requiring a visa extension in Kathmandu must go online and fill in the forms in advance, uploading a passport-style photo. Using the machine in the immigration hall is free of charge. All visas are currently multiple-entry, making visits to places like Bhutan, Tibet or India much easier than before. Check the up-to-date fees at www.nepalimmigration.gov.np. For comprehensive embassy listings, see: www.mofa.gov.np

Indian visa

Allow at least 7–10 days if you intend to get your Indian visa in Kathmandu and expect delays. It is currently much cheaper to do this in your home country than in Nepal. Fees in Kathmandu vary from US$50–$190 depending on nationality. E-visas are now available online; cheaper and easier! Do check the visa situation before travel; change is likely at any time! www.indianembassy.org.np

Tibet/China entry

For those planning a trip to Tibet/China from Nepal after a trip, it's currently of no use to obtain a Chinese visa in advance. The Chinese visa will simply be cancelled at the Kathmandu embassy, because travel to Tibet from Nepal currently requires special arrangements. It is necessary to prearrange the visa for Tibet in Nepal through a Nepalese agent. Allow a few days in Kathmandu to complete application well ahead of your arrival in Nepal if prearranging by email. Visas for travel across Tibet are normally issued on paper for the duration of the stated itinerary. Budget (not that cheap) tours are offered by Kathmandu travel agents for independent travellers, thus making that fabulous trip a possibility. The Chinese authorities frequently close the Tibetan border at short notice.

Following the earthquakes of spring 2015, the border road to Tibet via Zhangmu was closed. A new border post at Rasuwa/Kyirong (Gyirong) near Syabrubesi, Langtang area has opened for tourists. Check the latest information before planning a trip.

Money matters

> I now add worry about the cash supply to my collection of other possible misfortunes.
> ***Stones of Silence*, George Schaller**

The currency is the Nepalese Rupee (Rs). Notes come in the following denominations: Rs5, 10, 20, 50, 100, 500 and 1000, and occasionally coins: Rs1, 2 and 5.

Approximate exchange rates (Jan 2025)	
	Rs
£	170
€	140
US$	134
CHF	151

In Kathmandu and Pokhara, ATMs are now common, but not always reliable. Bring some foreign cash in case of problems. Moneychangers are very quick to change cash, but travellers' cheques are no longer usable in Nepal. It's a waste of time to head for a bank these days, as most rarely exchange money and if they do are generally exceedingly slow. Currently there are no banks or ATMs on the trails except in Jomsom. In the hills, you may find a self-appointed moneychanger offering poor rates for cash. Take more cash rupees than you think you will need, and then a bit more.

Practicalities

Language

The main language of Nepal is Nepali, but many people also speak some English. It is taught in schools across the country and is understood to varying extents by all staff involved in tourism. The main ethnic groups also each have their own language. Everyone understands '*Namaste*' – hands held together, with a smile.

Internet and phone

A full range of internet-based services are available in Kathmandu and Pokhara. International dialling code: +977.

Mobile phones have completely changed the nature of 'getting away from it all' on holiday anywhere these days and in Nepal it is the same. It's no big deal these days to call anywhere across the globe from Mustang and even high up the peaks! When disgruntled trekkers can call their travel agent at home to complain about the lack of hot water in their lodge, perhaps things have gone too far!

Wifi is available in many places, but not all. Foreign SIM cards may not work and, if they do, costs will be extortionate. With 3G and 4G networks in some parts of the country, trekkers who buy a local SIM card can become entangled in the worldwide web on their smartphones. But is that such a smart idea?

Nepal never really got past the first hurdle in developing landlines and thus avoided that vast investment. For a few brief years landline phones had great novelty value, with roughly one phone booth every four days' trekking distance. Nowadays people in the smallest village or trailside shack are busy keeping in touch with family down the valley. Monks seem very enamoured of phones, to keep in touch with the middle way perhaps!

However, there are some corners of Nepal where mobile coverage is absent or erratic. Make sure your staff are carrying a charged satellite phone. In the Mustang area, the situation is complicated. The major operator Ncell works in Jomsom and Muktinath and sporadically in Lo Manthang. Its coverage is expanding. Nepal Telecom works for most of the route, but in some places, only Sky will do. If you are contemplating buying a local SIM card, check with your trekking agency.

Postage

It's a long trek to find the Central Post Office now that it has moved to the Dilli Bazaar area. To send a letter or postcard it's normally better to use your hotel or a bookshop. To send home heavy souvenirs, check out the packing agents in Thamel.

Electricity

Electricity in Nepal is 220volts/50cycles, with most sockets having two pins of varying distances apart. Electrification of the countryside is progressing well, but power cuts (load shedding) in cities can occur. In recent years hydroelectric schemes have been installed across many villages in the regions, but occasionally some of those at higher altitude have frozen and not been repaired. Across the majority of the popular trekking regions, electricity is found in some form in most lodges. Charging your camera battery is possible in most but not all lodges – be sure to bring an electrical adaptor and more spare batteries than you expect to use.

National holidays

Sometimes there seem to be more official and unofficial holidays than there are normal days. As luck would have it, the busy trekking season in the autumn coincides with the biggest festival period. Enjoy the colourful festivities, but allow more time to get your permits.

National holidays
1 January	New Year
February/March	Tibetan New Year
14 April	Nepali New Year
23 April	Democracy Day
1 May	Labour Day
29 May	Republic Day

Plus many other religious festivals.
For comprehensive listings, see
www.qppstudio.net/publicholidays2025/nepal.htm

Trip planning

Permits and TIMS

Trip and trek permits of some form are necessary for most treks in Nepal. See www.timsnepal.com for the latest requirements. They are issued at the main office in the Bhrikuti Mandap tourist centre.

Currently there are two types of TIMS. The blue one is issued to trekkers organising the trip/trek through a Nepalese agency and costs US$10. The green TIMS card is issued to independent visitors/trekkers costing US$20 each. See www.timsnepal.com. The entire TIMS set up is currently under review, so do check the latest. Following a new constitution, more power has been devolved to the regions, and there is talk of new taxes, fees and rules for trekkers and visitors. Check the latest information before your trip.

Mustang permits

Despite widespread rumours that fees for Upper Mustang were going to be reduced to encourage more tourists, this has not yet happened. Currently the minimum fee is a massive US$500 per person for a 10-day period. Those needing more time can pay US$50 per extra day. The 10-day period is barely enough time to reach Lo Manthang and return, but try telling that to the bureaucrats. It's a pity the people in Kathmandu don't relax the time periods. Most locals would prefer the fee to be reduced, as they are keen to invest in their properties, but there is no point – or finance to pay for it – if tourists are unable to afford to visit. Perhaps a lower fee for the permit in winter could be introduced to extend the season a little more. The restricted area permit is only checked in Chuksang now. When we exited Upper Mustang at Muktinath, the authorities were completely uninterested in stamping our restricted area permits and only wanted to see our ACAP fee receipts. The same thing happened at the checkpost in Jomsom. For us this was a significant annoyance, as we walked long hours to cover everywhere we wanted to see in our thirteen days. We could still be in Upper Mustang now! Draw your own conclusions, but be aware that things may change.

Check the latest information: **www.nepalimmigration.gov.np**

The snags of the Upper Mustang permit

Of course the biggest snag with the Upper Mustang permit system is that foreign trekkers cannot know in advance what the terrain is like, how they will acclimatise to the altitude, what there is to see on a grander scale, whether a weather delay might occur or a landslide block a route. They might like an extra day in a fascinating place or need a day to rest after sickness, or be knackered from too much blasting along within a limited timeframe! It seems that no amount of lobbying the authorities in Kathmandu can change the system to allow more flexibility. It's extremely irritating for trekkers on the ground having to decide in advance the number of days required for a given itinerary. Some local trekking agencies are prone to offer very comprehensive, attractive itineraries that are, for some visitors, too optimistic for a given time period. Just like everywhere else these days, those who make the rules don't actually have any first-hand experience of the consequences.

Peak permits

Peak permit fees are currently levied at various rates according to the classification and altitude of the peak. The list shown on the NMA website is only a sample. Some major peaks and newly opened peaks are not listed. An additional 'garbage' deposit fee may be levied, refundable when the garbage is deposited at the registered depot for the particular climbing peak. Liaison officers are also sometimes required.

The Nepal Mountaineering Association (NMA) office is in Nag Pokhari near the Chinese Embassy. Check out the latest details, rules and fees at:

www.nepalmountaineering.org tel: +977-1-4434525, 4435442
Email: office@nepalmountaineering.org; peaks@nma.wlink.com.np
info@nepalmountaineering.org

National Parks
The general aim of the national parks is to regulate activities within the designated areas and to promote conservation. Prior to the formation of the national parks and conservation areas, there was fairly uncontrolled deforestation, since local people relied on the timber for cooking and heating. In association with local community development, the project seeks to develop ecological ways of improving the environment. Trekking groups are forbidden to use wood for cooking. The scheme aims to improve hygiene levels by establishing small health posts, toilets and safe drinking water depots. Bridges and basic infrastructure have been improved and new schools have opened. The preservation of the local culture has been another important contribution; evidence of this is seen through the restoration of key cultural monuments, such as the once-decaying monasteries.

Associated organisations
NTNC (National Trust for Nature Conservation)
www.ntnc.org.np; www.forestrynepal.org
TAAN (Trekking Agents' Association of Nepal)
www.taan.org.np
See also www.welcomenepal.com & www.tourism.gov.np

Annapurna Conservation Area
The Annapurna Conservation Area Project was established in 1986. Its aims, before the arrival of the dirt roads were much the same as those already stated above. It is unclear how the new road developments and the principles of a conservation area can coexist in the long term. Preservation of the local culture is still paramount; the monasteries and historic places continue to benefit from the original aims. The fee is Rs3000.

Important note
The **single entry** to the conservation areas of Annapurna does mean just one entry. This means that if you leave one part of the conservation area hoping to re-enter in another, you will be refused re-entry. This rule affects trekkers to Annapurna, where roads mean it's possible to shortcut some trails.

Choosing the season

Trips and treks to most areas of Nepal are best undertaken in either autumn or spring. The autumn period is usually the most stable period and thus will be the busiest time on the trails. Normally early October heralded the beginning of the season after the monsoon rains abated, but in recent years the weather has sometimes been more unsettled. Unseasonal rain and heavy cloud has intervened, causing the much awaited and colourful harvests to be delayed.

After mid-October the weather is usually better, with clearer skies and magical views. The ripened rice-terraced hillsides are ablaze with fabulous colours from gold to brilliant greens of all shades. November is generally the clearest month, with crisp and sparkling days. December is much colder at higher altitude, but routes and hotels/lodges are quieter. Just occasionally the stable conditions of autumn are disrupted when a storm blows in, bringing rain with heavy snow in the mountains.

Visiting throughout the winter is perfectly possible lower down but heading to the higher valleys during late December/January and early February may mean encountering more cloud, snow and colder temperatures. Ever more inhabitants descend to the warmer foothills for winter, so many accommodation options will be closed. Heavy snow will make some higher and narrow trails dangerous if not impossible, with a risk of avalanche.

The spring season, late February to early May, is the other popular season to visit. The weather is generally stable, but clouds often cover the mountains by mid-morning. The lower valleys (below 2500m) are sultry and hot. Crossing high passes before April could be tricky, with snow and ice a serious deterrent.

Haze will unfortunately mean those photographers who want their mountains crisp and clear might feel frustrated. However, keen botanists are sure to be delighted and satisfied with the prolific array of rhododendrons and magnolia. Heading higher, wind tends to be more of a feature, particularly closer to the Tibetan plateau.

For most, visiting at the height of the summer, July and August, is not really recommended, with mountain vistas a rare luxury. Monsoon cloud, rain and snow can be expected at any time from mid-June to mid-September. Incessant rain in the lower hills causes dangerous landslides, road and trail damage. Blood-sucking leeches are a plague.

The one positive advantage about a visit in the monsoon is that the valleys are green and the experience is totally different. The farmers are busy in the fields and some of the main festivals and colourful events are celebrated.

Areas that are commonly visited during the summer (monsoon) include Mustang and Dolpo, on the north side of the high mountains.

However, the approaches are through the weather-affected and landslide-afflicted middle hills. We personally are wary of trekking or visiting anywhere during the monsoon season (being addicted to the views), but others relish the different atmosphere and the many festivals that are celebrated during that period.

The most popular periods in Upper Mustang are autumn, spring and then the monsoon. The rivers are much higher in the monsoon and in October, so be wary of planning routes that use those deep gorges then. Winter is very cold between mid-December and mid-March. Many people migrate to Pokhara for the winter from Mustang, but some do stay on through the snowfall period.

Maps

> Frodo began to feel restless, and the old paths seemed too well-trodden. He looked at maps, and wondered what lay beyond their edges: maps made in the Shire showed mostly white spaces beyond its borders.
> ***The Lord of the Rings*, J R R Tolkien**

An amazing and varied number of maps are available in Kathmandu. The quality has improved dramatically in recent years, with excellent colour maps showing all the aspects and features that any casual trekker to Nepal might wish for. Place names on maps are often spelt differently from those seen on lodge signs and so on.

Most of the maps are produced by Map House (www.maphouse.org), who have a bookshop opposite KC's restaurant in Thamel. In Thamel there are a number of other map stockists, who also sell books on all aspects of the Himalaya.

A selection of titles is listed below:

Around Annapurna	1 : 125,000
Upper & Lower Mustang	1 : 90,000
Upper Mustang	1 : 65,000
Nar-Phu	1 : 75,000
Tilicho and Nar-Phu	1 : 125,000
The High Route to Tilicho	1 : 75,000
Pokhara to Muktinath and Jomsom	1 : 80,000

In the UK, Stanfords in Covent Garden, London is one of the best places to find maps of Nepal and the Himalaya. www.stanfords.co.uk

> **Notes on the Upper Mustang map (Map House)**
> Visitors should note that in addition to the yellow main trails, the local Upper Mustang map shows many side trails, marked in red and green. The red trails, defined as difficult, are in many places merely cross-country routes that are often poorly defined and little-used. They present some obvious dangers: exposure, landslides, erosion and wading in rivers. The green trails are a mixed bag; some are easy to follow, while others, longer and more remote, are less clear. Be sure to have a knowledgeable local guide if contemplating using any of these routes. Even a few of the less-used yellow side trails are poor, eroded and, in the extreme, dangerous; the Sakau Danda east trail is one at the time of writing. The main Jomsom–Lo Manthang road is marked in red, as well as side roads in white.

Photography

The Himalaya and anywhere in Nepal are a photographer's Shangri-La. The variety of the subject matter is mind-boggling. The mountains in all their aspects, the colourful people, the architecture and antiquities, bustling markets and every conceivable subject all offer wonderful opportunities. For much of the season the clarity of the mountain light is often brilliant. Keep all your photographic equipment in plastic bags, away from the unavoidable dust. Batteries do not like the sub-zero nights and need a warm up in the mornings just as much as the visitors!

You may need to sleep with your camera/battery when temperatures drop at night; keep the camera tucked up close to your body inside a jacket to warm it up before use. Bring cleaning equipment. Power supplies can be erratic, so pack extra batteries and memory cards.

Avoid taking photographs of any military-looking subjects, such as checkposts, some bridges and communication towers. You are strongly urged to ask permission of people before taking photographs, especially in the remote areas, where they still believe it will upset their spirits or ancestors. Yaks love having their photos taken, but not from a point blank range – watch those horns! If you manage to capture a snow leopard on digital, you'll probably be able to pay for your trek.

Budgeting

For full-service group of visitors, cyclists, motorcyclists or trekkers, there will be few extras other than a rare beer/drink at a lodge, the odd souvenirs, staff tips and meals out in Kathmandu. Independent visitors need to obtain the TIMS and park entry fees and calculate the costs with much more care. They will need to plan for additional staff/porters and food, as well as the above extras.

Organising your own guide and local staff through a recognised local agent is perfectly feasible. Allow at least US$35–40 per day for a guide, $25–30 for a porter-guide and $20 for a porter if needed). Be sure to confirm in advance whether or not these wages **also include** his or her expenses en route.

Don't forget **insurance** for local staff.

> **Costs on the road**
> Surprisingly, the prices in Kagbeni, likely to be your first night's halt, are generally higher than anywhere further north towards Lo Manthang. Expect about Rs3500–4500 per day for lodgings and foodings per person. Expect prices to rise around 10% per year from the date of publication of this guide. Take your favourite snacks and chocolate bars with you from home or from Kathmandu.

Take **more cash** than you have calculated, as there are few ATMs in the countryside nor are there many official places to change money. You don't want to spend all winter in a quaint but freezing gompa reciting prayers for deliverance!

Tipping

Since the 1960s, when trekking in Nepal was developed, there has been a tradition for groups and independent visitors to tip their crews at the end of a trek. It's no great hardship to budget for this and it's very rare that anyone is dissatisfied with the service. As a rule and through tradition, the head cook should get a little more than the local staff/porters, and any kitchen crew. The leader/guide would expect a little more again. Allow around at least 15% per cent of the wages or around one day's wage for each week on trek.

Style of trip

As much as anything, the itinerary you choose and the destination will dictate the style of trip undertaken.

Visitors will find adequate lodge facilities along all of the main trails of Mustang. However heading very far to the east or west of the main valley, camping is still necessary. Most routes traditionally connected the villages and apart from parts of Upper Mustang very little of Nepal is true wilderness. The routes/trails of the higher regions are generally less populated, apart from the occasional lost yeti.

However, the lower stages can be quite busy with local porters, people off to markets, children engaging visitors, wary and grungy dogs, banana-snatching monkeys, mad cows and 'mad' trekkers as well as mules and dzopkios.

Going independently does allow for perhaps greater interaction and a more intimate rapport with the inhabitants. It is also a cheaper way to visit Nepal and ensures that your cash goes straight to the local people. Those who have already been to Nepal or other developing countries will have the advantage of knowing roughly what to expect.

Independently organised trips

Those visitors who have a dislike for organised trips will find this an appealing option. It offers a good deal of freedom and flexibility. The trip can be tailored to the needs of the person, couple or small group of friends. Many visitors hire a local guide and driver through a reputable agency, paying their living expenses as well as the wage.

Make sure that the guide and any staff are insured and adequately clothed for the high altitude. Make sure also that the agency will cover any additional staff insurance if you hire extra services on the way.

Be sure to read the sections in this guide on altitude and mountain safety. The points may seem obvious, but every year people are evacuated from or die in these mountains.

Organising a trip through an agent in your home country or Nepal for a couple or a small group is not necessarily more expensive than a big company group trip. Naturally, booking the trip directly with a Kathmandu-based company is cheaper. However, unless you are familiar with the agency or have a recommendation, there may be snags. The main one is that you will not be covered by any foreign company liability if things do go badly. At the very least make sure your insurance covers a helicopter evacuation and is not limited by absurd altitude limits such as 'not above 1500m'.

There is a good selection of excellent local travel/trekking agents in Kathmandu who have years of experience in dealing with overseas trekkers approaching them directly. Sometimes getting an answer to your enquiry quickly does not happen because of the fickle nature of power cuts experienced in Kathmandu these days – just keep on asking. Choosing to arrange the trip with a Kathmandu agent means you can finalise the trip and pay the operators directly, but remember that if an internal flight is involved, the agent might ask for some advance payment.

Fully supported group trips

In the earliest years of trekking this was the main option (until guidebook writers came up with notes on the main trails!). For those with limited time, this option provides maximum security and the least amount of hassle getting permits, for example, in Kathmandu. The tour operators can smooth over the local difficulties and sort out any issues like transport, permits and porter strikes!

The big companies (foreign and Nepalese) can also organise any private helicopters or rescues more easily. The agent will arrange the permits and conservation fees. All day-to-day logistics such as accommodation, food and carriage of baggage will be arranged. Most trips are fully inclusive, with few added extras. Clients can admire the scenery in as much comfort as is possible in a high mountain environment. Trips by road use quite good lodges.

There are a few disadvantages to commercial group travel. Larger groups with the support of a Nepali crew can have more of an impact on the environment. The major disadvantage of an organised trip is the loss of flexibility concerning the itinerary and other issues.

Of course there is always the risk that your fellow travellers are on a different planet – although this is extremely rare. Perhaps the biggest snag of a group trip is the unnecessary danger posed at altitude by 'peer pressure' within the group. No one wants to be the first to admit to a headache or nauseas. At its worst, this pressure can overrule common sense, with some members ignoring symptoms of altitude sickness in the unacknowledged race to compete. **Do not fall into this lethal trap**.

It's wise to avoid alcohol of any description before any high pass or high terrain, since it adversely affects acclimatisation. A dinner of delightful goodies is served piping hot a little after sunset. Then the day is done, except for crawling into an uncooperative sleeping bag or on to a rock-hard bed.

Guides and drivers

Group trips will be led by an English-speaking Nepalese leader/guide who normally knows the routes.

As mentioned before but reiterated here, independent trekkers hiring a crew or a porter locally or from Kathmandu should ensure that insurance is obtained to cover any misadventure involving the guide/porters. They should also ensure that suitable clothing is provided for all guides/porters for the high altitude. Check out **KEEP** for guidance on the correct actions when hiring guides privately.

KEEP: Kathmandu Environmental Education Project
https://keepnepal.org

Following the Maoist insurgency, general wage levels for local staff and many other often poorly treated people throughout society have risen dramatically – perhaps the one benefit of that long reign of violence!

Trip planning

Accommodation

Lodges

Lodges are available and relatively comfortable across the Mustang region described in this guidebook. They generally have small but adequate twin-bedded rooms. Beds tend to be fairly hard and some dividing walls hardly provide a private boudoir – expect a lot of communal interaction. The lodges are now up to the standards found in the more heavily trekked areas such as the Annapurna Circuit. Mattresses are getting thicker each year, but occasionally they are rather thin and worn out in the middle. Some might wish to ensure greater comfort by carrying a Thermarest. Tibetan carpets look beautiful and soft, but just wait till you rest your weary bones on them for the night! Most Mustang lodges now have 'attached' en suite facilities; some are quite posh while a few still have mud floors.

Camping

Only the more remote areas in Upper Mustang require camping, like the route to Chodzong and Damodar Kund Lake.

Homestay

Homestay is a new but essentially old concept, where trekkers overnight in local people's houses. Normally a separate room will be set aside for the guests. Most homestays are basic, with outside toilets and primitive washing facilities – much as the first trekkers found. Mattresses may be thin or even thinner! Meals are provided by the household, using local produce. Nourishing dal bhat (lentils and rice) and potatoes are commonly available. Delicious, local organic vegetables are sometimes on offer!

One homestay in Lo Manthang is Tashi's Lowa Guest House in the northwest corner of the old city – quite popular with Nepalese visitors. Other householders may offer a place to stay in the winter when most lodges are closed.

Washing

> How can we be out of soap? Judging by appearances, we have not been contaminated by soap for weeks.
> ***Stones of Silence*, George Schaller**

Many lodges now have electric-powered and solar-heated water heating. Far fewer lodges still have gas hot showers. Apart from gas or solar power, other washing options are likely to be utilising scarce resources (wood or kerosene), meaning a conflict with conservation. Bucket showers are still offered in some places. The main issue is that hardly any lodges have heated rooms, so taking a shower is not always inviting.

Toilets

It's a certain bet that the subject of toilets is being discussed at any time, almost anywhere on trek across Nepal. In the more developed parts, lodges will have western-style toilets, often en suite. However, at higher altitudes the water freezes overnight, making the outside shed full of sawdust a more appealing option! Group campers will be privileged with a special toilet tent with appropriate hole – they're better than nothing! A trekker's worst nightmare is dropping their moneybelt down the hole, so be extra vigilant. Along the trails, toilet paper should be burnt and waste buried where possible.

> We have discovered, as have Tibetans long ago, that the luxury of warmth far outweighs that of cleanliness.
> ***Stones of Silence*, George Schaller**

Food

Across Mustang there is no need for lodge trippers to survive on dal bhat any more. Don't expect to be craving for variety now, although if you are on a trip longer than two weeks it might become an issue. Those on fully inclusive group or independently organised trips with full services will enjoy filling breakfasts, including porridge/cereal, bread/toast with eggs, plus hot drinks. Lunch is a favourite meal, especially the real chips. Other items are likely to be tinned meat/fish, noodles or cooked bread and something sweet to round off. At night campers are provided with three-course dinners: soup, noodles/pasta/rice/potatoes plus a dessert of tinned fruit (dream on, independents... you might just occasionally find a tin of fruit left behind by an expedition.) Plentiful amounts of hot water/drinks are available at all meal times to ensure dehydration is avoided, especially the higher you trek. As a rule, the food stocks dwindle the further you get from Kathmandu, as the fresh products are consumed. However, by now anything tastes good!

'Fried chaps'

The Nepalis' use of the English language is one of the most endearing features of the country. You'll see this on signboards advertising the lodges' 'faxsilities', such as inside 'to lets', 'toilet free rooms' and, on enticing teahouse menus, 'fried chaps', 'apple panick', 'banana crap', 'pumping soup', 'chocolate putting', 'palin chapatti', 'spleeping charge' and the like. Flash toilets invariably mean toilets flushed by water (or ice blocks) and it is a notorious fact that toilets and Nepal are not cuddly bedfellows.

Kathmandu has a good variety of supermarkets, but don't anticipate many treats elsewhere. New city malls are the latest trend in Kathmandu, with imported food items suitable for trekkers. Be sure to stock up on goodies – chocolate or power bars and any other cravings that need to be satisfied en route. There's not much on offer in the small shops unless you like chewing tobacco and rough cigarettes!

When visiting for a long period anywhere in Nepal and living in the lodges, the food can eventually get rather monotonous. It's worthwhile taking other food items if you have a porter or two. Muesli is a good standby for any time of day – even with water. Instant potato, soups or noodles and tinned fish are easily prepared as an emergency dinner at a high camp. Ensure that indestructible rubbish is carried out, or use the places set aside for disposal.

What to take

The following kit list is a guideline only:

Kitbag
Torch (flashlight) & whistle
Washing kit
Wetwipes, large and small
Toothbrush & toothpaste
Sun cream & lip cream
Water bottle
Trousers or cotton skirts
Shirts, T-shirts or blouses
Underwear
Boots and various socks
Sleeping bag + fleece liner
Toilet rolls
Plastic bags

Walking poles
Trainers or sandals
Fleece and woollen hat
Sunglasses & sun hat
Gloves and scarf/buff
Waterproof jacket/trousers
Warm sweater
Down jacket/trousers
Penknife and tin opener
Padlock for cheap hotel rooms
Ear plugs
Power bank and solar charger
Phone/Camera & batteries
Adaptor for electric plugs

Some of the equipment listed above will involve a considerable expense when purchased at home. Some commercial companies do now provide basic gear – sleeping bags, mattresses etc – but others do not. A few trekking gear shops in Kathmandu offer equipment for hire quite cheaply. Buying new gear is also good value, with excellent locally made items like sleeping bags and down jackets. We have been buying boots in Kathmandu for a number of years and most have proved quite durable.

The motto for mountain and wilderness trekkers and travellers around the world is:

Leave only footprints and take only photographs

Staying healthy

The main problems concerning health issues in Nepal are related to food, water, hygiene, the remoteness of the trekking regions, and the high altitude. Outside the main centres of Kathmandu and Pokhara, it cannot be emphasised enough that there are virtually no adequate medical facilities anywhere other than tiny, often barely functioning, health posts.

However, helicopter evacuations are possible from some parts of the mountain regions. You must have proof of medical evacuation insurance or payment before a helicopter will take off. (Helicopter quotes range from US$2000 per hour up to a whopping US$10,000, which might include a 'booking fee'.)

In general fewer bugs survive at high altitude, making the high zones of Nepal marginally healthier than the humid lowland destinations – a small comfort at least. Personal hygiene and what you eat really does matter. Unfortunately some local levels of hygiene still leave a lot to be desired by most standards.

Do your best to keep healthy:
Wash/clean hands regularly
Never drink untreated tap water
Avoid salads
Peel fruits
Brush teeth in bottled/cleaned water

Water sterilisation

Many difficulties concern the lack of clean running water. Just keeping your hands clean can significantly reduce the ailments transmitted through dirty water. The lodges and homestays on the trails are becoming more aware of hygiene these days. Group trekkers are at a distinct advantage, being regularly supplied with plentiful boiled water and hot drinks. Independent trekkers will need to be more vigilant as a rule. Antibacterial gel for hands and large baby wipes for other parts are extremely useful! Bring plastic bags for storing used items and carry out rubbish.

Water boils at a lower temperature at high altitude, so you might want to add sterilising tablets to the water as an added precaution. Iodine or chlorine tablets, or Micropur, can be used. Bottled drinking water can also be bought in Kathmandu and Pokhara. Along the trails, when available, it gets very expensive, especially the higher you go. Plastic water bottles have littered trails in the past but these days most are being carried out of the mountains by trekkers and crews. However, plastic pollution is becoming more and more of an issue worldwide, so we do not recommend it.

Staying healthy

The best option for independent hikers is to request boiled water from the lodges. Other options include bottles from www.watertogo.eu

> See also www.watertogo.eu and get a
> **15% discount using the code SB15**

Vaccinations

At present no vaccinations are legally required on entry to Nepal, but always check before travel in case of any recent changes. Your GP can advise you about the latest recommendations regarding vaccinations.

Be sure to allow plenty of time for the series of vaccinations – they cannot all be given at the same time and some require a number of weeks in-between. Keep a record of all the vaccinations, even though it's not a legal requirement.

The following are normally recommended by health professionals, but there could be others added at any time.

BCG tuberculosis Vaccination is often recommended by GPs.
Cholera Although not required by law or particularly effective, it might be recommended if an outbreak has occurred.
Hepatitis This nasty disease has various forms; hepatitis A is the main risk for travellers. New vaccines are being improved for all strains of hepatitis.
Meningitis/Japanese encephalitis Outbreaks do occur in rural parts of Nepal, often in the lower country. The risk is minimal and expensive vaccines are available. Clinics in Kathmandu can give vaccinations for a much lower negotiable fee than payable at home; the CIWEC clinic is highly recommended.
Rabies The disease is found across Nepal, but the vaccine is normally only suggested for those spending extended periods in rural areas away from the cities. The vaccination is expensive and the procedure lengthy, but it should be considered for remote areas of Nepal. Seek advice at least six months before the planned trip. The main thing for casual visitors is to keep a sharp lookout for suspiciously acting dogs and 'dog patrols'. Although not necessarily a risk for rabies, the guard dogs of herders in the high uplands can be rather intimidating and occasionally menacing if the owners are not present. A few monasteries also have guard dogs, so beware!
Tetanus/polio Recommended.
Typhoid/paratyphoid Vaccinations are strongly recommended, as there are possible risks.
Yellow fever Vaccination will give cover for 10 years. It is only required in Nepal if coming from an infected area.

Other nasty bugs

Giardia is a wretched bug to watch out for, since there is no preventative treatment apart from careful eating and drinking. Infected drinking water is the main culprit. Giardia lives happily in its host until sent packing by a course of Flagyl (Metronidazole), Secnidazole or Tinidazole (Tiniba in Nepal). Sulphurous foul-smelling gases, cramp and sometimes diarrhoea are the main symptoms, but let's not dwell on those.

Dengue fever outbreaks are much more commonly reported in Nepal these days, but the risk is generally fairly low in the high country, unless staying for long periods during the rainy season. Try to avoid mosquito bites, since there is no treatment other than rest.

Malaria

Fortunately malaria is not found in most of Nepal, being confined at the moment to parts of the southern lowlands bordering India. However, those trekkers travelling overland to India, or relaxing in Chitwan National Park, or anywhere in the Terai, will be exposed to malaria. Using insect repellent at and after dusk and wearing suitable clothing will give some protection against bites. The main drugs used in Nepal are Doxycycline and Malarone (Atovaquone/proguanil). For some users, Mefloquine (Lariam) can have very nasty side effects, so if prescribed, it is wise to test it out before travel. Some travellers may be recommended to take Proguanil daily and Chloroquine weekly, if going to a high-risk area. Doxycycline can be bought in Kathmandu if you need supplies. Do not ignore the risks of malaria. See also www.masta-travel-health.com and
www.ciwec-clinic.com/articles/malaria_advice.php

Common ailments on trek

The most common problems on trek are colds, blocked sinuses, headaches and stomach disorders. Common remedies (available from the chemist) for headaches, blocked noses, sore throats, coughs and sneezes should be easily accessible in any medical kit. The dry air often causes irritations. Take a good supply of decongestants and painkillers for headaches on any high altitude trek. It is necessary to drink more liquids in high dry regions. If the dreaded stomach bug appears, the use of Imodium, Loperamide or Lomotil is initially recommended if symptoms are not serious. These drugs will make a road journey much more comfortable. The antibiotic drugs Norfloxacin and Ciprofloxacin can be used in more debilitating cases, and are available from pharmacies in Kathmandu. Dioralyte will help rehydration in cases of fluid loss due to stomach upsets. Stemetil can be used for those prone to travel sickness.

It may seem obvious, but don't ignore the power of the sun at high altitude, despite the low temperatures; wear a suitable hat and cover your arms and legs; use sun cream on exposed parts of the body.

Staying healthy

Dental care

> A day may come when the courage of men fails… but it is not THIS day.
> ***The Lord of the Rings*, J R R Tolkien**

A visit to your dentist for a check-up before the trip is advised (unless you wish to rely on the 'tooth temple god' near Tahity Square in Kathmandu for treatment). Competent dentists do exist in Kathmandu, but you are unlikely to meet any serving time in the hills. If the 'tooth god' has failed you, try the excellent Healthy Smiles in Lazimpat in Kathmandu – it has the latest high-tech gadgetry.

First aid kit

The following list is only given as a suggestion:

Antibacterial hand gel	Insect repellent
Antibiotics (general)	Safety pins
Antihistamine cream	Scissors
Antiseptic cream	Sterile gloves
Aspirin/paracetamol	Sun cream
Blister prevention	Thermometer
Rehydration sachets	Water sterilising tablets
Dressings	Eyewash
Knee bandage	Wet wipes

Plus: Pocket First Aid and Wilderness Medicine
Dr Jim Duff and Dr Peter Gormly (Cicerone)
Cold and sinus remedies
Personal medications
Stomach upset remedies and Tinidazole

If this lot fails to sort you out, check out the local remedies.

Clinics

Consult one of the specialist clinics or their websites listed below for the latest medical advice for travellers. Your doctor should also be consulted.

CIWEC Clinic Lainchaur, near the British Embassy in Kathmandu, www.ciwec-clinic.com
International Society of Travel Medicine www.istm.org
Hospital for Tropical Diseases Travel Clinic www.thehtd.org
MASTA (Medical Advisory Service for Travellers Abroad) www.masta-travel-health.com

---

RISK: Remember altItude Sickness Kills
descending is the only safe cure, day or night!

> **Lipstick**
> Add a touch of glamour and protect your lips at the same time! For many years I simply used colourless lip protector sticks, but returned from Dolpo with a horribly cracked lower lip despite frequent use. Since then I have worn a standard coloured moisturising lipstick... and it works!

Altitude sickness & precautions

All mountain trips presents hazards, but in the high regions the biggest danger comes from the dehydrating high altitude, severe cold and bitter winds. Be careful on the rough and rocky routes; bear in mind that the next hospital is many miles away. The real problems of altitude sickness occur at heights above 3000m (10,000ft), especially if you climb quickly.

There are generally two levels where the effects of altitude kicks in, 3500m and again around 4500m, so these two stages of upward motion should be carefully planned. Even before you reach 3000m, it is beneficial to gain height as slowly as possible, including extra nights. The recommended daily height gain is only 300m, with 500m per day being the upper limit. Obviously in some areas this is difficult, so you must monitor your condition closely.

Serious altitude problems occur in the highest mountain regions of northern Nepal. Kathmandu is at 1317m and presents no problems. To combat the problems of altitude, it is important to learn about its effects before you start hiking along the trails. The most common symptoms of altitude are headaches, nausea, tiredness, lack of appetite and disorientation. It is often difficult to sleep and breathing becomes erratic (Cheyne-Stokes breathing). The heart might thump a bit disconcertingly at times.

Be very careful not to overexert on arrival at any destination; symptoms often only begin to appear after an hour or more. Having some of these does not mean abandoning the trip but watch out for any changes as altitude is gained. Mild symptoms, perhaps just a slight headache, are acceptable so long as they do not get worse or persist all day and night. One real nuisance is the need to urinate more, especially at night at a high camp, but it's a good sign as a rule!

It is vital to walk about very slowly at altitude, especially when climbing any hill. If in doubt, be sure to admit any problems and don't be pressured by your fellow trekkers. Altitude sickness does kill. If you are having any serious effects before a high pass, it might require another intermediate night or at worst an immediate return downhill.

Staying healthy

Minor effects of altitude above 4000m are felt by most – maybe slight nausea and extreme lethargy – but symptoms will improve on the descent. Continuing to ascend with any persistent symptoms can lead to the serious risk of Pulmonary and Cerebral Oedema or even death. Deaths occur each year in the Himalaya and Nepal, despite all the warnings. Complications from altitude sickness can strike very quickly.

Glacier Lassitude

Even today some aspects of mountain sickness continue to pose puzzles for the medical profession, climbers and trekkers. In 1899 Freshfield's party around Kanchenjunga still thought it was a sort of glacier lassitude, caused perhaps by the atmospheric conditions surrounding high altitude icefields and glaciers.

Freshfield does, though, try to consider some alternatives as he writes:

'The Gurkha seemed, as I watched him through field-glasses, almost to run up the last slope, a remarkable performance at over 20,000feet, and a fact which should be taken into account by theorisers on mountain sickness, who like most theorisers are very often slow to recognise facts which do not fit in with their preconceived theories.'

As an aid before the trek, some start a course of Diamox (Acetazolamide), a diuretic which thins the blood, making you urinate more – which is generally considered good at altitude. It can have the disturbing side effect of pins and needles in the fingers. Another option is to try homeopathic coca, a version of the substance used by natives of Peru and Bolivia. Coca is available as homeopathic tablets that some trekkers (including the authors) swear by.

Others swear by ginkgo biloba tablets, which appear to work for unfathomable reasons. It is suggested that these can be taken twice a day for five days before arrival and one tablet a day during the trek. However, there are some side effects when taken with some prescription drugs and other substances so check with your GP.

Gamow bag and oxygen cylinders

A Gamow bag is a large bag used to temporarily relieve the effects of high altitude. An ill person with serious altitude problems can be cocooned under higher air pressure for a limited period to mimic a lower altitude. Oxygen cylinders are quite common in the Everest region but not so prolific elsewhere.

It's better to proceed slowly in terms of the altitude to avoid problems before they develop.

Mountain safety

> Man has pondered the transience of existence since he became man, yet such reflections recur in high and lonely places.
> ***Stones of Silence*, George Schaller**

It's not just the altitude that visitors need to watch out for; all mountain areas present hazards. In Nepal, apart from the high altitude, severe cold and bitter winds are another menace to guard against. Just after sun up, be sure to keep well wrapped up and during any day always carry enough warm clothing.

In the deep gorges the sunlight disappears early in the afternoon (sometimes as early as 2.30pm) and temperatures plummet. Breathing through a scarf at high altitudes can help to retain fluids and will help protect against dust and icy winds. The high passes can sometimes be notorious for deathly cold winds.

Unnoticed dehydration is easily overlooked; you may not necessarily feel like drinking – remember that tea and coffee are both diuretics, so keep vital fluids up. Electrolyte powders can be added to clean water if lethargy arises (apart from when going up steep trails, when a little tiredness can easily be explained!). Noting the colour of your urine is one good way to be aware of dehydration. If it's very yellow, you are not drinking enough. Always concentrate and take care on the trails – the nearest hospital is just a distant dream. At high altitudes you may not be thinking as clearly as normal. Leaping carelessly about is an easy way to fall foul of snags.

Remember too that evacuation by helicopter is not guaranteed: you might be too high, there could be bad weather or there might easily be no serviceable helicopter in Pokhara or Kathmandu. Porters with cut-out baskets on their backs and ponies do occasionally carry out visitors in an emergency. To avoid this rollercoaster ride, it's best to try not to fall over!

As mentioned, unruly dogs in Nepal are a less obvious menace. Normally these dogs are docile and easily controlled. However, during a night-time visit to the toilet, watch out! Ideally, plan on not going out at night at all, but improvise some sort of suitable receptacle. Find a large-necked plastic container and make sure the lid seal is good! Of course there is no need to be put off by all the above advice; just take care and enjoy the trip!

Weather

No man or woman yet has tamed the weather although forecasts are pretty accurate these days for the coming week or so. Today there are some high-tech sages who can predict, with surprising accuracy, the weather patterns to come. Perhaps the gods will be on your side, but as a road visitor it's not normally of so much consequence, unless there is a landslide due to unexpected or excess rain. Motorcyclists and cyclists will need to be prepared for frequent cold spells in Upper Mustang at any time of year.

Security

Once upon a time, as the fairytale goes, there was virtually no crime in Nepal, but those days have long gone. However, it is still an amazingly safe country for foreigners to visit. It is unlikely that anyone will encounter any danger in Kathmandu, even well into the night (though night owls might want to avoid grungy dogs in the early hours). Isolated incidents and attacks have occurred in the hills, and tent theft has increased. Take the usual precautions that you would observe almost anywhere these days.

Narsing canyon

Kathmandu – gateway to the Himalaya

Kathmandu (1317m) is the normal gateway to all parts of the Nepal Himalaya. Trekkers should spend a few days exploring the magical parts of the city. It's a friendly, welcoming place, despite some obvious distractions. The longer you stay, the more of a home away from home it becomes. There is a wide range of excellent hotels and guesthouses to suit all tastes and an astonishing array of eateries and restaurants. Despite the obvious modernisation, the city and the whole valley still have some enchanting places to discover.

The Kathmandu Valley probably has the greatest concentration of temples, shrines, monasteries and idols of anywhere across the globe. Kathmandu is the trading crossroads of the Himalaya between India and China, through Tibet. The city is a great melting pot of migrating peoples. The religious mix of Hinduism, Buddhism, Tantra, Vajrayana, Tibetan Buddhism, Bon and Shamanism is intoxicating. Legends, folktales and myths influence every Nepalese ritual and festival, as well as everyday actions. Idols once outnumbered people, but that is not quite the case today, although they do still outnumber tourists.

Kathmandu Durbar Square

No visit to Nepal would be complete without a thorough exploration of the **Durbar (palace) squares** of the three great cities, Kathmandu, Patan and Bhaktapur. In Kathmandu, be sure to investigate the Jochen Tole alley also known as **Freak Street**. It's still there, bearing a faded resemblance to its glorious past. Those 'idle' hippies were the eccentric pioneers of Nepal's tourist industry. The bustling byways of **Asan**, Kathmandu's old market streets, are a kaleidoscope of colour and confusion. Brass pots, fabrics, metal and woodwork crafts and everyday items almost block the narrow lanes.

In Asan is **Jan Bahal**, a fairyland of glittering temples and devotional artwork. The enigmatic Seto (White) Machhendranath idol with the strangest mesmerising eyes resides here, surrounded by goldleaf. **Itum Bahal** is a typical Newari courtyard housing complex, hidden in a maze of dark mysterious alleyways close to Durbar Square; finding it is quite a mystery as well. **Sano (Little) Swayambhunath** and the temple of **Nara Devi** lie north of Durbar Square.

Kathmandu

To the south, down a small street from the Kasthamandap temple, are a number of tiered temples, like **Jaisi Dewal** and other shrines or stupas set in quiet courtyards – bahals.

A day in Kathmandu

As a misty dawn stirs over the valley's stupas and temples, the dog patrols fall silent. A chaotic cacophony erupts; pedestrians lose the battle with bicycles, cycle rickshaws, motorbikes, taxis and minibuses in the vibrant, colourful streets and alleys. Yet in quiet corners, little has changed; a few holy cows linger beside a grotesque, gargantuan gargoyle or a serene, stony-faced idol. Hidden in the intricate maze of the old cities, potters spin their wheels by hand; antique sewing machines spin their cotton threads. Buddhists spin their prayer wheels. The rumour mill is in full swing; Bob Dylan or Cat Stevens are in the low-roofed, dingy café around the corner. People offer devotions to the golden Ganesh idol near the old 'pie and pig' alley of the 1970s, behind the Kasthamandap temple. Trekkers scurry about trying to find the current location of the immigration department. Others seek out the cheapest sewing shop, getting a T-shirt embroidered with their latest trekking route, or 'Yak Yak Yak'! And the dog patrols lie dormant, gaining strength for another night of barking...

Patan Durbar Square

Patan is a city of artisans and quaint, quiet lanes. The Durbar Square here is perhaps the most exotic of the three such squares of the valley and the number of impressive temples and palaces merely adds to this dimension. Deep in the old quarter are the **Kwa Bahal** (Golden Temple) and the temple of Rato (Red) Machhendranath, plus many other exquisite temples and shrines.

Bhaktapur, 11km east of Kathmandu, is the least modernised city of the valley, although a new multi-lane highway makes the journey there less of a Himalayan expedition today. Its **Durbar Square** is intriguing, with some impressive restoration after various earthquakes destroyed the once vast complex.

Be sure not to miss the other squares: **Nyatapola Square** displays a five-tiered temple and topsy-turvy temple cafe. **Dattatreya Square**, some distance to the east, magnificently illustrates the fabulous artistry and skill of the Malla-era builders. The whole scene is of overwhelming grandeur, with intricately carved wooden windows and fine brick structures. In the quiet mediaeval streets of Bhaktapur, time stands still – it's a living relic of a forgotten era.

On a hill to the west of Kathmandu is **Swayambhunath** (the Monkey Temple), a picturesque Buddhist stupa surrounded by shrines and temples. It's quite a climb up, but the views are stunning – it's a good workout for the trek to come. The great stupa of **Boudhanath**, with its all-seeing eyes and peaceful atmosphere, is east of Kathmandu. Pilgrims, monks, Tibetans and tourists circle the base in a clockwise direction, turning the prayer wheels, breathing the sweet aroma of juniper incense and enjoying the relaxing atmosphere.

Bhaktapur Durbar Square

Close to Boudhanath is the great Hindu temple complex of **Pashupatinath** beside the holy Bagmati River. Non-Hindu foreigners cannot enter the main shrine, where stands the great golden bull of Nandi – Shiva's vehicle. Across the river in a forested monkey-infested area, sadhus congregate and show a few surprising tricks. Along the riverbanks is a more sobering sight, where Hindus are cremated before passage into the next life.

'*There's a green-eyed yellow idol to the north of Kathmandu*' (so says the famous poem), but today only an image of Vishnu covered in snakes and reclining in a pool can be found – at **Budhanilkanta**.

Further afield in the valley to the south of Patan are **Bungamati** (with a quaint square hosting the Red Machhendranath temple) and **Kokhana** (with old brick houses and the Shekali Mai temple). Southwest of Patan are **Pharping** (Buddhist monasteries and Guru Rinpoche cave), **Shesh Narayan** (a temple devoted to Vishnu) and **Dakshinkali** (where pilgrims offer live sacrifices to the bloodthirsty goddess Kali).

If you have plenty of time, seek out other enchanting places: **Changu Narayan, Kirtipur, Vajra Yogini** near Sankhu, the boar-headed Vajra Varahi temple garden of **Chapagaon**, quirky Bishankhu Narayan and the mountain viewpoints of **Nagarkot** and **Kakani**. A few kilometres to the east along the road to Tibet are **Dhulikhel**, **Panauti** and **Banepa**, with some little-visited temples and shrines.

Accommodation

Changes will continue to occur following Covid; some hotels and restaurants may not reopen. The main Kathmandu tourist enclave for hotels and restaurants is Thamel. However, the fast-regenerating Freak Street should not be disregarded, with much lower prices. The excellent Hotel Moonlight is in Paknajol near Thamel. The famous Kathmandu Guest House, originally the backpackers' favourite, was damaged during the earthquakes and has now been remodelled as a more upmarket establishment. Other hotel options include Metropolitan Kantipur, Acme, Newa Home, Garden Home, Northfield, Marshyangdi, Manang, Avataar, Potala Guest House, Utse and Vaisali.

For a taste of Tibet, try the Hotel Tibet in Lazimpat; nearby is the Ambassador. For similar luxury, lodge at the Nepali Ghar or the Malla. The Hotel Shankar (a former Rana palace) and the palatial Yak and Yeti hotel suit more well-heeled guests. En route to Swayambhunath is the traditional-style Hotel Vajra. Around Boudhanath there are many hotels to suit all budgets. The heritage-style boutique hotel of Dwarika's is near the airport and restored Ram Mandir temple. In Patan, the Hotel Heranya La:Ku and Temple House are located close to Durbar Square, and in Bhaktapur is the Hotel Layaku Durbar, also close to Durbar Square.

Eating out

For returning trekkers, Kathmandu and Pokhara are a paradise of over-indulgence. Choose your food very carefully before your trek – there is nothing worse than bumping along Nepal's 'main roads' with an upset stomach, except lurching along a 'side road' with an urgent need! Even in the better restaurants, avoid salads and unpeeled fruit as a precaution. The following are a few of the popular eating places in Kathmandu (in no particular order; exclusion does not imply any criticism): Northfield Café, La Bella Café, Avocado Café, Hotel Marshyangdi, KC's, Rum Doodle, Yin Yang and Third Eye, Dechenling Garden, Kathmandu Guest House, Pumpernickel, Black Olives, New Orleans, Nargila's, Gaia, OR2K, Himalayan Java Café, Roadhouse Café, Delima Garden, Electric Pagoda, Utse, Fire and Ice, and Utpala in Boudha. A reasonable meal will cost from Rs600–Rs1200 per person for a main dish, pizza, steak, curry... Popular watering holes are Sam's, Tom & Jerry and various Irish Pubs.

Tourist office

This office is located in Bhrikuti Mandap, near Ratna Park bus station. National Park/Conservation Area permits and TIMS are issued here.

Pokhara – after the trek

Pokhara (900m) has boomed over the years into a sprawling but still pleasant town. It was once a sleepy village surrounded by rice fields and dense jungle. Lakeside is the main tourist area, where hotels, restaurants and shops are found. There are not many historic sites in Pokhara, but it does have an old bazaar street and the Pokhara Mountain Museum.

High above the placid Phewa Lake are the Peace Pagoda and Shiva Temple. Tibetan refugee camps are located around the town and to the southeast is the narrow ravine of Devi's Falls.

Of course it's easy just to eat, sleep and muck about in a boat on the lake after a hard trek. Sarangkot, now accessible by the Annapurna Cable Car, is a spectacular vantage point to watch the sunrise or sunset on the Annapurna ranges. Sarangkot is also the place for paragliding and ziplining.

Accommodation

Pokhara has hotels and guest houses to suit all budgets. The expensive Fishtail Lodge is a good place for afternoon tea on the lawn. In Lakeside is the beautifully designed Heritage Hotel and Suites, along with many old favourites such as the cosy Peace Eye Guest House, Three Jewels Hotel, Hotel Elegant, New Tourist Guest House, Snowlands (once a thatched farmhouse), Hungry Eye, Rising Moon Guest House and many more. For a quiet retreat overlooking Lakeside, stay at the Bar Peepal Resort.

Further along the lake, try the Waterfront Hotel; on the Sarangkot ridge are Himalaya Front, Bhanjyang Village, Pristine Himalaya and many others.

Eating out
Pokhara Lakeside has places to satisfy every cuisine and taste of returning trekkers, tourists and idle, ageing hippies. There are some great new places, too many to name. The long-established Punjabi Restaurant is popular with Indian food lovers, including ourselves! Boomerang, Moondance, Maya, OR2K, Roadhouse and the Harbour are a few other popular haunts.

Tourist office
This office is located in the Damside area of Pokhara. Permits and TIMS are normally issued here.

Other places of interest

Those with more time often visit the following places after a trek. In the west, Nepalganj is not really a cultural highlight, but there is a certain atmosphere to be enjoyed!

Bandipur
Up in the hills just south of the road from Kathmandu to Pokhara is the small traditional hilltop village of Bandipur. With great mountain views, fresh air and many beautifully restored old buildings and temples, this historic village is fast becoming a popular getaway and stopover. Try staying at the **Old Inn;** www.rural-heritage.com. Just north of Bandipur along the Besisahar road is the **Riepe village** complex near Chowk Chisapani; www.annapurnahomestay.com

Bandipur high street and the Old Inn

Gorkha

Gorkha has a reasonable selection of hotels, so it's worth stopping overnight here to visit the famed Durbar Palace. Gorkha has rapidly expanded from a two-horse country bazaar into a sizeable town with hotels, guesthouses, bus syndicate wheeler-dealers and wily horse-traders. The views of Himalchuli from above town are stunning.

Gorkha Palace and the Annapurna peaks

Bhimkhori (Kavre district)

East of Kathmandu is the Bhimkhori area, where the hilltop village of Manegaun offers a warm welcome and a genuine rural experience. Overlooking the hills above a tributary of the Sun Kosi, it is 40km southeast of Dhulikhel off the BP Highway. Call Binay 9841797526; www.sacredhimalaya.com

Temal (Timal)

Temal is historic for the Tamang people and hosts many hilltop Buddhist and Hindu shrines, as well as a celebrated cave used by Guru Rinpoche. It's accessed from Bakunde Besi, on the same main road as Bhimkori. There is one hotel – the Temal **Shangri-La**. Call Rajan on 9886586022; www.temal-hotel-shangri-la.jimdosite.com

Nuwakot

This ancient settlement sits almost pristinely on the ridge top, just 8km off the road to Langtang. Its ancient palace has been a fortified stronghold for centuries. Being in command of the important trading crossroads of the Trisuli Valley, it exacted tolls and duties on goods flowing between India and Tibet. Stay at the delightful **Famous Farm** for a touch of class at good rates; www.rural-heritage.com

Other places of interest

Nuwakot Durbar

Chitwan National Park
The most popular and easily accessed national park, Chitwan is located south of the Kathmandu–Pokhara road not far from Narayanghat. Rhinos, sloth bear, deer, a variety of birds and gharals are most frequently sighted. Elephants are no longer used for safaris. Jeep safaris, jungle walks and canoe rides are available.

Rhinos are seen in Chitwan often

Using this guide on the routes

The following route descriptions indicate approximate distances, timings and altitudes. Maps of the routes sometimes show different figures for altitudes. The days described mostly correlate to day-to-day itineraries, but not at every stage. The itineraries shown in the appendix summary section reflect the possible routes and durations.

With time and energy, it's perfectly possible to combine the routes described. The times shown are an attempt to give the average time for the drive or ride, with extra time added to cover a few photo stops and pausing for those quick visits into the sparse vegetation.

Remember a trip in the Himalaya should be an enriching experience, while also a holiday. We have not attempted to list all the lodges along all the trails! There is often little to choose between them – it is usually determined by where you happen to be by late afternoon and which place catches your attention.

This guide is not intended to reflect every twist and turn on the route, but to give the overall flow and interest of the day. Some junctions change, landslides intervene, bridges are improved, moved or even destroyed, and routes are redirected.

New 'roads'

As a rule, the effect of a new road in Nepal is rather negative, with the creation of noise, pollution, dust clouds and chaos for pedestrians. Inevitably the destruction of the once-pristine environment is noticed quickly. Most of the 'new roads' are little more than farm tracks, meaning rough rides, dust or mud, delays due to avalanches, floods and bridge washouts. The journey time is never set in stone. Bear this in mind when planning your itinerary.

Trekkers who visited Nepal some time ago lament the coming of roads, but from a Nepalese point of view this is progress. There is no more humping of heavy loads along narrow, exposed trails or crossing precarious log bridges, not to mention the leeches. Generally local people are in favour of new roads, since they significantly reduce food and commodity prices, and enable easier access to medical treatment. The main downside of the new country roads is that some people who earned money from passing trekkers have perhaps lost their most valued asset… but the trekker today has to take the treks as they are now.

And the roads now bring a new market to countryside tourism: jeep tourists who are not inclined to trek, or who can no longer trek as easily as they could. Motorcyclists and mountain bikers are also taking to the roads in greater numbers, exploring the hills in ways that were just not possible before.

Using this guide

Nepal is there to change you, and not for you to change it. Experience so far suggests that very few hikers are put off by the quiet, almost traffic-free, jeep roads close to trails – just look at the Annapurnas, where the number of trekkers has increased. You would hardly think there is any need to define a road in so many ways, but in Nepal nothing ever quite conforms to the norms.

Sealed road: A tarmac highway – but expect potholes and even broken-up sections.
Jeep track: Any side road used by jeeps and tractors.

Of course roads will change – sometimes surprisingly fast!

Spies on the roof of the world

Today GPS and satellites can give us an accurate altitude for any given point but 150 years ago there was another way. Water boils at a lower temperature at higher altitude and this may be noticed by trekkers. What is less commonly known is that the measurement of that boiling point can actually be used to determine the altitude with surprising accuracy. When the British colonial administration in India felt threatened by the Russians and Chinese during the 'Great Game' in the 19th century, they sent spies into Tibet to discover the geography of that great blank on the map. These spies, known as the pandits, were Indians, who could easily travel in disguise as pilgrims, measuring miles with rosary beads and altitudes with thermometers. The most famous pandit was Sarat Chandra Das, a Bengali and Tibetan scholar, whose exploits are recorded in his book A Journey to Lhasa and Central Tibet. He measured the boiling point of the water at Kambachen (Kanchenjunga region) as 187°F, calculating the height as 13,600ft (4145m). Today we have all manner of dubious listening devices, so little has changed!

Pre-trek checklist

Don't trek alone: hire a guide.
Don't set off without your national park, conservation area and restricted area permit(s).
Register your journey with your embassy (if trekking independently).
Have adequate insurance for yourself and your staff.
Carry a photocopy of your passport/visa details page.
Carry a first aid kit and medications.
Be forewarned about the dangers of altitude and act accordingly.
Treat porters properly.
Register with the checkposts.
Respect the culture, the environment and local sensibilities.
Dress appropriately. Watch your step!

Enjoy your trip!

THE ROUTES

Not all those who wander are lost.
***Lord of the Rings,* J R R Tolkien**

MUSTANG EXPLORER

Introduction

Mustang is still a magical and mysterious destination, despite the encroachments of the modern era. The vast majority of the wild, rugged kingdom north of the Annapurnas still hides quaint, picturesque villages, exotically located monasteries, historic treasures and a rich cultural heritage This one tantalising region – Upper Mustang – remained firmly shut long after Nepal opened its borders to outsiders. Apart from some privileged anthropologists, few other visitors were permitted until 1992; we were lucky to count ourselves among the first 200 trekkers in the region.

Planning

Most trekkers now approach the area by plane on a fully supported lodge group trek. Increasingly, smaller parties are discovering the Mustang region as well. Some on lower budgets use the road transport between Pokhara and Jomsom/Kagbeni at least one way. It's a lot cheaper, but with the high permit costs, it may not be of relevance to most visitors.

If time is not an issue, it makes some sense to hire a vehicle from Kathmandu to Lo Manthang for two weeks or so, to have the most flexibility once in Upper Mustang. This is a good option in high season, when vehicles hired in Jomsom or even Lo Manthang are at a premium.

A number of good lodges have sprouted up along the main valley trail and a few on some significant side tracks. With ever-better lodging facilities along the main Mustang trail, hardly anyone camps. Only those seeking to proceed east of Lo Manthang (for some distance from the Mustang Khola River) need to carry tents and take camping crews, either locally or more commonly from Kathmandu.

Normally the basic Mustang route can be done in two weeks, which allows a day or two for rest or side trips and acclimatisation. This includes time getting to Kagbeni and out again. Having a 10-day permit for Upper Mustang does not really lend itself to a leisurely trip with so many places of interest to explore. Side trips are mentioned in the appropriate sections, but most are from Lo Manthang.

Everyone should plan to take time acclimatising before entering Upper Mustang to get the maximum enjoyment from the trip. That means spending a few days in the Lower Mustang areas above

Kalopani (2650m) adjusting to the altitude. Visits to Tukuche, Marpha, Kagbeni, Jomsom, Jharkot and Muktinath provide excuses to delay the height gains and climb up into Upper Mustang.

The first big hill in Upper Mustang is located above Chele, after Chuksang. At this stage some could find the altitude effects quite noticeable. Sleeping in Samar, just after the climb, usually sorts out any lingering altitude gremlins by the next day. Those who are well acclimatised could continue to Syangmochen, but beware the telltale signs of altitude even so. Don't leave Samar unless confident of being well in tune with the height gain already.

The biggest headache, apart from the altitude en route, is getting to Jomsom or taking that long road approach along highways that are occasionally prone to blockages or slow-going. Allow time in Pokhara or Kathmandu at the end for potential flight and road delays to and from Jomsom.

The optimum period to visit Mustang is early autumn, when the skies are clear, the monsoon rains have abated and the harvest is in full swing. One possible drawback is that flights to Jomsom can still be disrupted by bad weather, entailing delays and cancellations. After late November, it gets too cold for most; most lodges close and many residents migrate south for the winter. Late spring is attractive – the higher altitudes offer pleasant trekking, generally clear views and cool temperatures – although winds can be a negative factor. The monsoon is often cited as the main season to visit, due to the rain shadow effect of the Himalaya, but cloud is likely. Flights and roads to Jomsom from rain- and cloud-engulfed Pokhara are severely disrupted. Avoid the monsoon unless festivals are the main attraction.

In general, along the main routes the lodge food is sustaining and plentiful. That is, unless you visit after mid-November, when even the supply of eggs could run out. In this book we do not have a Mars or Snickers Price Index, since there were none left for sale anywhere in Upper Mustang by late November!

Although the region is less remote in places than before, it is currently necessary to visit here with a guide (and driver of course). Finally, don't underestimate the level of fitness required for the trip. Little of the region is flat and, even for non-trekkers, there are some steep ascents and descents to negotiate when visiting caves or monasteries. The nature of the terrain also adds to the effort needed where paths are eroded, damaged by landslides or just plain tricky.

Itinerary and routes
Road development has brought massive change to Upper Mustang. Although it is no longer the remote Shangri-La of the past, the region remains as enticing as it was when it first opened to visitors in 1992.

From Kagbeni, the 'improved' and widened dirt track has finally reached fabled Lo Manthang, from where a restricted Chinese-built road crosses the Kora La (4660m) at the northern border. A number of side tracks also head to main settlements adjacent to the main valley, as well as to Yara, Luri, Tange and even Old Samdzong.

Generally the altitude gains and the distances between villages or lodges determine the itinerary and night stops for lodge visitors. Most villages along the main trail now have lodges of varying standards. Between Chele and Ghami, altitude (3000–4000m) becomes a factor in deciding the night stops, particularly in the early stages of the tour. However, once acclimatised, the main route is relatively moderate in terms of ups and downs. Planning is exciting, since so many wheeled transport options have become a reality.

Most do the standard itinerary, Kagbeni to Chuksang, Chele and Samar, but from here there is quite a lot of choice, mostly depending on how many days you chose to pay for in the first place (especially not knowing the terrain, and how well or how quickly you will acclimatise.) After Samar it depends on your acclimatisation and timeframe whether you choose to stay in Syangmochen, Geling or Ghami before Tsarang. After Tsarang there is only Lo Manthang (3810m) left to reach.

The main choice of routes is to be found from Ghami: either via Drakmar or Tsarang. Having wheels means it's possible to visit Drakmar easily, inbound or outbound. Most choose the main route to Tsarang on the inbound route to Lo Manthang, unless planning to visit Yara and Luri. Ideally no one should miss Ghar Gompa (Lo Gekar) if the road is open.

Once in Lo Manthang, there are quite a few options for side trips, 4–5 days could easily be spent around the sights here and beyond. These are described in the Lo Manthang section, including some options further east.

The astonishing eastern trail (only for trekkers) from Tange to Tetang is highly recommended, but road access is not possible here. Getting to Tange, though, is an intermittent, recent option via the Dechyang Valley route south of Yara and accessed from Tsarang. Do check before planning this, as it's quite a formidable drive with few jeep owners likely to be very keen.

The basic trip can be done in 14–16 days, with 10 days (9 nights) within the permit area. Using a private jeep, 9 nights is enough, unless more remote areas are contemplated. Travellers on public transport will need more time, but it is perfectly possible for those seeking a more intimate trip with local interaction!

The following stages are described in short sections that can be linked together to provide as many options as required.

It is possible to drive from Jomsom to Lo Manthang in one day. Levels of acclimatisation could modify some days. Allow a day for flight delays between Pokhara and Jomsom on the return, or take a jeep or bus out. A comprehensive summary of routes and itinerary options for the trek is given in the appendix.

Mustang Explorer Summary	
Start	**Jomsom** (2720m)
Finish	**Jomsom** (2720m)
Distance	approx. 200–220km (125–140 miles)
Time	14–16 days
Maximum altitude	**Chogo La** (4280m/14,040ft)
Trip style	Lodges
Transport	Flight, bus, jeep, private jeep

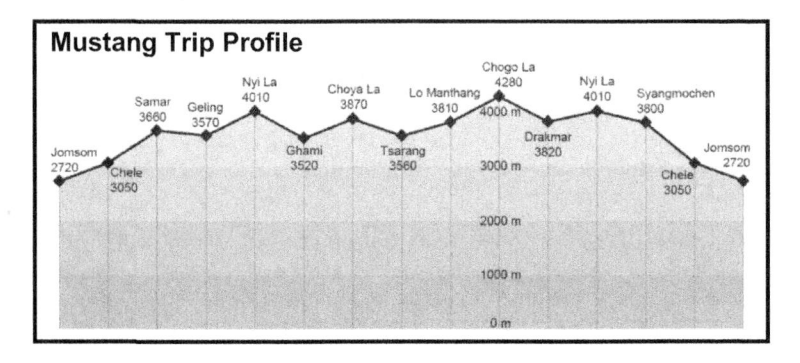

Mustang Trip Profile

Kathmandu – Pokhara (25mins flight)
Kathmandu – Pokhara

For most visitors, taking the road approach both ways to the region is really too time-consuming and too uncomfortable for the trip to be called a 'holiday'. The flight from Kathmandu to Pokhara takes less than half an hour, once it's airborne. The views are sensational en route, passing Ganesh Himal, Himalchuli, Manaslu and the Annapurna peaks to the north.

Kathmandu – Pokhara (7–9hrs drive)
Kathmandu – Mugling – Pokhara

Taking private transport makes some sense for those who want to experience the low country of Nepal, but it won't save any rupees. A selection of good tourist-class buses run between Kathmandu and Pokhara, but avoid the flying microbuses, a dangerous option. Taking a private jeep will be more costly all the way from Kathmandu to Pokhara (and on to Jomsom and Lo Manthang) but does allow an amazing degree of flexibility and comfort to admire the views.

Currently delays are common between Kathmandu and Pokhara due to ongoing road widening. It used to take 6–7hrs, but now it's more likely to be 8–10hrs. A narrow new road between Swayambhunath and just below Naubise cuts about an hour off the time by the main, busy, congested Thankot road.

Pokhara – Jomsom (20mins flight)
Pokhara – Jomsom

There's no greater adrenalin rush than taking the early morning flight from Pokhara to Jomsom: an early 'high' for the trek already!

In fact it's all over very quickly, this mountain-dodging flight through the Himalaya to the stunningly located airstrip of Jomsom. As the aircraft edges between Annapurna and Dhaulagiri, high above the Kali Gandaki gorge, the views are sensational.

Once on the ground in the more rarefied atmosphere of Jomsom, most trekkers need more than a few minutes to catch their breath. It's essential to have a long brunch break in Jomsom, with plenty of tea or suitable fluids before proceeding to Kagbeni.

Pokhara – Kalopani or Jomsom (1 day bus)
Pokhara – Kalopani – Jomsom

Although it's perfectly possible to make it all the way to from Pokhara to Jomsom by local direct bus, it's a long, hot, sweaty adventure, taking 8–10hrs or so. As the road continues to improve, the journey times are falling. Some choose to go by taxi or private car to Beni, stay the night and then continue on the bus to Jomsom. A private jeep on this sector might cost from Rs10,000.

By private jeep it takes around 1hr from Pokhara to **Kusma** via Nayapul. The route heads around to the north, crossing the Kali Gandaki in about 20mins. After the bridge the current route climbs up to **Baglung** a further 30mins.

The main valley road has suffered devasting landslides; it now awaits tarmac and is only used by local village buses. In all it might take 2hrs to **Beni** on this west road over the hump. In Beni is the notable Hotel Yeti.

The route continues passing the Hotel Yak and in 10–15mins reaches **Galeshwar**. A couple of hotels are found here, Paradise and Hotel Taj. After town is the pleasant Kali Gandaki Resort.

The road is a mix of sealed and dirt and quite fast to the junction of the Kali Gandaki valley and the way to Ghorepani. The original Hanuman Temple has been washed away but a new simpler one has been built on the east side, still with an image of the monkey god.

Mustang Explorer

Tatopani is around 2–2½hrs from Pokhara. Apart from the new Hotel Natural Spring, look for the Hotel Annapurna, Old Kamala, Hill Top and others. The road bypasses old **Dana** and in 25mins reaches the viewing area of the **Rukse Chhara** waterfall, where locals gather for pictures and selfies. Then it's on up through **Ghasa**, which has remained mainly intact as before, to **Lete** and **Kalopani**.

Kalopani is a good place to stop for the night, with its stunning and rare views of Annapurna I, especially at sunset. To the west soaring high above are Dhaulagiri, its ice fall and Tukuche Peak. Top of the range here is the long established but modernised Kalopani Guest House – rooms from Rs3000 (US$25). Top rooms $140, $90, all with 25% discount in winter and during the monsoon. Heated dining and electric blankets all round – a super place, especially after a rugged trek. Adjacent is Pine Forest Lodge. Other hotels include The Black Horse (Rs2000), Four Peaks, See You Lodge, Natural Inn, Angel Lodge. Menu food everywhere is around Rs400–500 main, Thakali dishes Rs400–600 and full breakfast Rs550–650.

Those continuing to Jomsom head on around **Larjung** and **Kobang** to **Tukuche**, which retains its charming old main street complete with the stylish and traditional Tukuche Lodge / Guest House. Along beside the open flats of the Kali Gandaki and up around the bend is Marpha, again with its traditional main street, charming houses, lodges and shops. **Marpha** is another good place to overnight; try Tampopo Guest House. Finally the road climbs a little to **Jomsom**, a rapidly growing town of new hotels, shops, ticket offices and the enlarged monastery on the north side of the settlement. Some hotels and lodges are Om Home, Mustang Taj, Nilgiri, Marco Polo, Majesty, Snowy Desert, Xanadu Home and a number of others along the main street north. It's Rs1300 bus to Pokhara and Rs3600 by jeep to Lo Manthang.

Jomsom – Kagbeni (20–30mins)
Jomsom – Eklobhatti – Kagbeni

Fortunately most visitors do not suffer any ill-effects adjusting to the sudden altitude gain experienced on landing at Jomsom. For most heading to Upper Mustang, a long brew of tea with apple pie is in order to get adjusted to the height gain. Many visitors now drive between Jomsom and Kagbeni, taking 15–20 mins by local jeep.

As you leave Jomsom there is a new and imposing monastery. The road keeps to the east side of the wide stony riverbed climbing up above the banks.

Watch out for the first Rigsum Gonpo of Mustang, where three small grey, red and white chortens and a tiny gompa appear on the bank below.

Soon after this on the right is a valley that leads to **Lubra**, a mysterious Bon settlement which is a highlight to be taken in such is the rarity of Bon culture. A dirt road leads off to the right (east) to access the village and monastery above. See Lower Mustang page 227.

The new dirt road to Chharka is on the left soon, marked by a road sign for Dolpo – how fast things change! The road climbs gently on above the settlement of **Eklobhatti** (2740m). Soon one route descends to the riverbed and circles around beside the river into lower **Kagbeni** (2800m).

There is a good variety of lodgings, including the Paradise Lodge and Asia. Above town 10mins up path or road Dragon Hotel (Rs Rs2000), Happy Hour Lodge and Aabha Hotel. The cost of food in Kagbeni seems to be higher than almost anywhere else in Upper Mustang. For quirkiness check out the YacDonalds café (rooms Rs2500). Kagbeni, like many villages in Upper Mustang, has low tunnel alleyways that give protection from the wind. Despite the initial injection of concrete buildings seen on arrival, the old Kagbeni can still be discovered behind this modern façade.

Kagbeni monastery
The large, red-coloured monastery was founded by Tenpe Gyaltsen in 1429. It now has a couple of additional building that are used for housing monks and visitors. The monastery is known as Tubten Samphel Ling. Images include the earthly Sakyamuni Buddha, a four-armed Chenresig and a white Tara. Also present are the Four Harmonious Friends, some wise arhats and an image of the Sakyapa lama Tubten Samphel Ling.

The female Kheni guardian of Kagbeni & typical back alleys

Exploring old Kagbeni

Until a devastating flood recently, this classic Mustang-style village had typical mysterious alleys and tunnels that led deeper into a maze of mediaeval courtyards. All is not lost, although first appearances are hardly enticing. Behind the new hotels on the riverside lies the original mud settlement. At the entry, a female Kheni introduces visitors to the old city. Going clockwise, the enlarged monastery is next and then it's into the old square and around to the male Kheni on the north side. Continuing around is the Annapurna Lodge, an old time favourite, and then along the street is the Red House Eco Lodge and museum. Non-residents are charged Rs100 for entry. A large chorten is found on the southside of town near the Asia Hotel and Paradise Lodge, with paintings including Chenresig, the Medicine Buddha and Guru Rinpoche up inside the low entrance.

Stage 1 Map: Jomsom to Chele

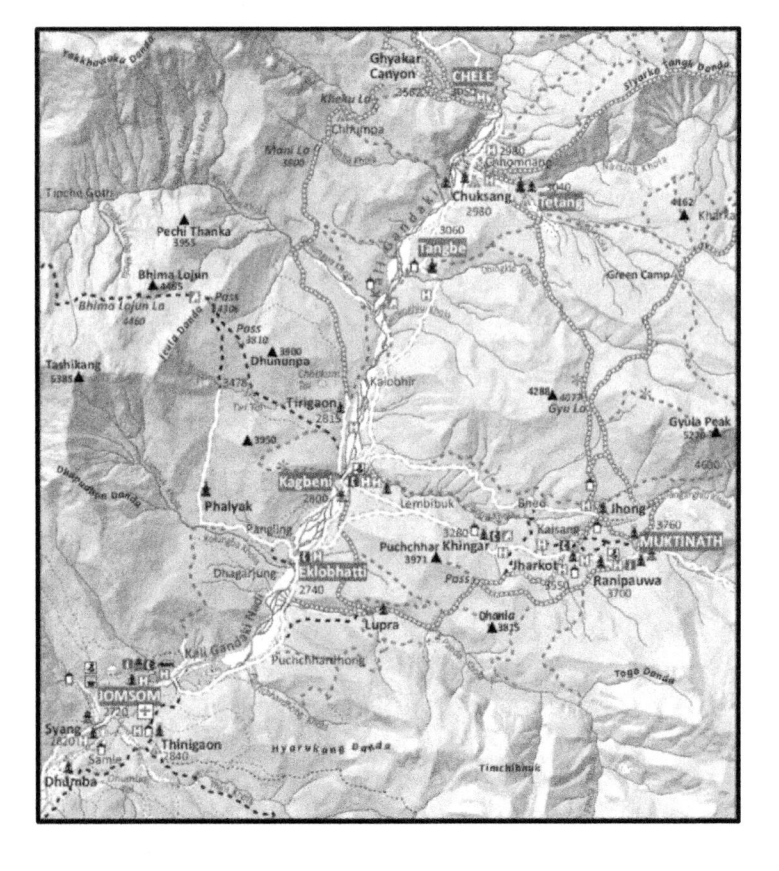

> **The Khenis of Kagbeni**
> Guarding the north and south entrances to the old part of Kagbeni are the Kheni images. Originally there were no buildings outside the old city walled area. The northern one is the male image and the southern one the female version. These two strange-looking images ward off the evil spirits and more correctly are the 'ghost eaters'. The origins of these weird images lie with the pre-Buddhist Bon people. The northern gate is also protected by a shrine where ghosts are afraid to proceed. Other safeguards are the tiny doorways that protect against taller 'zombies'.
>
> These days, as superstitious beliefs have been overwhelmed by texts and Facebook, most of the houses and lodges have spread way beyond the old walls.

> **Rigsum Gonpo**
> These three small chortens appear at the entry and exit of almost all the villages of Upper Mustang. Usually coloured in white, red and grey, they represent Chenresig (Avalokiteshvara) in white, Jampelyang (Manjushri) in red and Channa Dorje (Vajrapani) in grey or sometimes a greenish grey. Through their presence, the village is protected from bad spirits found in the sky, earth and underworld.

Acclimatisation day: Kagbeni or Khingar

Those planning to take a jeep to Lo Manthang need to consider a day off around Kagbeni or higher up in **Khingar**. There are four lodges here (for pilgrims and visitors to Muktinath, suffering from the altitude perhaps) – Hotel Nirvana, Tri Ratna, Blue Sheep Guest House and Hotel Green Hill. It's worth going on up to Muktinath for those with wheels on this day off. The new sealed road climbs steeply passing the new **Selfie Park**. It's a 10mins drive to Khingar and about 20mins to **Jharkot**. When visiting Muktinath at this stage, be careful of the altitude – it's around 3760m.

Old Jharkot village

Old Jharkot is a great place to explore starting from the west side. A new hotel is almost open on this side plus the Himali Hotel nearby. Jharkot is a typical Mustang village with great atmospheric alleys and flat roofed white houses. The monastery is probably closed but the courtyard is normally accessible. There are superb views of Dhaulagiri and Tukuche Peak. Walk uphill from the north side of Jharkot to rejoin road. Muktinath is a few minutes further uphill and has expanded a lot to cater for the Indian pilgrims. Its supposedly traffic free. The Bob Marley Lodge is still going strong with new deluxe rooms in a different building for Rs6000. The Hotel Grand Shambala offers more comfort. A new Guru Rinpoche statue sits high above the town. The checkpost is still on the left. See more on Jharkot and Muktinath in the Lower Mustang section.

Kagbeni – Chele (1–2hrs)
Kagbeni – Tangbe – Chele

Originally the entry formalities into Upper Mustang were done at the north end of the mani wall in the old city, but now there may be a checkpost on the river road; if so, check here first. When driving in we did not see it, but there is a new road checkpost in Chuksang.

Almost immediately the road loops around and climbs steeply up from Kagbeni. There is a short section of tarmac at first. The route follows the quiet dirt road and around the bluffs. In about an hour the archetypal gullies, characterised by eroded turrets and dry cliffs, can be observed.

Looking back, Kagbeni is framed by the tremendous, fluted spires that drape the north face of Nilgiri. Watch out for any local horsemen splashing happily along the riverbed.

Oozing salt and brightly coloured canyons are on display from the road.

Across the valley to the west is the deeply cut Ghilungpa Khola, which drains from the mountainous ramparts that hide another remote and enticing region of Nepal.

A trail/track can be seen high above the canyon westwards; this is the route over the Jungben La pass (5550m) to Chharka, in the mysterious land of Dolpo.

The road climbs quite a lot and comes to the Green Tangbe Organic Apple Farm. Apples are a common food source in much of Upper Mustang, providing the choicest ingredient for all those sustaining apple pancakes.

The road loops around into a deep furrow of the Dhingklo Khola canyon with steep and eroded slopes. The village of **Tangbe** (3060m) is well hidden below the road. It's a typical Mustang village, with narrow alleys, whitewashed walls, chortens and prayer flags.

If time allows, a short detour is in order, but be prepared to walk to explore here. It's around 30mins from Kagbeni to this village.

For lunch, keep to the road and look out for the Hotel Alisha restaurant, run by an astute business-like Tibetan lady!

From Tangbe the dirt road continues around the hillsides with increasingly amazing views ahead of the sheer, red-walled Kali Gandaki canyon. Across the river from near Tangbe is the notable monastery of Gompa Kang, more correctly called **Kunza Choling monastery**.

There is a new suspension bridge near Chuksang for those in need of a cultural injection at this early stage, although it's quite a long detour. A rough road crosses the river in the low water season.

Kunza Choling Monastery

This significant monastery is located across the Kali Gandaki. It houses some old statues of Guru Rinpoche and a large Maitreya image. There are many faded wall paintings and an unusual image of Vajrapani, as well as a forbidding-looking dark image of Samantabhadra in Yab Yum. Vajrasattva, an esoteric vehicle for meditation, resides on a wall here. Another icon is Vajradhara, often coloured dark blue, a primordial Buddha linked to the five Dhyani Buddhas so often seen in monasteries. This monastery is rarely visited except by Buddhist students and scholars.

The route takes around 15mins from Tangbe to the next settlement of **Chuksang** (2980m). Chuksang hosts some reasonable lodges for those needing a bed. A stunning, white-walled fortress dominates the north side of the village. The new Upper Mustang checkpost is located here adjacent to Mentsi Cave Monastery. (It is 14km to here from Kagbeni.)

Lodgings include the Cave Monastery Guest House, Bhrikuti Guest House, Prabisha Guest House, Alice Guest House, Annapurna Hotel and Braka Guest House. Chuksang also appears on maps as Chhusang and guards the entrance to one of the most mysterious canyons in all of Upper Mustang, but that is a story for later.

Chuksang Fort and Mentsi Lhakang Cave

Even at this stage the hidden but significant side canyon of the Narsing Khola offers views of some of the amazingly eroded landscapes that characterise Upper Mustang. The multi-coloured soft layers of rock have been modified into chimneys, 'organ-pipe' features and fairytale gullies. Anyone wanting to get a peek at the dramatic Narsing Khola could divert to Tetang from here and stay the night en route to Chele.

See **alternative** on page 138.

Otherwise, either before leaving Chuksang or on the return trip, be sure to visit the amazing **Mentsi Lhakang Cave** set in a strange-looking outcrop just up the road to Tetang on the right. The path to the cave is near a cliff and once in the first hollow a couple of tricky ladders lead to the main sanctuary. This alone is worth the effort to see even if it is closed. On our last visit it was less obvious where the actual entrance is now as some stones have been erected by the old entrance – it seems it is rarely ever open.

The man with the key was absent during our visit, but according to various scholars the above can be seen within.

Mentsi Lhakang Cave

The cave of Mentsi Lhakang is known as the temple of the holy medicines. The name Mentsi is associated with the famous monastery of Braka near Manang; one persecuted clan moved from there to the remote Narsing Valley. However, scholars link the cave shrine to Lama Mentsun Yonton, a sage associated with the famous Kagyu-pa masters Atisha, Marpa and Milarepa.

There is a possible connection to the famed translator Rinchen Zangpo, one of the major figures of the Buddhist revival of the 11th century and linked to the Guge Kingdom.

The presence of Vairocana (the main icon here) lends some credence to this theme. The main Dhyani Buddhas, Ratna Sambhava, Akshobhya, Amitabha and Amoghasiddhi, are also in residence. Translated as the neck of the horse, the wrathful icon called Hayagriva is also of note. The altar hosts the bird-faced deity Garuda.

Some of the oldest wall paintings are said to date from the 12th century.

From Chuksang the road keeps to the east bank above the river to the red cliffs that hide the Kali Gandaki River as it squeezes through the narrow defile between sheer walls. The road swings around a loop and climbs to **Chele** village (3050m). Chele is around 20mins from Chuksang.

Chele village has a few lodges; take your choice from Hotel Mustang Gate, Bishal Guest House and Eagle's Nest. For eating there is the Mina Cafe and Camp, and Butik restaurant.

The setting of Chele is quite dramatic and there is a large prayer wheel housed on the south side, together with the painted eight auspicious symbols. It has a few narrow alleys and various chortens.

Beware of any growly dogs here, as visitors are rare these days.

Mustang Explorer

> **The Kali Gandaki/Mustang Khola Canyon**
> During the late autumn and winter period, some local people travel along the actual gorge of the Kali Gandaki/Mustang Khola between lower Chele and Geling or Tsarang. The first part of the gorge is almost too narrow to pass, with towering sheer walls on both sides of the canyon. The sunlight is virtually shut out. The colours and features of the canyon are stunning, from photos we have been able to see taken by local friends and guides. Taking ponies obviously makes some sense along this gorge, but jeeps and tractors also use it. If walking through this canyon appeals to you, then seek sound advice with your planning and enjoy the trip with experienced local guides and crews.

Alternative: Kagbeni – Tetang (1–2hrs)
Kagbeni – Tangbe – Tetang

Being slightly off the main route, it might seem a strange choice for the first overnight stop, but the sensational village of Tetang is one of the most evocative, spectacular, brilliantly located and historic villages of the entire Upper Mustang district. We would go so far as to say it should never be omitted from any itinerary. The new Hotel Salt Born is certainly no hardship to stay at. Even if your itinerary does not include any of the other eastern Mustang trails, Tetang should definitely not be missed!

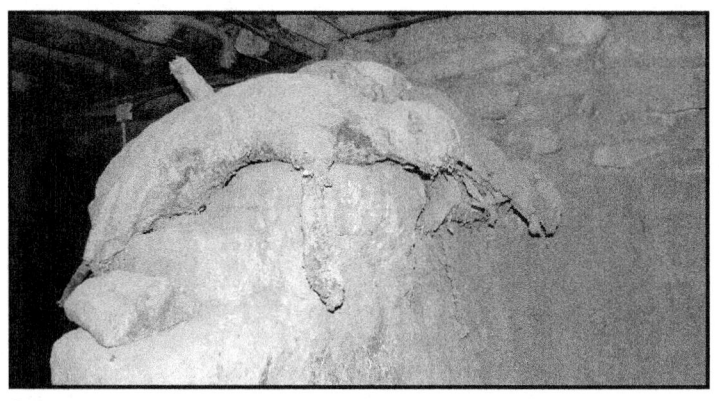

Strange images at Tetang

A gently graded dirt road climbs up from Mentsi Lhakang Cave and the checkpost. There are plenty of reasons to stop, as the scenery is ever more sensational, forcing the camera to overheat en route. The 2km detour takes around 10–15mins to **Tetang** (3050m). It's also located at a good altitude for acclimatisation. The two-part settlement is about as mediaeval as the imagination can stretch. There is a deep chasm between the two parts of the village, with the ancient monastery attached to the eastern area. The eastern part is a maze of dark alleys and high-walled houses, most of which are uninhabited.

In fact a lot of the structure is in need of urgent repair, especially a few with cracks from the April/May 2015 earthquakes.

The western part is still inhabited and is also a fabulously evocative series of alleys, dark corners, secret passages, mysterious doorways and more high-walled houses. During the sunny hours the local people, mostly the old and the very young, gather in the small square.

Various mani walls, small chortens and prayer walls surround the settlement.

Tetang Gompa

Originally a Nyingma-pa gompa, the Tetang shrine is now aligned with the Sakya-pa sect that has dominated Upper Mustang since the visits of Ngorchen Kunga Zangpo during the 15th century. The monastery, one of the oldest across Mustang, houses some extraordinary sights. Just by the entrance are what look like two dried-out snow leopards. On the left side is an amazing painting of a flying chained tiger, the traditional vehicle of Guru Rinpoche. However, the icon close by is more Mongolian in style, perhaps an after-thought painted in place by the Sakya school lamas. Unusually the guardians are found inside on the left wall, together with the harmonious friends, including the elephant. Four of the auspicious symbols are found on the left side, as well as some books and texts. Hidden behind murky glass the central icon is Guru Rinpoche, flanked by Sakyamuni Buddha (left) and Manjushri (right). A photo of the Dalai Lama is prominent. On the right side wall are paintings of the other four auspicious symbols, and a plaque with scripts. From the lodge the monastery can be accessed via the lower part of the long mani wall, across a small water course, and up.

Towering above the valley, a vast wall of brilliant yellow sculptured turrets and organ pipes dominate the scene. It's a brief window on the fantastic scenery of the **Siyarko Tankt Danda ridge** that only trekkers can gaze in astonishment at – such is the fairytale vistas on the ridge.

Apparently around an hour from the village, upstream along the waters of the Narsing Khola, is a salt mine. The salt is gathered where water issues from two main hollows or caves. To visit, take a local guide and expect to get wet feet, as the route goes along the sensational narrow chasm of the Narsing Khola.

For overnight comforts stay at the Hotel Salt Born. Its name comes from the above-mentioned salt mine.

The Hosts of Hotel Salt Born
The lodge is simple, clean and well run. For such a remote and little-visited lodge, the story of its owners is surprising. The lady of the house worked for the UN in Korea for five years and speaks that language well. Her husband has relatives in Slough outside London, where he went to study Hotel Management. Together with their daughter, Sonam, their personal enthusiasm and local knowledge bode well for the visits of future trekkers.

Tetang village

Chele – Samar (20mins)
Chele – Ghyakar canyon – Samar

Due to the considerable height gain further on its worth considering staying in Chele or Samar depending on acclimatisation. Anyone suffering from the altitude should stay in Samar, since the trail ahead is generally above 3700m. The stage negotiates a dramatic canyon with glimpses of rarely visited villages across the gorge. Going on to Geling is another option where the altitude is around 3500m. The dramatic peaks of the Damodar and Khumjungar Himal are visible to the east higher up near the Dajori Pass.

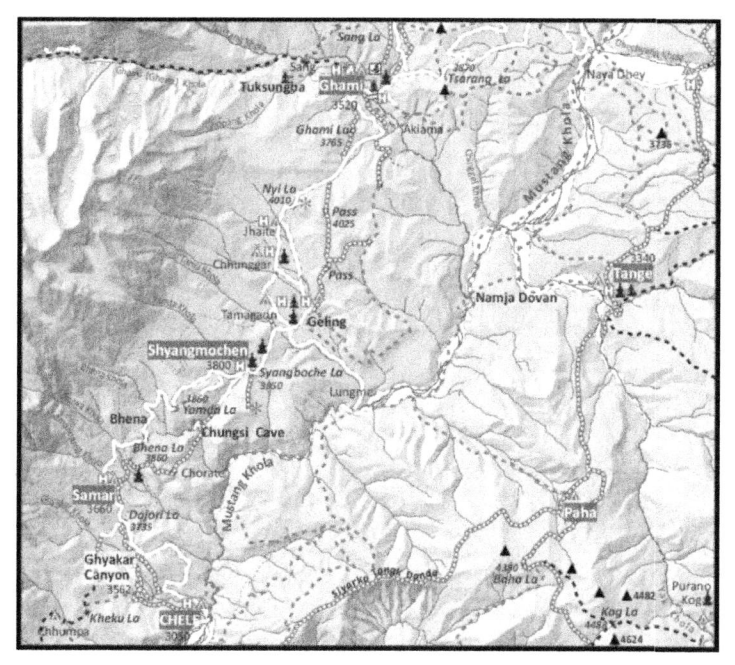

Stage 2 Map: Chele to Ghami

The road begins a dramatic climb to the Dajori Pass climbing on a series of zigzags in a cutting. This might hide the views, but the drops are sensational, so this cutting does offer respite to those who suffer from vertigo. Higher up and out of the cutting there is a panoramic view across to the Thorong La peaks of Khatung Kang and Yakawa Kang.

The village of **Ghyakar**, set among fields of buckwheat, lies across the main gorge. It's rarely visited and can be accessed on foot across a suspension bridge above Chele for those who have time to explore.

Mustang Explorer

The dramatic climb is rewarded by more panoramic views to the south from the **Dajori La pass** (3735m). The other peaks revealed are the Nilgiris and Tilicho Peak. A short descent, on the road leads to the settlement of **Samar** (3660m).

Lodges on offer here include the Himali Hotel and the Hotel Annapurna, with a new block. Rooms cost from Rs1500 to Rs3000–6000, depending on the season and room. It is about 35km here from Kagbeni.

There is a Nepalese-style monastery above the village, but it is rather out of place since the style does not conform to the usual Mustang designs.

Samar – Syangmochen (1hrs)
Samar – Bhena La – Yamda La – Syangmochen

It's another superb drive of constantly inspiring panoramic views to savour. Geling has a small monastery set above the village. If you visit in October, the buckwheat harvest will be underway and fun to watch. It will be all hands on deck, so you might get some unexpected work if there is any surplus energy in your system!

The route continues from Samar and negotiates the upper reaches of a couple of deep side canyons, the **Samarkyung Khola** and the **Ihuwa Khola**, which drain from the mountains that separate Mustang from Dolpo. These hillsides still host some vegetation. There are a few isolated ever-decreasing areas of ancient juniper and the remnants of a long-denuded woody glade. The road climbs to the **Bhena La** (3860m) before descending to Bhena.

The Bhena Khola has to be crossed before another pass, the **Yamda La** (3860m), interrupts the flow. About 5mins from Samar on the descent is a lone teahouse.

After yet another canyon is the place originally called **Eklobhatti** (3820m). Meaning one house stop, it is now marked as **Chungsi** on maps.

From here the dirt road crosses a small pass at 3870m before dropping now to **Syangmochen** (3800m).

This is actually a great place to overnight for the well acclimatised, since there are superb sunset views to be bagged; see Side trip below.

Enjoy your afternoon tea (but no cucumber sandwiches or further delights, that is unless you've loaded your car with a secret stash of Huntley and Palmer biscuits. The early expeditions to climb Everest from Tibet lived on them, but none succeeded!)

For those staying in Syangmochen, there is the Hotel Dhaulagiri plus the Hotel Nilgiri and Chungsi Guest House close by.

There's nothing much else here, apart from the viewpoint.

Side trip: Syangmochen Sunset viewpoint

This walking side trip is a stunner on a clear afternoon, with tremendous panoramic views of the Khumjungar and Damodar peaks as well as the more familiar stars of the Annapurna northern barrier, the Grande Barrière. It's marked as the Kali Gandaki Viewpoint on most maps.

From the hotel, follow the dirt road up around the hillside and on along it as it heads south briefly. The road has cut the old trail, so just try to head off right and then climb easily along the ridges.

Mostly the easy path is on the east side of the ridge, which is where those fabulous views are very distracting. Further up the path is steeper and zigzags up to the higher hilltop viewpoint. It takes around 30mins or so to reach the viewpoint.

There is a small **concrete viewing tower** here with a cracked narrow stairway and seemingly made of dubious quality materials. Beware the wind up here; it's strong in the afternoons and bitter as sunset approaches.

The view is mind-boggling, down into the chasm of the now tightly enclosed, raging waters of the Mustang Khola. The Geling valley is to the north, and it's easy to pick out the Yara and Tange valleys to the east.

Also to the east and southeast are the rolling hills of the high trail to Damodar, the barren wastes of the Kog La and the peaks of Sano Kailash, Bhrikuti (6476m), Futi Himal, Lena Peak, the highest peak Khumjungar (6759m) and Yuri peak. **(Photo below).**

Identifying each individual peak is quite a task. More to the south, but probably hazy, are the old favourites of the Annapurna Circuit: the northern ramparts of Yakawa Kang and Purkung Himal, Khatung Kang, the snowbound Muktinath Himal ranges, Annapurna I, the Grande Barrière peaks of Tilicho and the Nilgiris. The return to the hotel takes about 20mins.

Damodar peaks from Samar

Alternative: Samar – Syangmochen via Chungsi Ranchung Cave

If you are fit and wanting a trek on foot, this is the trail to take to visit the Chungsi Ranchung Cave complex. At this early stage of the trip it's a tough day, due to the delays of becoming properly acclimatised to the altitude. It's not an easy trail; the route dives down steeply and climbs wearyingly up, steeply. The trail departs from Samar and rejoins the main trail just before Syangmochen and its lodges.

Samar – Syangmochen/Geling (5–7hrs trek)
Samar – Chungsi Cave – Syangmochen/Geling

This is a spectacular alternative to the main route via the Bhena La, but it does need some effort; ideally trekkers should not be feeling any effects of the altitude. Some will undoubtedly feel slower than normal, even if not suffering headaches. The location and scenery surrounding the cave is stupendous, with a touch of mystical charm.

If your planned itinerary is along the eastern trails back to Muktinath, it is strongly recommended to take this option between Samar and Syangmochen or Geling.

The trail begins gently up through the village, where a few prayer wheels will speed you on the way. Once beyond the kani gate chorten of Samar, the route drops into a rugged-looking canyon; the lower part of the **Samarkyung Khola** river. Juniper bushes still cling to life around here. The trail drops steeply to the stream before an equally steep climb out of the gloom. Above is the old trail to Bhena near the new road.

About 30mins from Samar is a junction with signs for Bhena La to the left and Chungsi Gompa / Syangmochen to the right. Again the route descends into a deep, eerie chasm: the **Ihuwa Khola** this time. The stream is crossed on a stone bridge and once more it's steeply up to the plateau area above. This place is called **Chorate** on the maps. The sheep and goat pens are guarded by two large growling dogs, but they seem to be chained up for the most part – so it is said. The old trail to Bhena is visible, climbing up to the west just below the new dirt 'highway'.

Meanwhile this trail to Chungsi climbs gently up below some impressive and quite distinct outcrops, almost glowing in the mellow morning light. Now follows a 30mins steeper climb to a junction. Guess what, the correct trail heads even more steeply upwards to the left. If in doubt, isn't it always up!

This path is very steep and draining, but of course the views are sensational from the **'topside'** at about 3900m. The path contours around to the east on a narrow ledge and in 10mins the view is yet more inspirational.

Syangmochen is visible ahead, although a vast abyss blocks the way to it; below to the east, just out of sight, are the turbulent waters of the narrow Kali Gandaki gorge. Far to the east are the snowy peaks of the Damodar and Khumjungar Himals, a knotted collection of little-known spires awaiting adventurous climbers. The great Himalayan giants of the Annapurnas sit in the misty southern glow.

It's hard to leave this wondrous panorama, but a cave is waiting below. The trail passes a solitary juniper tree before descending in a series of steep but pleasant turns on and on down into the depths of the canyon. Sheer cliffs guard the left side with a large cave lower down. Further into this ghostly chasm, the path is narrow and a little exposed.

The valley walls begin to creep inwards, as if to shut off the exit forever. Finally the deepest depths are reached beside the Syangmochen Khola, gushing below a deep orange and yellow cliff. Once across the stream the path climbs a little to the **Chungsi Ranchung Cave** turnoff, 3–3½hrs from Samar.

The access path is a bit of a shocker, as it climbs steeply up the side tributary on a rough, narrow and steep path with some steps. The top area just below the cave needs some care, as the exposure is real enough, although very brief.

Chungsi Ranchung cave interior

View of the trail to Chungsi Ranchung Cave

Chungsi Ranchung Cave

This isolated cave (also spelt Rangchyung) is almost covered by prayer flags at its entrance portal. A small donation will be appreciated from visitors, although the meditating lama is often absent. There is a basic kitchen area, but it is the cave itself that commands all attention. The shrine is dedicated to Guru Rinpoche, who is said to have meditated here on his way to Tibet. Visitors can take the darkly lit kora clockwise around the shrine. Heading up on the left side, the path is slippery and steep but mercifully very short. There are various natural blackened images; some as they were formed and one or two modified from the original calcite formations. Each represents a deity of unknown name. One larger and strange-looking black image is said to be Atisha, the great sage and Buddhist master of the Kadam-pa sect. Around the back of an amazingly formed calcite stalagmite structure, the small circling path descends back into the sunlight. It is very slippery going down; beware! The front of the shrine hosts four painted icons. These include Sakyamuni Buddha, Amitabha, Guru Rinpoche and Chenresig. Adjacent to the right are the famed more than 180 images of Guru Rinpoche, all arranged in lines one upon the other. The excursion from the junction to the cave and back could easily consume a fascinating hour.

From the cave turnoff, the trail begins an immediate climb around into a side chasm that seems to have no exit. The walls tower high above, but the path is good.

Slowly height is gained and the chasm turns into a wider canyon; steadily the walls retreat like curtains opening on another gala performance. Your own performance might begin to drag as the never-ending climb out of the abyss continues.

Once almost out of this canyon on a steadily rising route, the end seems in sight, with a fleeting glimpse of a Syangmochen lodge ahead. But is this just an apparition? There is still more up until, about 1–1½hrs from the cave turnoff, **Syangmochen** (3800m) is 'discovered' to be in hiding behind a small hillock. As mentioned earlier, there are three lodges here and an optional side trip to the Kali Gandaki Viewpoint for sunset.

If you have energy and a tight schedule, **Geling** (3570m) is a little over 1hr further (15mins up over a small pass followed by a 45min descent).

Syangmochen – Geling (15mins)
Syangmochen – Geling

This short stage is described separately here for those who want to take in the cultural delights of Geling. Geling has a few lodge options. Geling is often spelt as Gheling on maps.

From Syangmochen it's an easy ascent to the pass of the **Syangmochen La** (3850m) by road. Near the top is a colourful chorten (also called *Lhato* by more scholarly folks than us). It has encouraging views down to the village of Geling. However, a further 5mins are required to reach the settlement, because another side canyon interrupts the rhythm. **Geling** (3570m) has some intriguing, dingy lanes and a monastery to explore, so it makes a good stopover.

Lodges are Kunga Hotel and Dargeling Hotel; on the road out to Ghami is the Tibet Hotel and Norbu Ling Guest House.

Geling Gompa
Known as Tashi Choling or more correctly Pal Sa Ngor Tashi Choeling., the monastery was founded in the 15th century by Ngorchen Kunga Zangpo, a wise Buddhist master of the time. It belongs to the Sakya-pa sect of the Ngorchen. A superb chorten guards the entrance. The main structure houses an image of the founder as well as Mahakala, Sakyamuni Buddha, Chenresig and other lesser-known icons like Chakrasambhava/Heruka and Hevajra. The five Dhyani Buddhas are also to be noted. This chamber may not be open, but the newer area hosts smaller images of Maitreya, Buddha and books. The other smaller building above is the Gonkhang, where the protecting deities are normally found. Quite often these commonly seen shrines across the Buddhist high country are not open to female visitors. This one apparently houses covered images of Mahakala and Gonpo, linked to Shiva in Nepal. The small chamber has paintings of Jambala, two dancing skeletons and the boar faced Yamantaka! Ancient muskets are also found in here.

Geling – Ghami (45–50mins)
Geling – Nyi La – Ghami

It doesn't look that far on the map, but with the first high passes to cross, the road has some twists and turns. Here the route to Tsarang is split into two stages. The Nyi La is the highest so far, a shade over 4000m.

Leaving Geling, the route climbs up through the fields, meadows and dry scrub in a northwest direction. The pass is almost visible for much of the way. On the trail just before the summit of the **Nyi La (**or **Nyika La)** at 4010m was a rock painted with a smiley face, that greeted visitors with joy as they topped out the pass; it is no longer visible from the road. There is a long descent ahead as the dirt road drops down for some 15mins. Miles ahead there is also a view of the dramatic red cliffs of Drakmar.

Ghami (3520m) has some picturesque mani walls and small chortens to photograph as well as a monastery to visit, but beware of big growling dogs if you stop over here after dark.

Lodgings on offer include the Royal Mustang and cosy Lo Ghami Guest House.

Ghami Monastery
The entrance or kani (gate) chorten of Ghami (Ghemi) has some notable stone carvings. Belonging to the Sakya-pa, the monastery contains a significant chorten and an image of Chenresig. Otherwise it's noted mostly for some newer paintings. Nearby is a large prayer wheel in a building called the Mani Lhakang.

Ghami – Tsarang (1hr)
Ghami – Choya La – Tsarang

Before the arrival of the motor vehicle in Upper Mustang, this used to be the main trail to Tsarang. Since there are two options between Ghami and Lo Manthang, it makes sense to follow both routes at some stage of the trip. Tsarang has an exotic, ancient ambience displaying the cultural uniqueness of Mustang and should not be missed.

From **Ghami** the road passes a trio of chortens, and then crosses a deep gully by a bridge. About 10mins from Ghami is a very long mani wall – the longest in Upper Mustang. From the junction, the dramatic, red-walled cliff area in the direction of Drakmar captures all the attention. About 20mins from Ghami is a small pass, the **Choya La** (3870m), sometimes marked as the Tsarang La. From the pass the road drops down to the fields of the oasis-like village of **Tsarang** (3560m).

The mud-walled ramparts of the tremendous fortress-citadel and the monastery dominate the village. Tsarang is also dominated by a number of impressive large chortens and a new large monastery.

Lodges here are Lumbini Guest House which stays open longer and is good – Rs1500–2000 or dorm beds at Rs500. It has a new block above the bank next door, with posher rooms at Rs3000–6000. The owner lived in Switzerland for 10 years. Also look for Dolma Guest House, Tsarang Guest House, Norbu Guest House, Paradise, Damodar Kunda Guest House, and nearer the monastery, Royal Mustang Holiday Inn/Maya. Tsarang is often spelt as Charang on maps.

East of Tsarang and the Kali Gandaki (Mustang Khola) is the village of Dhi (Dri). Beyond Dhi are the dramatic Yara caves and the Luri Cave retreat en route to Damodar Kund, a sacred lake. See more on options for these areas later.

Stage 3 Map: Ghami – Lo Manthang

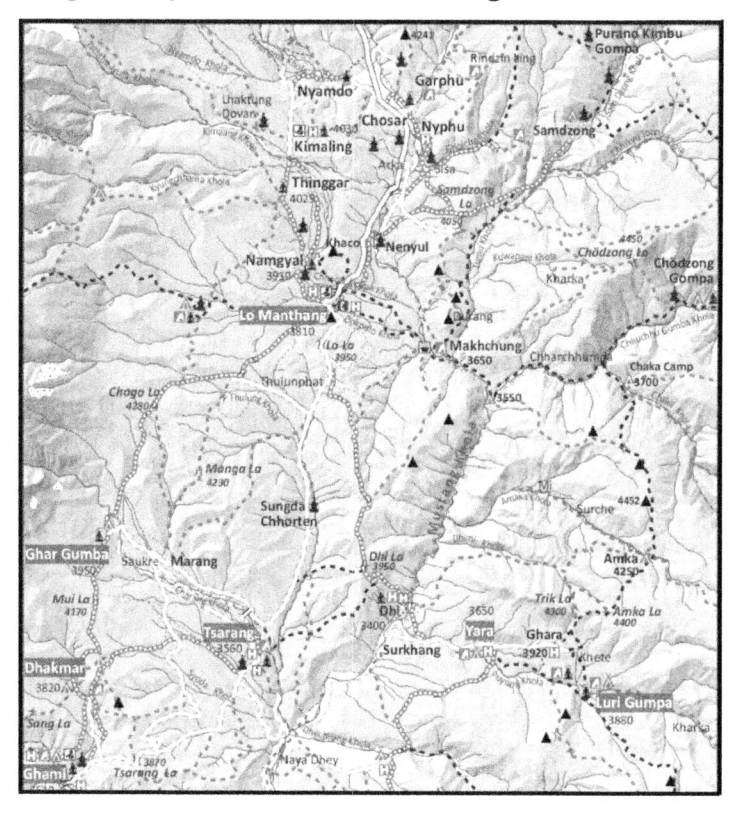

Tsarang Monastery

The stunningly located Thubten Shedrup Dhargyeling monastery has some amazingly intricate murals and mandalas that have mostly been restored since our first trek in 1992. Belonging to the Ngor Sakya-pa sect, it is said to have been founded in the 16th century. Maitreya, the Buddha of the Future, is the main image. Flanking this image are the Sakyamuni Buddha and Vajradhara. A much-revered, wooden statue of Chenresig (Avalokiteshvara) in the gompa was brought from Lhasa. The Thousand Buddhas are in evidence as well as the directional Buddhas: Vairocana, Amitabha, Akshobhya, Ratna Sambhava and Amoghasiddhi. The new monks' quarters are painted in the distinctive Sakyapa colours and are south of the gompa.

Samdrup Gedphel Palace

Samdrup Gedphel Palace was the kings' residence and is now used to house museum pieces and other odd remains. That said, a few notable icons are in residence, such as the bronze Maitreya. Another is the rarely seen wooden image of a little-known icon, Phagpa Lokeshvara, linked to Srongsten Gampo, the acknowledged founder of the Tibetan state. It is thought that Srongsten Gampo sought out sandalwood trees to make such images to placate the demons, and that the images were to be placed in 108 shrines or temples across the Himalaya and Tibet. One of the kings of Mustang, Agon Zangpo, is probably one of the icons on display. The famous monk Ekai Kawaguchi, who spent some time living in Tukuche, also lived in Tsarang for a while before sneaking into Tibet for three years.

Tsarang – Lo Manthang (1hr)
Tsarang – Lo La Pass – Lo Manthang

The anticipation of reaching the fabled walled city of Lo Manthang makes this a fabulous stage full of long-promised anticipation.

The deep canyon beyond **Tsarang** today ensures that the drama continues and the prospects of reaching Lo Manthang ahead are delayed for a short spell. Climbing out of this substantial ravine reveals a splendid Himalayan panorama to the south: Annapurna I, Nilgiri and Tilicho; and the Damodar–Bhrikuti Peaks to the southeast.

About 30mins from Tsarang the road comes to the much-photographed, isolated and beautiful **Sungda Chorten**. The gently ascending road soon passes spectacular caves and crosses a stream. Cliffs of yellow conglomerates and dark bands flank the route as it climbs to the last obstacle – the pass of the **Lo La** (3850m).

Suddenly this window opens to reveal the much-anticipated splendours of Lo Manthang – the fabulous city below, a spectacular sight greeted with incredulity. The walled city is still an extraordinary sight, with its white houses, red monasteries and palace.

This viewpoint reveals other treasures: Thinggar (Tingkhar) and Namgyal Gompa – the red, cream and grey-coloured edifice on a promontory.

On the hill above are the ruined forts of Khacho Dzong and Khartsun Dzong. The Mustang Khola, hemmed in by a veritable sea of coloured cliffs, lies to the east. To the northwest, the Mansail peaks rise in a crescendo above the barren hills to rugged ramparts and white-capped summit.

The rapid descent to **Lo Manthang** (3810m) is short and, once across the river, the gates of the city (and jeep park – so exotic!) are reached.

Alternative: Ghami – Lo Manthang via Ghar Gompa

When Mustang first opened in 1992, there was so little literature available, apart from the writings of Michael Peissel, that few people knew much about optional routes to reach Lo Manthang. Today another half-day road route links Ghami to Lo Manthang via Tsarang, Ghar Gompa and the Chogo La. It may be better to do this on the way back down the valley, because it's a rougher, slower, newly constructed dirt road option. Ask your driver/guide to check the road condition before making a decision. It would also be possible to just detour up from Tsarang to visit Ghar Gompa and then return to the main road north to Lo Manthang.

Lo Manthang approach

Lo Manthang

> **Lodgings in Lo Manthang**
>
> There are several lodges here to choose from, including the Mustang Mystique (Rs2000, 9844738000, 9857650866). It has a cosy, heated dining area. Others are Lotus Guest House, Hotel Peace off to the southeast, Hotel Tibet (Rs1500 cold concrete building but good food), Lo Manthang Guest House, Everest Guest House, Kora La Guest House and Mustang Guest House. Around the northwest corner are Golden Gate Guest House, Tashi Delek Guest House, 3 Sisters Guest House, (the Horse Power Workshop – repair shop), Jambala Guest House. Uphill a little out of town is the top notch Royal Mustang, Hill Town Guest House and the cosy Tri Bhadrika Guest House (meaning 3 'rulers – the king, the high lama and the high government official). The Lo Kunphen Medical School is opposite, and on the northeast corner is the Himalaya Hotel.
>
> Passing the large chortens, off to the south is the Snow Lion Guest House, with the Ancient City Guest House, Mona Lisa Hotel and Hotel Caravan in the area. The Potala Hotel is near the main gate. The more upmarket Hotel Mandala is near the Mustang Mystique, with rooms for Rs2000–3000, mid-range Rs4000–5000 and suites on the top for Rs10,000–13,000. Also in the old city NW corner is Lowa Homestay Rs1000 (no attached) in Tashi's house, along with his View Tower rooftop with great views and yak head. His artist's shop with thangkas etc and Map House guidebooks is just inside the main gate to the right.

Old Royal Palace in Lo Manthang

Map of Lo Manthang

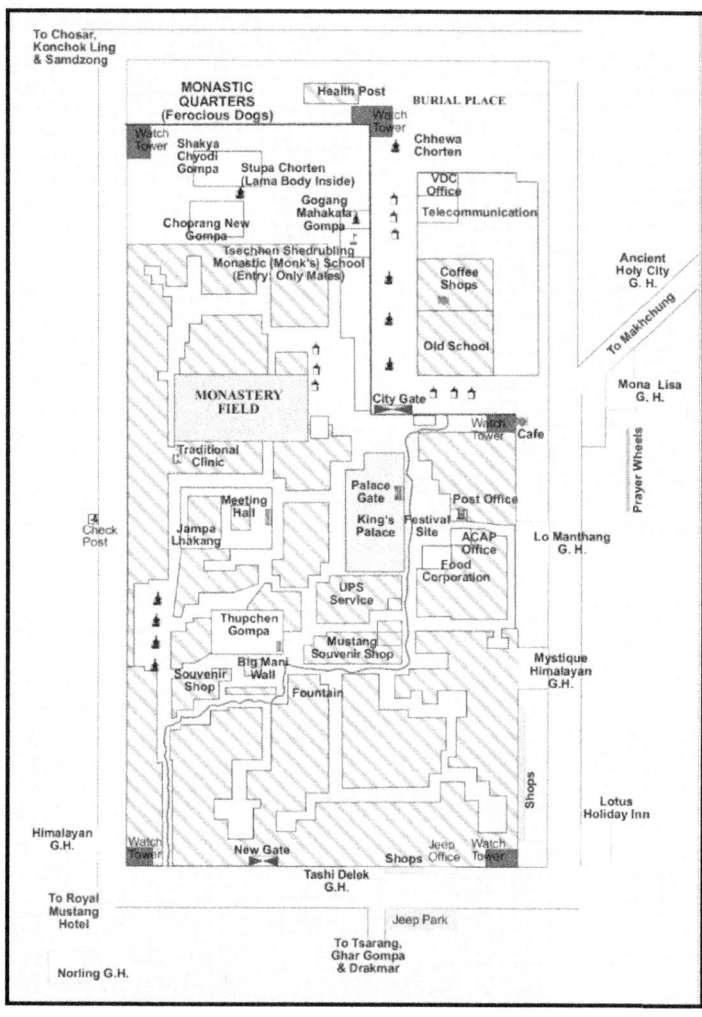

Jampa Gompa

The East Gate Chorten area

The old Choide monastery

Typical alleys and lanes in the old city

Some of the old walled city has covered passages

Lines of large chortens on the city 'Kora walk'

Lo Manthang from near Lho Lo pass

Time in Lo Manthang

> Lo Manthang contained all the mystery and charm of a lost world that spoke of war and battle against both the elements and time. The capital was surely man's last fortress against nature and the changing world.
> ***Mustang: A Lost Tibetan Kingdom*, Michel Peissel**

The extraordinary walled city of Lo Manthang has been on the Tentative List to receive UNESCO World Heritage Site status for some time, but things are never that simple in Nepal. There are roughly 140 houses within the 8.5m-high walls built by the Amapalas. The big chortens of Lo Manthang house relics of the Buddha or his disciples.

The four-storey palace of the Mustang monarch, King Jigme Dorje Dradul (his Nepalese name is Jigme Palbar Bista), was constructed in 1441. Apparently the chapel of the former king houses a gold example of the Tibetan texts, the Kangyur. The King of Mustang resigned his position in 2008 and died in 2016. In the early days of trekking when Lo Manthang first opened, he and the Queen of Mustang invariably entertained visitors at the Royal Palace; its quaint mediaeval atmosphere was impressive. Unfortunately it was damaged during the earthquake.

We were among those early visitors fortunate enough to be given an audience with the gracious monarchs. Delighted by this act of generosity, we obediently quaffed their quality Tibetan butter tea. One cup was sufficient to show gratitude; anyone leaving their tea decades ago might have seen the inside of a dank dungeon!

Ideally explore the alleys, chortens and sights by walking clockwise around the 'kora' route. Outside the city wall is the Lo Kunphen Mentsi Khang, housing the traditional Tibetan herbal medicine clinic with a school attached. It was established in 1998 and is run by traditional Amchis (traditional medical sages). One of the most famous Tibetan icons, Milarepa, the Kagyu-pa hermit and poet sage, came to the Lo region, so it is said.

A couple of lines of large chortens grace the Kora path in the old city

Monasteries of Lo Manthang

As the oldest, the red-walled, three-storey Jampa (Champa) Gompa is devoted to Maitreya, the Buddha of the Future. The Sakya-pa structure was consecrated in 1448 under the auspices of Ngorchen Kunga Zangpo and the king, Agon Zangpo. The gold-painted clay image of Maitreya was completed in 1663. The monastery is famed for its abundant mandala images, originally produced by Newari artists under King Kunga Zangpo, which have undergone restoration. Many were covered in centuries of grime and butter-lamp soot. It also hosts a special Thousand Buddha mandala and five Pala art Buddhas painted in fine detail. The lokapalas are painted on the inside wall, due to lack of space outside. No new repainting has been allowed in here.

The Sakya-pa Thupchen Lhakhang (Mahamuni) or 'Great Sage' Gompa was initiated in 1468 under King Tsangchen Trashigon. The north wall was destroyed by an earthquake 200 years ago, and partly rebuilt. It has a magnificent image of the fifth Dhyani Buddha, Vairocana, facing east above the entrance. There are prominent images of Guru Rinpoche, Amitayus, a White Tara, Vajradhara and a bird-like Kirtimukha. The main icon is Mahamuni (Sakyamuni) in copper, flanked by Chenresig as Shadakshari Lokeshvara and Manjushri made in clay. Other icons are the five Dhyani Buddhas, with Ratna Sambhava a notable one on the left wall. The four lokapalas (guardians), unusually here in the form of statues outside the main chamber, are very impressive. A major restoration programme started in 1999 under the auspices of the American Himalayan Foundation. Some completely new painting is still being done here below the main deities' feet.

Ngonga Choide Gompa (also called Dragkar Thegchen Ling was initiated by King Tsewang Phuntsok Tsugyen Norbu. The original gompa probably dates from the time of Amapal, but a more recent incarnation began in 1710. It features a silver image of Tara and, probably locked away, an impressive Mahakala. Some deities from Choprang were moved here, including an image of Vajrakilaya (a fearsome blue deity, crowned with skulls and arms out wide, who 'battles' the obstacles to compassion) after a fire.

Choprang Sakya-pa Gompa is the newest structure and is in effect part of Choide Gompa. Adjacent to the monasteries is the museum, initiated in 2008 by the community of Choide Gompa. It houses artefacts, masks, scriptures on wood and some 3000-year-old Bon texts from Mardzong Caves. Currently closed, a new building has been constructed and it will be open again soon. All these sights are located in a corner of the city famed for its ferocious guard dogs.

A US$10 (Rs1000) fee covers entry to all the sights of Lo Manthang.

Philosophy of the American Himalayan Foundation restoration programme with Luigi Fieni
www.himalayan-foundation.org

Since 1999, the Upper Mustang Cultural Heritage Conservation Project has been restoring and preserving the 14th- and 15th-century Newari (Pala) art on the walls of the monasteries in Lo Manthang, Lo Gekar and Tsarang, among others. The expert Italian restorer Luigi Fieni has spent 17 years in Lo Manthang working on the restoration of the monasteries, along with the American Himalayan Foundation and many talented local artists.

'We arrive in a country that is not our own, with a culture that is not our own, and we try to convince the locals that art is more important than religion. My vision has evolved as I have seen how important religion is to these people. Our project is one of development as well as restoration. We have to study the present, work on the ancient, and all the time bear in mind what the local people want and need.'
Luigi Fieni

The generally accepted view of restorers around the world is that no new painting should be done; old paintings should simply be restored by removing the grime of centuries from the surface, or regluing surface paintings to the supporting walls that they have peeled away from or fallen off. However, in Mustang the opinions and needs of the local population have to be respected and taken into account.

'We need to pray. The monastery of Thupchen is very important to us and we need to finish it.' So said the inhabitants of Lo Manthang to Luigi Fieni.

The local people feel that paintings, statues and holy places that have fallen into disrepair are no longer sacred and cannot be worshipped. But as the paintings have been restored, so the people have returned to the monasteries to pray. The monasteries are no longer simply 'dead' museums of the past, but a living, breathing part of their cultural heritage.

Chorten gate on the east side of Lo Manthang

Artists of Lo Manthang
A big development since our first visit here in 1992 is the profusion of souvenir shops. Although all the familiar items are on offer, there are also quite a number of thangkas on sale. Most of these are painted locally by internationally trained and accomplished artists. The quality of the thangkas ranges from simple to very intricate and the general standard of the work is high. Prices vary from US$30 to US$60 for the smaller sizes but of course larger ones cost much more, up to hundreds of dollars.

When painting a thangka, the canvas is prepared by coating a soft cloth with glue, drying and rubbing it till it is hard and not flexible, but can still be rolled into a tube. Paints are made from expensive mineral pigments. Certain colours cannot be painted in the cold autumn weather because of the way the pigments react to the temperature. In the depths of winter it is too cold to paint at all in Mustang, so the artists go to Kathmandu for training by master thangka painter Mukti Singh Thapa. It's a 5-year course, including the iconography and painting style particular to these gompas.

Many of the thangkas on sale are copies of the art in the monasteries that the local artists are working to restore, thus keeping the old style of art alive. The thangkas more commonly found in Kathmandu are of a later style, from the 17th–18th centuries.

Thanks to Tashi Gurung of the Lowa Art Gallery in Lo Manthang, for his explanations and excellent guided tour of the monasteries.

Time around Lo Manthang
With ever more visitors arriving by road, there is time within the 10-day permit to explore more of the fabulous sights around Lo Manthang. Top of the list is Chosar, with the **Sijha Jhong Cave** complex now accessible. Close by are the **monasteries of Nyphu (Nyiphu) and Garphu**. Taking longer is the amazing trip to the **Konchok Ling** cave art and stupendous scenery.

In the same valley as the Jhong Caves, higher up is **Rinchenling**, relatively recently opened, and hidden in a side canyon the **Nupchokling Caves**. The road loop to **Nyamdo**, **Kimaling**, **Thinggar** (Tingkar) and **Namgyal** monastery can be added to excursions to the above.

Those with wheels might persuade their driver to cross the Samdzong La pass to the abandoned village of **Old Samdzong** set in more sensational scenery. Even further afield is the monastic art and indescribable scenery of **Chodzong** with the Bon outcrop of **Mardzong** en route, east of Lo Manthang. Nepalese citizens are permitted to head north to the border with Tibet/China on the **Kora La pass**, but foreign devils will be stopped near Nyamdo.

Chosar, Nyphu and Garphu

This popular half-day side trip can be done from Lo Manthang by jeep, returning via the Nyamdo, Kimaling, Thinggar and Namgyal alternative road loop back to Lo Manthang afterwards. Taking in Konchok Ling the same day is really too much, although it's included in the Jhong Cave/monastery ticket which currently costs Rs1000.

Very few visitors trek the route following the road to Chosar now, but ponies are available for those who don't use a jeep. Ponies cost around Rs4000 per day, plus pony man Rs2000. The above is quite a lot to do in one day, but with days in the Upper Mustang permit period in short supply – Ke Garne – what to do?

Chosar (Choser) is the general name of the village in the area. The road (and trail) north leaves Lo Manthang from its northeast corner and crosses the Chhorak Dokpa Khola. The route heads beside the diminishing waters of the river, passing a long mani wall and isolated buildings on the west bank for most of the way. About 15–20mins drive from Lo Manthang is the cave village of Chosar on the right across the river, with a checkpost to buy tickets. The red monastery of Nyphu is set in a rock face beyond. There is also just a view of the monastery settlement of Garphu further north.

There are two options to stay in the vicinity – the Lo Choser Guest House on the left up the road to the Jhong caves and around to the south of Nyphu, the cave hotel of Shelkar Guest House set high in the cliffs above Chosar. Costs are from Rs5000 per night.

The road continues into the side valley, with great views north of the incredible multi-coloured turrets and erosion features. It takes about 10mins to reach the Sijha Jhong Cave complex on the right (south side) of the valley. Access to the caves is up a wooden stairway to a small doorway. Various steps and steep ladders lead up through narrow, dusty tunnels to the five levels within the 50m cliff that are normally accessible. It's quite tricky in places, so boots are advised. Drinks sellers keep all refreshed.

Sijha Jhong Caves

The caves are northeast of Nyphu and are perhaps 3000 years old. A visit to the Jhong caves is a surreal experience, not knowing what the lives of the ancient inhabitants were really like. Suggestions that the people practised human sacrifice here are still not confirmed although evidence suggests it might have been carried out in other areas of Upper Mustang. There are around forty chambers in all in the complex, but not many are easy to reach. Some small chambers and side rooms are decorated with kata scarfs. Eerie tunnels and a number of gaping holes or windows look out to the surrounding hills and cliffs. There is no art to be seen in the currently accessible parts.

The Sijha Jhong Cave complex

Cave dwellers

Many of the geological strata across Upper Mustang are soft and friable. There are thousands of caves. Some of the more elaborate caves are at Nyphu (Niphu), Yara, Chosar, Tange and Drakmar. The extensive Chosar cave system (including all the Sijha Jhong (Sija Dzong) cave complexes) dates to 800BC, with 40 or more chambers.

In the Mardzong (Makhchung) caves anthropologists discovered 13th-century paintings and manuscripts executed in silver and gold. More recent excavations have revealed that a substantial civilisation inhabited much of the Trans-Himalayan region, encompassing the Lo region, Damodar Himal and Tsaparang in Western Tibet.

From 1992–97, digs around the Mehbrak caves revealed the grave of a mother and baby along with food offerings. It was dated to around 450BC. Over 60 more such corpses have been discovered, some with food items in ceramic vessels. Initially the finding of mass graves or burial sites was attributed to burial by landslides, but that theory was soon discounted.

Now scholars believe it is almost certain that the cave dwellers practised sacrificial rituals, but at which place, and how long the practises may have lasted, is not known.

Inside the Jhong cave complex

Nupchokling Caves
In the nearby cave of Nupchokling across the valley from Jhong there some murals that probably date to the 13th century. Trying to locate the caves is difficult, as the locals are fairly reticent about visitors exploring the sight. There is a very dramatic canyon almost opposite the Jhong caves, where fabulous, coloured cliffs dominate. We understand that the cave is close by here, where blue sheep can quite often be seen. Those interested can check out the art on offer from photographs by Michael Beck in his book **Mustang: The Culture and Landscapes of Lo** published by Vajra in Kathmandu.

Nyphu monastery

Returning down the valley its around 5mins to the Nyphu monastery and settlement. There is a new monastery west of the cliff Gompa.

Nyphu

The Nyphu (Niphu) cliff complex belongs to the Ngor-Sakyapa school and is known as the Cave of the Sun. The age of the first structures here is unknown. The current site is believed to have been founded by Lo Khen Chen, a prince of Mustang and Sakyapa sage who visited the site in the 15th century. He meditated here in the cave for some time before constructing the monastery. A newer structure painted in the traditional colours of the sect has been added since our first trek here in 1992. Steep steps lead up to the entrance. Entry is included in the Chosar area ticket. The upper chamber houses utensils and two horns, a prayer wheel and a box of small icons including Chenresig and Buddha. There are also some books. The lower chamber hosts, from left to right Vajradhara, Manjushri, the 1000-armed Chenresig, Buddha and his disciples, plus the familiar four-armed Chenresig and a Green Tara. On the left side are, apparently, covered Buddhas, and on the right side a drum. The interior of the 16th-century shrine also houses some damaged murals and artwork, which may or may not be seen.

From Nyphu monastery it's a short drive or walk around the cliffs north to Garphu and its monastery. The village has quite a dramatic setting below well eroded cliffs and ruins. There are quite a number of houses and ponies that some groups use for trekking east of Lo Manthang.

Garphu Gompa

Garphu Gompa is close by to the north. It is one of the oldest monasteries in Mustang and called Lo Garphu Kanying Samten Choeling. The Kanying school is an obscure sect of Tibetan Buddhism. It was established in the 9th century by Lama Zenji Gyatso Duecho. There is a footprint said to be of Kathok Rinchen Tswang Norbu, one of the earliest lamas of the monastery. Inside, the monastery has blackened walls that tend to hide the artwork. The usual protectors are located each side of the entry door. Images of the boar-faced icon of Yamantaka can just be made out, along with a Mahakala. On the left wall the paintings are hard to discern, including probably the 1000-armed Chenresig, but there are books further along. The main paintings here are Zenji Gyatso, Tsewang Norbu, Tsewang Lhundup – the three main mentors, plus a Dorje Chang in yab yum with his consort, Guru Rinpoche and his consorts, Sakyamuni Buddha with his disciples and a picture of the Dalai Lama. The right wall has books, some learned Arhats, and some thangkas. Ngyugne, Mahakal Puja and Ghutor Chemo are the main festivals celebrated here.

> **The Kabum Chortens**
> There are four such shrines across Upper Mustang. Most are either well-hidden or inaccessible. The example near Garphu is impossible to locate without a local guide and then is only accessible with ropes and safety equipment. One that is open is the Luri Cave chorten; another was the Tashi Kabum cave chorten near Luri along the river to Yara, but the access trail appears to have been damaged during the earthquake. The other is near Tange but few ever visit, such is the reticence of the local people to point the way. It apparently also has a decorated dome of note.

The valley beyond Jhong also hosts the recently opened Rinchenling Cave complex. This sight also appears on maps as Ritseling, Rinzing Ling and locally as Rinchhenling. It is described later as it needs further acclimatisation before attempting a visit, such is the altitude gain to reach the site.

North of Lo Manthang

Nyamdo, Kimaling, Thinggar and Namgyal (1–2hrs)

Those not taking in Konchok Ling the same day can return to Lo Manthang by road through the little visited sights of Nyamdo, Kimaling, Thinggar and Namgyal. The trek would take 6–7 hrs.

From Garphu the road heads north towards Tibet for a few minutes before turning west (left) at **Nyamdo**. A checkpost just to the north prohibits all foreigners from going any further to the border. The road west goes below the hillside, with an impressive new chorten located on the hilltop with eight smaller chortens around the slope below. There is also an old fort and lone square chamber, but all was closed this late in the season. A Nepalese stupa is located below the hill in the village near the road.

The road sweeps around and climbs a little on to a plateau area to continue to **Kimaling**, a settlement of spread-out buildings and the large clinic on the right. It is about 5km to Lo Manthang from here.

A large, ruined fort is soon seen uphill on the right, then the route goes gently down to **Thinggar** (Tingkar) village, a typical Tibetan-style village of flat-roofed and white-walled houses with black windows. The former king of Mustang had a summer palace here – the highest flat-roofed structure we believe. No entry is possible here thus far. Just 30m down the road is a lane on the right. It is well worth exploring, climbing up the steep lane below the palace area to get views of the village. The route continues on down the broad valley to **Namgyal Monastery** (3910m), a large red and cream structure on the bluff.

> **Namgyal Gompa**
> Known as Namgyal Choide Thubten Dhargyeling, this shrine stands on a hill northwest of Lo Manthang. It too once belonged to the Ngor-Sakyapa sect and was founded in 1465. However, today's structure only dates from 1953. All the decorations and imagery are thus relatively modern, with Buddha central. Foreign visitors will almost certainly not be able to see inside the Gonkhang that hides the protecting deities. A vast amount of rebuilding and additional space has been added to this monastery recently.

En route there are good views of the two ancient forts that dominate Lo Manthang. Trails climb to each from Lo Manthang if the energy levels are high. The road goes around to the south where better views are obtained. The complex is rarely open. It's a short drive on down the road to Lo Manthang.

Kora La Pass

The road from Tibet is encountered along the way; Chinese trucks are not generally permitted to bring goods south of the border post on the **Kora La pass** (4660m). The views from the border are sweeping and windswept, with few particularly interesting features other than the general bleakness of the location. We were lucky to see some videos taken by a local Nepalese tourist. Today up to a thousand people are said to live in the new settlement at and north of the border. Foreigners are not permitted near the border.

Northwest of Lo Manthang

The high country of the Mustang Himal northwest of Lo Manthang has recently been traversed by climbing groups, but the routes are technical and not for regular trekkers. However, trekkers do have the 4–5-day option of visiting Mansail Base Camp from Nyamdo, including a camp at Longkyok Tso Lake. Currently the climbing permits for peaks in this area and others are actually cheaper per person than the US$500 that trekkers are being charged.

Khacho Fort and Mansail Himal from Lho La

Side trip: Konchok Ling (6–8hrs)

Between us and the monastery (Konchok Ling) there was a steep slope of land eroded into shapes that suggested a thousand stalagmites sprouting from the earth like gigantic needles. The tantalising monastery, standing upon its lonely ledge, surrounded by this quite lunar sea of pinnacles and columns, just stared at us.
Mustang: A Lost Tibetan Kingdom, **Michel Peissel**

Trail to Konchok Ling

Some say that the day trip to Konchok Ling is the most spectacular and beautiful adventure in Upper Mustang, including these scribes. Making a side trip to Konchok Ling in a day from Lo Manthang is one of the more unusual choices, but don't discount this fantastic fairytale destination unless you hate exposure or suffer from even mild vertigo. The paintings in the small cave have suffered greatly from time, but there are enough images to make it worthwhile even for those with only a casual interest in Buddhist art. It's the stupendous, geologically unbelievable scenery of the location that makes this such a sensational place. It's hard to judge the timings on this option because of the eroded nature of the path.

The following description is for those who care to walk all the way between Lo Manthang and Konchok Ling, but of course the new road has made it a much shorter trip, with only a 20min drive each way. The road also goes higher and closer to the entry gate area, cutting out more time walking. Allow half a day using jeep transport.

The trail leaves from the northeast corner of Lo Manthang around from the big chortens near the main gate. Drop into the big gully and climb out along the wide road. The main border road leads the way around below the Khacho fort and soon a path goes to the right after a downhill stage. This goes down to the upper reaches of the Mustang Khola, now known as the **Nhichung Khola**. A bridge or two lead to **Nenyul** (3800m) after a short zigzagging climb. It's about an hour from Lo Manthang to here.

Heading northeast from Nenyul, the trail reaches the new settlement of **New Samdzong**, where the people from the stricken Samdzong village have been resettled. A scarcity of water in old Samdzong forced a planned general evacuation of the village.

Many villagers were reluctant to leave their families' ancestral homes permanently. It's a pity that water could not have been brought to old Samdzong as locals lament, but many people migrate from Upper Mustang in winter in any case.

Further around the low hills is **Bharcha,** also marked as **Sisa**, decked out with some prayer wheels you need to turn for a safe passage to the cave grotto. This is the place to find the man with the key to Konchok Ling and it's also a tea house. Already there are tantalising views to the east along the side valley of the **Ghoiche Khola**.

The trail is easy on the lungs for the first part but the visual fantasy really stirs the heart. The colours, shapes, variations and sheer drama of the valley are mind-blowing. With sheer, eroded outcrops painted in cream, orange, yellow, deep red, purple and greys, the whole vista is like a fleeting apparition, dancing in the shadows, hardly credible or believable. Nowhere in Mustang are the towers and turrets, fin-shaped spires and stalagmite-like walls so vividly painted by nature. And this is only the first page of the story.

Not long after passing below a starkly orange-coloured outcrop below towering cliffs, there is a junction. Two options lead up the cliffs to the right; one is used by anything with small wheels or four legs; it is wider and less steep. The other is the original trail, steeper, narrower and enticing. Take your choice, as both soon meet higher up, where only those with two legs can venture further. For most it's less than an hour to the **'gates'** of Konchok Ling.

However, the 'gate', a locked wooden door that blocks the passage to the narrow exposed trail around the bluff, is not the end of the folktale yet. On the skyline, high above the sea of fin-shaped slumbering eroded turrets, is a red-painted mud-walled square building, but this too is not the fabled cave.

Once through the gate, the path contours around briefly above some gaping chasms, then drops into the turrets on a path that seemingly is heading nowhere but into the depths of the abyss.

Trakpuk Konchok Ling monastery ruins

Slowly but surely on this crumbling, narrow pathway the way becomes clearer. The trail begins to climb up through more gashes and chasms between the turrets on to a more substantial but exposed pathway to heaven. This stage can be seen from a small shelf just before the gateway. With some engineered steps in the soft mud, the route climbs up to the red-painted structure seen from below, the remains of **Trakpuk Konchok Ling Gompa**. There is also a weathered, barely discernible, chorten here.

The views are amazing across this vast never-ending sea of organ pipes and coral-like, multi-coloured outcrops. To the south yet more turrets and spires stretch towards a dark grey cliff, sculpted by aeons of weathering, that sits almost directly above the unseen village of Samdzong. The adrenalin-pumping path along the top is extremely exposed and narrow, yet strangely exhilarating. The way skirts weird formations and winds above the abysses on both sides. Fleeting visions of shadowy sentinels, etched in sand and mud hundreds of metres far below, are tantalising. Demons and ghosts move in the dark tempestuous dungeons glimpsed below through gaps in the gothic-like walls. The path drops through a narrow defile on steps and comes to the edge of another abyss.

Formerly, without the two strong-looking and confidence-inspiring iron cables, there would have been no way down to the Konchok Ling treasure. Now a better approach has been fashioned with bright red wooden steps and handrails, but it still needs care.

The final couple of minutes are accomplished along a narrow path, along up and around below the cave. Prayer flags and some 'auspicious' wire netting guard **Konchok Ling Cave** (est. 4100m).

The surprise of the trip is that the cave is quite small. Why anyone would want to meditate in this inaccessible and remote cavern is inexplicable.

Konchok Ling

The cave 'grotto' of Konchok Ling was only 'discovered' by outsiders in 2007. Quite a lot of damage is evident here in this former meditation cave. The cave is associated with the ancient monastery of Trakpuk Konchok Ling. Some of the paintings are thought to date from the 13th and 14th century; they are now protected behind glass panels. The main paintings depict some of the Mahasiddhas, who were tantric masters and ascetics considered to be sufficiently empowered to act as teachers. There are 84 major Mahasiddhas: Nagarjuna, Indrabuti, Tilopa and Naropa are probably the most notable, but we do not know which are seen at the cave. Other larger, quite faded images on the left depict a four-armed Chenresig, a central Vajradhara and a Green Tara to the right. The white four-armed Chenresig is the manifestation called Shadakshari Lokeshvara, linked to the mantra 'Om Mani Padme Hum'; he is a particularly compassionate icon who sits on a moon disc in his paradise. Some lamas are also depicted on the northern wall. There are also paintings of some cooking utensils and pots. Visitors and their guides should avoid touching the paintwork, due to its fragile nature. It is especially important to protect this precious site.

Reaching the cave is only half the story. Paradise it may be for Shadakshari, but for mortals there is still the need to retreat to a safer place of rest, so be very careful on the return stage to the gateway, and don't mellow out until you are on the way back to Lo Manthang.

Konchok Ling cave
entrance

inside

and an image of a Mahasiddha

Contrary to the Map House map, there is sadly no safe way down from Konchok Ling to Samdzong. Even with a rope it would be quite a task to descend into the Tumu Khola valley side canyon that leads to the Samdzong village.

Image of a Mahasiddha, Konchok Ling caves

The ridge top trail to Konchok Ling

Side trip: Samdzong (3hrs)

The road trip to Samdzong (Samjong) departs from near Dhuk not far from New Samdzong. The route is briefly in the main valley passing the Konchok Ling valley to a sign for Old Samjong. To the west is an ancient fortress in ruins.

The route climbs steadily up on a narrow but soft road negotiating the gullies and ridges quite easily. The **road pass** is at 3988m with panoramic views all around… to the south the Himalayan barrier, to the west over to the Kimaling Valley, to the north towards Tibet and the mountains and to the east the Samdzong Valley with the Nepalese white dome on a high hill to the northeast. The trail from Dhuk to the Samdzong Valley is just north of the road pass and drops dramatically into the valley eastwards.

View west from Samdzong La pass   **Crossing the pass**

The descent is steeper and dramatic, as the road drops quickly to negotiate a side chasm before dropping to the valley floor. The route now climbs very gently along the valley, with amazing outcrops, fairytale chimneys and the endless etched turrets that characterise both sides of the Konchok Ling ridge. The actual cave of **Konchok Ling** is not obvious, set amongst this mirage of heavenly artistry.

The trail from the trekkers' Samdzong Pass appears on the left, cutting dramatically through the turrets and outcrops.

A lone herder was seen here with his yaks and goats, so there must be some water somewhere around.

The outcrop on the east side of the canyon and icicles

The road drops a little into a side stream and then climbs out through a very narrow defile.

Here the main river squeezes through eroded cliffs. The road hardly exists here and there are icicles (in late autumn) on the east, shadowy side as well as a weirdly sculptured outcrop which appears to have inaccessible caves very high up.

The road is good and climbs gently on around a bluff to **Old Samdzong** (4100m), taking just over 1hr 15mins from the Chosar valley. Samdzong is an eerie lifeless spot.

Old Samdzong village

Old Samdzong
The village of Samdzong lies northeast of Lo Manthang and suffers from perennial water shortages. In 2011 a team of anthropologists under Peter Athans discovered the human remains of 27 people in a cave near Samdzong. It was partially this discovery which fuelled speculation that the ancient inhabitants of Lo practiced human sacrifice. The caves were used to house the remains of these unfortunates long before they were used for habitation. Today there is little chance to access any of these caves. Perhaps that is just as well as some further information suggest even more macabre activities in this region a long time ago.

Old Samdzong is quite a large village, set against dramatic cliffs where erosion has again carved out fanciful shapes and structures. Above the village are some cave hollows and one we presume is a small cave monastery retreat. There are maybe twenty-five houses or so, with a small mani wall and prayer wheel building before the main area. A small grove of trees is set below the village. The village has been abandoned due to lack of potable water – the village tap is forlorn and dry. The nearby river is toxic with salt and probably sulphur as well. The houses remain intact, a forlorn and ghostly silence pervades the air. Will Old Samdzong ever rise again, or will it fall into decay and ruin?

The salt pans and cliffs at Old Samdzong village

Old Samdzong village

The return trip to Lo Manthang takes around 1hr 30mins, with views of blood red cliffs down the Samdzong Khola river, which later becomes the Tumu Khola valley towards the north side of the white Sakau Danda rocky ridge.

Side trip: Mardzong Bon Caves (2–4hrs)

Also sometimes referred to as Makhchung, the Bon Cave shrine east of Lo Manthang makes a great half-day excursion for those with time to explore beyond the norms. This cave outcrop complex was explored in more detail in 2008, when a considerable find of ancient texts and historical records (later referred to by some as the Mardzong chronicles) was found. The trail is described below but it's much easier to drive there in about 20mins from Lo Manthang.

The trail out of Lo Manthang departs from the southeastern side and heads across the fields in a direct line towards the vast white-mountain outcrop of **Sakau Danda**. The Dokpolo Khola river is some way over on the right side of the path at first.

In 20mins there are some old mud ruins and the route heads down left of these to a much wider track that gets steeper and stonier. The Dokpolo Khola is much closer now. Towering high above are the startling and brilliant white towers, turrets and strange-shaped eroded features that make up the massive Sakau Danda hill. Other colours add to the mix, including the beautiful red, orange and brown shades of the Mustang Khola valley.

Once across the shallow Dokpolo side stream, there is an unexpected bonus in 5mins. Hot water is bubbling up and captured in a couple of pools for local bathers at **Tatopani Springs**. Close by is a small bridge that leads over the tricky flows of the Mustang Khola, but it's a forlorn hope to use this path in its current state. Almost immediately after the bridge is a dangerously exposed, loose area. The path is said to lead to high yak pastures, but it looks a near impossible task to take this high eroded route to Samdzong in its current state.

For the Mardzong Caves, keep to the south side of the Mustang Khola and continue down the valley. There is no well-defined path, but this is not an issue. It's a short hike to the imposing **Mardzong Bon Cave** outcrop.

A new suspension bridge cuts out all the hassle and wet feet that were to be endured before.

Cave chamber at Mardzong

Mardzong Bon outcrop and caves

Mardzong (Makhchung) Bon Caves

The Mardzong Caves are sometimes referred to as Makhchung, but they should more correctly be called by their Tibetan name Mardzong. Apparently the historical chronicles of Mustang mention the Mardzong Bon monastery cave complex along with a Buddhism monastery in the vicinity. According to one legend, a fracas broke out between the two opposing monasteries. Each sent their respective powers of magic to attack the opposition. An earthquake shook the area and the Buddhist monastery fell into ruins. As recently as 2008, some scraps of texts and ancient manuscripts were recovered from the cave complex by a couple of western teams that included Ngaru Geshe Gelek Jinpa, a local Bon scholar. The strange-shaped outcrop is where the Bon master Rong Tokme Shipko is said to have meditated. During this time he met Sherab Gyaltsen, also known as the Great Yangton, the father of the founder (Trashi Gyaltsen) of the Lubra Bon community that remains to this day. There are many openings in the strange-shaped outcrop, but none are easily accessed without the safety of a rope. Constant erosion has exposed what were once secure inside chambers. The remnants of an ancient 'kora path' remain, but it's all too loose for general access.

On our previous visit it was impossible to access any of the caves and tunnels of the outcrop, but in recent years a concrete and stone stairway has been added.

The concrete steps go up in up two levels to the first cave opening hollow. Here are some simple well-worn paintings and coloured walls, but not much detail remains.

Entrance to the mysterious Bon Caves of Mardzong

Mardzong cave views

A narrow ledge leads further around to the next cave hollow and tunnel further in. **Beware, it's extremely dangerously exposed here!** We did not go round here; thank you Sanjib!

A second chamber is reached and then a tunnel stairway leads to the third chamber above east. There is no particularly clear artwork left in these two cave hollows, so it's not vital to risk the tiny ledge to get to them.

The ancient 'kora' around the whole outcrop is also scary.

Life on the edge at Mardzong, Tanka and Bob

Sanjib negotiates the narrow ledge to the 2nd and 3rd caves

The eroded Mardzong 'Kora' trail is definitely disused!

Side trip: Demons' Chasm – Tumu Khola Canyon

Warning: Be aware that during the day the water levels in the canyon will rise, making the tiny trickle of the morning grow into a more significant stream later in the day as meltwaters increase higher up.

If there is time it's worth explore the narrow defile of the Tumu Khola, the canyon that drains from Samdzong. We had hoped to find a way to Samdzong up this streambed and make the day into a long route. However, there is a revelation in this small, deeply cut gorge, but be very careful in this chasm of the demons.

Passing below the Bon shrine outcrop, just a few minutes further along the initially easy streambed reveals some amazing features. The streambed itself is red in colour, lined by oozing black salty mush in places. The water is very salty and sulphur-smelling.

It's not long before the sheer-sided and crumbling-looking walls of the canyon creep inwards, choking off the stream and creating small waterfalls to negotiate. Be careful higher up.

It's slippery and this place feels very remote. Finally the main canyon is blocked by a much bigger waterfall, but to the left is a weird-looking rock formation where water drips over the overhang. Ahead is a small pool whose waters are never going to slake anyone's thirst. This **goblinesque water cavern**, where the cliffs threaten to cut off the light, is very dank and eerie; a true hiding place of the ghostly ghouls. Climbing down one of the smaller waterfalls on the way back needs some care.

Entrance to the demons' canyon

Further **east** the cliffs have some very inaccessible-looking caves near the confluence of the Mustang and Chhuchhu Kholas.

Demons' canyon   **Road access to Mardzong**

Side trip: Rinchenling Cave Trek (2–3hrs)

Only recently opened, the trip to the Rinchenling Cave outcrop is another stunning destination not to be missed for those with time and energy. Rinchenling has a couple of other spellings – Ritseling and Rinchhenling. From Chosar the drive is less than 15mins (about 30mins from Lo Manthang). The man with the key is also the guide; he needs to be found and driven to the trek start point. There is about a 400m height gain on this trek, so it's best not done immediately on arrival in Lo Manthang unless already acclimatised. Previously one needed to take one's own ladder to access the cave!

Rinchenling Cave outcrop

The trek begins at about 3900m and immediately begins a steep ascent, initially on dirt and then on steps. There are great views to the north of more multi-coloured turrets and outcrops painted in red, yellow, grey, white and orange. The trail gets ever steeper for about 20mins to a more level area, where an alternative trail down is reached. Continuing upwards, the route becomes more level to a **knoll outcrop**. There are views northwest to the distant Mansail range along the Tibetan border. The trail climbs to a flat 'rock' seat and then climbs on a zigzagging path. To the west the Nyamdo and Kimaling Valley can be made out.

There is **a cairn** at 1hr 10mins up as the trail gets steeper. Finally a bluff is rounded and there is the first view of the **Rinchenling cliffs and caves**. It's a little further to the base of the cliff and the new stairway to the caves (4295m). This ascent might take from 1–1½hrs, depending on acclimatisation. There are views of the Damodar peaks, the Arniko Himal, Mansail and the border range to the north. Tilicho, Annapurna 1,

Nilgiri and the Muktinath Himal with the Thorong La peaks are visible to the south. The trail to the Chogo La and Lo Manthang are also in the frame. To access the caves there are two staircases, and once inside, a bit of a scramble up a wooden ladder. The main chamber hosts amazing artwork; this is where the monk meditated in retreat. A small hole connects this room with the black-ceilinged kitchen next door; his food was prepared and passed through the hole so he was not disturbed. The artwork is very well preserved here, with particularly good images of a Garuda figure and fat Guru Rinpoche. Nepalese temples feature in the main paintings.

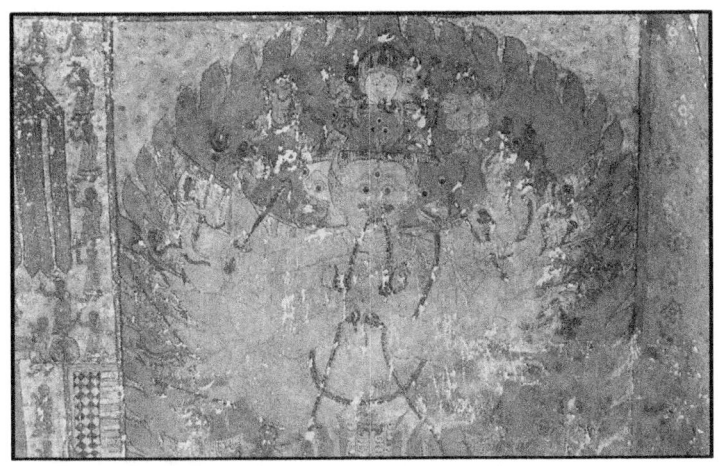

Wall murals at Rinchenling

Paintings in the Rinchenling Cave

More paintings at Rinchenling

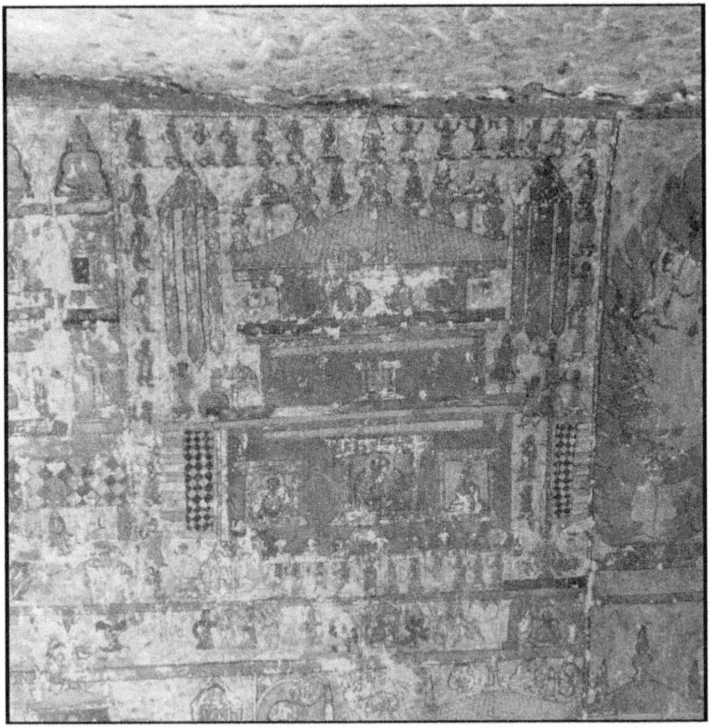

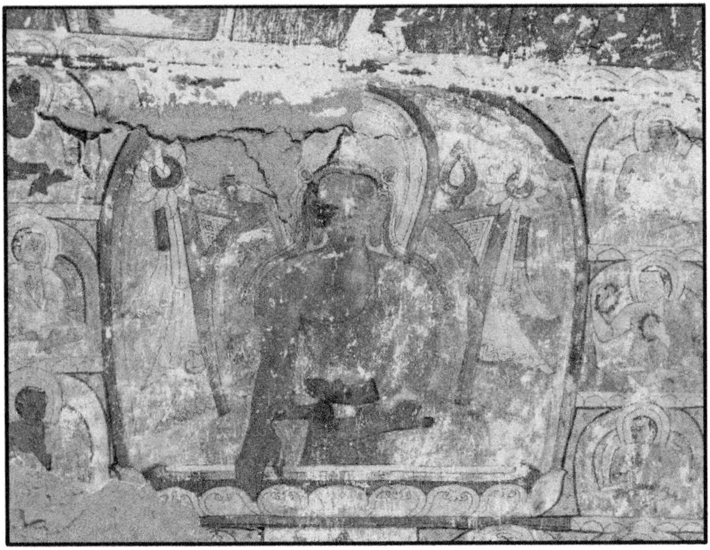

Kitchen area at Rinchenling

Rinchenling Col (10mins each way)

Before leaving, it's worthwhile to walk southeast to the ridgeline for a panoramic view across to Konchok Ling and beyond. A narrow but OK path cuts around the bluff and up to the col on the ridgeline.

Konchok Ling from the Rinchenling Col

The return trek back to Chosar is quicker, taking around 50mins – 1hr. The cairn is reached in 15mins, the knoll in 20mins and the junction in 25mins. Go ahead left here on a different route down to the mani wall, keeping on the west side of the main ridge. The path is OK but ever steeper and a bit loose in places. Follow the ridgeline into a red-coloured area of small turrets. Care is needed near the bottom area, which is steeper and looser underfoot.

On our trek we glimpsed Blue Sheep across the valley.

Views northwest on the trail to Rinchenling

Side trip: Chodzong (6hrs pony + 2hrs trek)

One of the most remote and strangely exotic outposts in Upper Mustang, the Chodzong cave monastery valley is as sensational for its scenery as it is for its acclaimed Buddhist art. It's possible to trek to this remote valley from Garphu over the Samdzong La pass to the Samdzong Valley and then over the Chodzong La to Chodzong, but it requires a full camping crew from Kathmandu, as few in Lo Manthang are available for such a venture. The only other alternative is to take a pony and pony man for a long day-trip east along the Chhuchhu Gumba Khola from Lo Manthang.

A pony costs Rs4000 per day plus Rs2000 pony man wage. Entry to the famed 'troglodyte' cave paintings is a whopping Rs15,000 plus Lama costs – his pony and his fee.

First views of the Chodzong Valley

The trip begins with a short 15min drive from Lo Manthang to Mardzong. Once astride the ponies, the route is along the upper Mustang Khola deep canyon east under cliffs of caves to the junction of the **Mustang Khola** (or upper Kali Gandaki) and the Chhuchhu Gumba Khola, taking about 40mins. The route goes around into the side canyon, and is quite wide with towering cliffs. Three river crossings follow, as the trail comes to a small ridge; it is necessary to walk the stage over a small rise around a chasm where the water flows to the left for 10mins. Some multi-coloured features are seen here, salty and icy crustations clinging to the cliffs that never see sunlight.

Once astride the ponies again, the route heads into a narrower ravine area with around 18 crossings of the water required before the valley widens with sheer sandstone cliffs and turrets. (The water is icy, and trekking along this valley would be quite a task). A further 8–9 more crossings are required before reaching the **Chaka Khola** canyon, which heads south here. The ride takes around 1½hrs to this river confluence.

The entrance to the next canyon is narrow, but the valley opens out with spectacular, sheer sandstone organ pipe-like features. On the left (northwest) are **multi-coloured veins** in the cliffs, with one strange-looking flat-topped outcrop with coloured veins 'dripping' and draped down its cliffs. The colours are not dissimilar to the Sakyapa monastery walls of the Upper Mustang region. There are more staggeringly contorted, eroded turrets and gullies on view to the north.

The route comes to a **saltwater waterfall** and ahead the canyon is impassable, with deep chasms hiding the river with sheer cliffs each side. The ride to here took 2hrs and it was a relief to dismount!

From here the trail is very steep, narrow, dusty, loose and zigzagging up a white slope. Ponies cannot negotiate this ascent with jockeys, so it's back on two legs for a while. The exposed trail snakes up between crumbling, small turrets into a side stream gulley. From here a narrow path climbs very steeply through the maze of outcrops for a while. The climb is around 200m up to 3900m, taking 30mins or so, where the trail emerges on to a grassy sloping plateau area. The ponies are in action again as the route crosses the top of the bluff and bend of the river for a few minutes. The indistinct trail to the Chodzong La pass climbs from here, meaning it's actually a detour east to reach the Chodzong monastery.

Amazing outcrops en route to Chodzong

The chorten kani gates to Chodzong Valley

There are views to the right (south) into the abyss of the Chhuchhu Gumba canyon and then the views begin to open out as two chortens appear below. This is the notable viewpoint of the Chodzong Valley that entices all to seek out its wonders. The two chortens are effectively the **gates of the Chodzong Valley**. The trail descends on new steps which the ponies find difficult, so it's back to two legs for this 80–100m descent to the valley floor. Once down it is an easy stroll for 5–10mins east along the rather unusual-looking raised plateau area above the river.

Just before the shelter a small gully hides the route up to the famed Chodzong monastery. The very narrow chasm with sheer cliffs winds around and climbs to a steeper stage. A tricky section follows, ever more steeply up around turrets and outcrops. After about 5mins the final climb to **Chodzong Gompa** appears, with some painted images on the cliff to the left. The steep top stage is a bit loose underfoot, with minor exposure, so take care, especially with wobbly legs or bruised backside after the pony ride.

To be honest, the tin-roofed structure is not overly attractive, standing below a turret outcrop. The gompa was locked but the entry area hosts some quite eroded, ill-defined wall paintings of the Lokapalas. The main door, as expected, was locked.

The famed chamber with the mysterious artwork is evidently within this locked area and also locked, unless a monk (and Rs15,000 paid in advance) has accompanied the visit. It's a good spot for lunch, this lofty perch (at 3897m) above sheer chasms each side. We took 4hrs to reach the gompa from Mardzong.

Bob approaching Chodzong Gompa

Chodzong monastery and cave outcrops above

Chodzong Monastery

Being remote and little-visited, Chodzong (Chhuchhu or Chhujung) gompa is a place of mystery with a surreal, mystical charm. It is known as the 'Castle of the Dharma'. Because of its isolation, Buddhists refer to it as a place of paradise, a 'beyul', or hidden Shangri-La. It is located above the river, accessed by a small path that forces a passage into a very narrow gorge. Constructed after Luri, Tashi Kabum and Konchok Ling, it was built in the 14th or early 15th century along a trade route with Tibet. An ancient Kagyu-pa shrine may have been here earlier in the 11th century, linked to the sage Atisha, who probably visited Mustang in 1041AD. The artwork follows the Indo-Newari style that combines imagery from the Nyingma-pa and Kagyu-pa sects. This once-abundant style of painting appears to have died out across Mustang by the end of the 15th century. Apart from covered icons, there are apparently three statues of Mahakala, Yamantaka and a Buddha, otherwise it's the wall paintings that are the main feature. These are mainly the protector deities, Mahakala, Yamantaka, Chakrasambhava and others in yab-yum poses. There is a white 8-armed deity, perhaps Chenresig. Records of the art and interior here are illustrated in the book, Wonders of Lo by Erberto Lo Bue, published by Marg Publications, Mumbai 2011, now unfortunately out of print.

Above the gompa is a large stone wall, which presumably encloses the valuable paintings mentioned within. A small, steep path climbs up beside this wall to a plateau area and steeply on up again to caves hollows above. In the contorted outcrops above up the steep loose path is the **retreat cave**. It's quite a tricky access to the wooden door, which was not locked.

Upper outcrops hiding the retreat

The whole site of Chodzong Gompa, the retreat cave and the visible outcrops is actually detached from the main cliffs and slopes, making it almost impregnable to intruders – even today – so be very careful up here near the top. Inside the retreat cave are a couple of beds for the lamas, some simple thangkas, an altar and an alcove.

The upper retreat cave (photo: Sanjib)

East side outcrops at Chodzong Gompa

More cave outcrops near Chodzong monastery

Looking down into the abyss from Chodzong monastery

There are more cave hollows looking east. The valley trail continues east on to the Salde camping area and the more subdued rolling border hills beyond. The old trade route to Tibet followed this route before the border was closed.

Cliff artwork just below Chodzong monastery

Chodzong Valley looking east

It's an easy walk back now to the stairway then a hard ascent to the **chortens.** After a good rest, the ponies are back in action, as far as the steep 200m descent which must be walked on two legs again; the descent is perhaps harder than the ascent, with many slippery stages. Take care on this 200m section When the saltwater waterfall is regained, the worst is over; it's back up on the ponies for the return river ride down the canyon. The afternoon light is a little more co-operative for pictures of the stunning canyon back to **Mardzong**.

Chhuchhu Gumba Khola canyon leading back to Mardzong

Stunning cliffs on the route back to Mardzong

See **Monastery Cave Circuit Trek** for more photographs of the Chhuchhu Gumba Canyon.

The return trip to Jomsom

Taking a local or private jeep for most or part of the way allows plenty of scope for variations within the 10-day permit timeframe. Jeeps generally depart daily around 8am from Lo Manthang for Chuksang and cost from US$35 per foreigner. This figure might vary widely according to demand.

Lo Manthang – Jomsom via Drakmar
Lo Manthang – Drakmar – Syangmochen – Jomsom

Ideally take the recently built dirt track from Lo Manthang via Ghar Gompa to Drakmar and then Ghami on the return trek. From Ghami it's the same as far as Syangmochen, where another (trekking) option is on offer via Chungsi Ranchung Cave. From Samar the route is the same to Kagbeni. This routing is about as much as one can fit into the standard 10-day permit allowance.

Lo Manthang – Drakmar (1–2hrs)
Lo Manthang – Ghar Gompa – Drakmar

For those who came to Lo Manthang via Tsarang, this is the obvious choice of route for the return trip, but check if the road is actually open. The climb up to the high Chogo La is the first major obstacle. No one should miss Ghar Gompa (Lo Gekar), though, as it is one of the oldest and most historic of the monasteries across Upper Mustang. Take a packed lunch.

From Lo Manthang the road climbs steadily up around outcrops and into troughs between hills. Samdrubling remains are on the way but there is little to see. There are a couple of minor cols en route, which offer the last views of the ancient settlement. Once around a bluff it's a steeper ascent to the **Chogo La** (4230m).

> ### Samdrubling
> Samdrubling (4090m) was once a sacred Buddhist centre, founded in the 12th century by a disciple of King Nyingpo. Once belonging to the Kagyu-pa, it is still a noted place for sky burials. The sky burials are infrequent and not necessarily a sight to contemplate watching for any number of reasons, including the solemnity of the occasion for the grieving relatives. There is a cave for meditation nearby.

Initially the gradient is quite gentle, almost flat, but soon the descent begins. It's not so far down, though, to **Ghar Gompa** (3950m), also previously known as Lo Gekar.

The monastery is a superb place to visit. There are sometimes refreshments in the kitchen area by the monastery, but food is rarely available. Bring your own supplies.

Ghar Gompa (Lo Gekar)

Ghar Gompa is said to be the oldest monastery in Mustang, dating from the 8th century. Its greatest historic connection is with the Nyingma-pa sage Guru Rinpoche. His image is found in great profusion in the shrine. Ghar Gompa has strong links to Samye in Tibet, another shrine linked to Guru Rinpoche.

According to legend, when Samye monastery was being built in Tibet, all the day's work was being destroyed by the magical powers of demons every night. The lamas dreamt that Guru Rinpoche could help them, so they called him. He came to Tibet, destroying all the demons in his path. Then he told them that they would not succeed in building Samye until a monastery had been built on the site of what is now Lo Gekar. He returned to Mustang and killed the demon, whose blood was split on the rocks of Drakmar and whose intestines became the long mani wall. Lo Gekar was built according to his instructions and Samye was then constructed without further problems.

The monastery is surrounded by many long lines of prayer wheels, and a separate prayer wheel chamber. The four Lokapala guardians are in evidence before the main chamber along with Mi Tsering, the wise man. Inside the first room are paintings of the protectors, Hayagriva (Tamdrin) left, Vajrapani, and Mahakala on the right. One thousand Buddha images grace the right side. Also on the left wall are the twenty-one Tara images and eight Medicine Buddhas. Eighty Mahasiddhas or wise disciples appear on the wall before the next chamber.

In the second chamber things get even more evocative. The white Tara appears as a natural image in the immediate left corner. Further along the left wall are the first of the eight manifestations of Guru Rinpoche. Here are Pema Gyalpo, Loden Chokse and Dorje Drollo. Along the main altar wall are Sakyamuni Buddha and Guru Rinpoche, flanked by his usual consorts, on the left Mandavara and on the right Yeshe Tsogyal. To the right of these three are two more of the eight forms of Guru Rinpoche: Padma Sambhava (his usual equivalent in Sanskrit) then Padma Jigme Jungne in red.

Along the right wall are the last three of Guru Rinpoche's forms: Shakya Senge, Nima Ozer and Sange Dradok. Another figure sits in the right corner – the second Nyingma-pa Lama after Guru Rinpoche, apparently. Other visitors of note to Ghar Gompa were Tibetan poet sage and meditator, Milarepa, and Rinchen Zangpo, the 11th-century translator who initiated 108 monasteries. Apparently some of Guru Rinpoche's texts (termas) were concealed around the shrine for future generations to discover.

David Snellgrove visited the gompa in 1956.

Following the exquisite atmosphere of the gompa, the road fails to get the same rave reviews. The road descends the relatively gentle slopes of the wide valley through Saukre and on to skirt around above **Marang**.

The route then keeps above the Tsarang (Charang) Khola on the northeast side. It then drops down to the major hairpin on the main road in the gorge just below Tsarang.

From Tsarang it's back to the main road over the **Choya La** (Tsarang La) pass and down to the junction for Drakmar. Heading right, passing the chortens the road climbs a little to the village of **Drakmar**. It's a sensational conclusion to the day and Drakmar does not disappoint with its scenery.

A new side trip here is to climb the narrow path above the village up to the series of caves in the red cliffs. A **Buddha 'park'** has also opened around in the north area, with outcrops and caves to explore, all watched over by a golden Buddha.

The legend of Drakmar
Once upon a time the good people of Drakmar were fearful of the demoness called Balmo. It was said that only the great master and sage Guru Rinpoche could vanquish such a powerful evil spirit. During their tussle, so it is said, her blood was spilt, thus creating the red-coloured cliffs of the village. Her intestines transformed into a long mani wall. A chorten holds down her heart, with smaller chortens covering the spots of her spilt blood, hiding the remnants of her powers.

Drakmar Gompa
The small monastery is not far from the upper lodge, Red Hill Guest House. It houses a startling wooden head of the protector, Mahakala, and imagery of Vaishravana/Kubera, one of the four guardians (lokapalas) seen at the entrance to most monasteries. Another deity is an exquisite image of Vajradhara with crossed arms. Vajradhara is the figure who gave rise to the five Buddhas of wisdom, the Dhyani Buddhas – see the glossary for more on these icons.

Around the western bluff outcrop are yet more imposing cliffs and turrets. The Tenzin Hotel & Guest House and the Red Hill Guest House are located uphill further to the north. Red Hill is almost the last building along the base of the cliffs. It's a little unfortunate that the lodgings are tucked away around here, so far from the rest of the village and the main part of the cliffs. The morning light is absent from the cliffs above the lodges, so try to explore here in the afternoon.

Time in Drakmar

A day off is a very real temptation in Drakmar, but that frustrating permit time restriction is not conducive to a change of plan. Anyone with enough time can easily discover hidden canyons and lost paradises in the maze of towers and turrets. Those with nerves of steel might try to climb to the enticing cave shrines on the west side of the village above the lodges; but beware! This area is now enclosed by a fence where a golden Buddha sits in serenity. There might be a fee for entry by now. Another trail leaves from near the lodges bound for Marang; this would be a good option for some relaxing but exciting exploration, as it climbs the cliffs south of the main path to Lo Manthang via Ghar Gompa (Lo Gekar). Ask the local people for the exact starting point of this trail, as it is not obvious, even from the signpost in upper Drakmar. There are superlative views south over the cliffs towards Ghami.

Drakmar Buddha 'park' area

Buddha 'park' in Drakmar

Drakmar cliffs and view from the top

Drakmar Caves Trek (1hr)

Warning: Be very careful near the top of the walk about 3–5m below the chorten, where the steps are eroded and the route loose with no handholds. Going up is OK with care and maybe a guide's helping hand! The top area is very small, with a cave hollow to escape the vertiginous drops and vertigo. Only about 4–5 people can safely stop here at once. Getting down is currently very dangerous and best done sitting down gently over the eroded steps. Maybe it's best not to negotiate this last 5m or so; it's definitely not for anyone with even the mildest vertigo.

Climbing to the Drakmar cave complex trail

Mustang Explorer — Drakmar

The trail begins on a wet, grassy area between two houses in the village going north. Head around to the right behind the east house and start climbing gently below the towering red cliffs. The trail climbs steadily and after 10mins it's on new steps. It's all wonderful until **the last zigzag**, which is a bit loose underfoot, and then to the last 3–5m as mentioned above. It might take 30mins to the chorten here. The top **cave hollow** does not have any defined artwork, but the views of the cliff are amazing, with its higher inaccessible cave hollows. What mysteries are hidden there?

The return trek takes around 15–20mins from the dodgy area.

The difficult top stage to the chorten

Lo Ghami lodge

Drakmar – Samar (1–2hrs)
Drakmar – Ghami – Syangmochen – Samar

This is a long haul and could be spilt by overnighting in Ghami. Those not taking the option via Chungsi Cave to Samar can stay lower in Geling.

Leaving Drakmar the road heads down to the long mani wall before dropping across the wide valley to Ghami. Following welcome refreshments in **Ghami** the route again climbs, and this time it's considerably longer, to the **Nyi La** (4010m).

There's a small ascent before **Syangmochen** and then it's a short drop into the settlement and its cosy lodges. The road route goes around via Geling before crossing the **Yamda La** and the **Bhena La** (3830m) to the sunny shelf of **Samar**.

Samar – Jomsom (1hr)
Samar – Chele – Kagbeni – Jomsom

The return route to Kagbeni is the same down to **Chuksang**. If you missed **Tetang** on the way in, do head up there for a stunning finale to the Upper Mustang Trek! Otherwise the route to **Kagbeni** and **Jomsom** is familiar territory.

Jomsom – Kathmandu
Jomsom – Pokhara – Kathmandu

Most trekkers by this stage are only too happy to hop on the next flight to the hotspots of Pokhara, but for those with the time and inclination there are a few interesting sights in the vicinity. See under **Lower Mustang** for some of these, such as Thini and Syang, the closest to Jomsom. After all that bumpy journey it's off to the comforts of Pokhara and Kathmandu, which invariably means the end of the trip. Oh, deary me!

Mustang Explorer

For more details on the remote treks in Mustang, see **Mustang: The Untrodden Trails** by Paulo Grobel, Sonia Baillif & Etienne Principaud, published by Map House, Kathmandu, 2023 and also available on Amazon worldwide.

Drakmar cliffs cave complex is now accessible with care

Buddha Park area

Dhaulagiri from Upper Mustang

Typical festival mask

OTHER CLASSIC MUSTANG ROUTES

Wherever one heads in Upper Mustang, there are revelations and surprises in equal measure, but the eastern trail between Lo Manthang and Muktinath defies all descriptive powers and is just mind-blowing. The scenery is like one vast painted thangka – a star-studded jewel of nature. It is surely the intricate work of the gods to totally bewitch us, mere mortals. Currently it's possible to visit Yara, Luri and Ghara by rough dirt road, which is expected to be extended to Damodar Lake one day! See the camping-based Monastery Cave Circuit Trek for more choices.

Until quite recently, only trekkers could explore the spectacular Buddhist art found near Yara at Luri and Tashi Kabum as a detour from Lo Manthang or Tsarang. New dirt roads and lodgings in Yara have opened up this part of the eastern side trail between Lo Manthang and Muktinath. These fairytale landscapes are the stuff of dreams. Since the scenery cannot be described adequately in flowing prose, you will just have to come and see it for yourself! For those with permit time restraints, it's best to get to Lo Manthang as soon as acclimatisation allows. The following are some of the side trips now aided by road construction.

Side trip: Yara, Luri and Ghara (6–8hrs)

Ideally these fabulous sights of Upper Mustang should be included in any road trip itinerary. The scenery of Yara, the cultural and historic importance of Luri and Tashi Kabum Cave are highlights.

Yara cliffs and caves

Lo Manthang – Yara (2–3hrs)
Lo Manthang – Tsarang – Dhi – Yara

The road route to these sights is from Lo Manthang via **Tsarang**.

Descending from Tsarang to the east, the road drops to the Kali Gandaki Valley. It's a colossal chasm, this defile between the soft grey strata and sheer cave-lined cliffs. Across the valley is the settlement of **Surkhang** (3400m), with some new buildings. Nearby northeast, ahead is **Dhi** (3400m).

In Dhi are a couple of lodging options. The Hira Hotel is a very amiable watering hole for lunch, with good apple pancakes. The Potala Hotel is another choice.

Dhi village from above

Once across the river the road then climbs up the drama-filled Yara valley, with amazing sheer columns and fantastic fairytale organ pipe features etched into the sheer cliffs. Within these cliffs are hundreds of now-inaccessible caves and cave hollows. The cluster of four or five caves seen in cultural books on Mustang is quite a sight. The more extensive group of caves in the separated outcrop seen higher up is as sensational in real life as in the picture books.

The Yara cliffs are rightly a big highlight of Upper Mustang. The village of **Yara** (3650m) is a delightful place, with a setting to match. For lodging try the Saribung Hotel or the Roof Top Guest House next door. It's easy to stay overnight if a day off for cultural exploration is planned.

In some ways it's better to explore the sights on foot, but the dirt roads are generally usable to get as far as Luri, if not Tashi Kumbum.

> **Yara Caves**
> There are quite a few theories about who lived in these apparently inaccessible caves, and what they were used for apart from shelter. Its thought that the caves were used by Tibetans as shelter, for meditation and storage. The caves here are generally rectangular or square – a more unusual feature in Mustang. The walls are quite smooth and some were painted. A number of caves are interconnected, and most are quite low at the entry area. Quite a few artefacts – tools, pottery, religious objects, manuscripts texts and even some tangkas have been found here. The caves were evidently also a pilgrimage site in ancient times for Bon and Buddhists. See the Cave dwellers box for more.

Side trip: Luri Cave and Monastery (5–6hrs)
Yara – Ghara – Luri – Tashi Kabum – Yara

A cultural 'rest day' – This is one of the most spectacular days for cultural highlights in the whole of Upper Mustang. The scenery is full of drama; how could it be otherwise, with imposing cliffs and outcrops surrounding the whole valley. The cultural offerings grab most of the headlines today, though: Ghara, Luri Cave, Luri Monastery and the elusive Tashi Kabum. It's best to go to Ghara first, since the lady with the key to Luri Cave and Gompa lives there. The new dirt roads will modify some of the text below, and give closer access to the sights for those who have neither the time nor the possibility to walk here.

Before leaving Yara it's not a bad idea to climb up to the northeast side of the village for a great sunrise (or later for those who find rising early a chore or those who dream of coffee in bed) view across the village to those imposing Yara cliffs.

The route for Ghara is up through fields near an irrigation channel with a red chorten nearby; it soon joins a wide track. Although it is an easy track, the climb to Ghara seems quite long.

There is a surprising glimpse of Dhaulagiri and Tukuche peak miles to the southwest, reminding us all that the Himalaya are still around. It takes 1–1½hrs to reach **Ghara** (3920m), if treating the day as a 'rest day'. Rest days invariably end up harder than normal days, but not on this occasion. In Ghara tea is on offer at a house near the new Luree Karbung Guest House that was closed for winter (late November).

High above the village, dominated by red outcrops, is the **Trik La** (4300m), a pass that leads to Chaka Camp via a camp at Amka (4250m).

You might think it would be all down now to Luri, but no! The trail climbs out of Ghara near another water channel and various chortens and a ruined mud structure of old.

Other Classic Mustang Routes

The trail for Damodar Kund can be seen snaking up the hills opposite; it doesn't look inviting.

Eventually, after an ancient fort-like building, Luri Cave is seen ahead, and in what an astonishing location! The key lady was absent from Ghara, but luckily we met her en route, as she normally does prayers each day in Luri Gompa.

It takes only a little over 45mins to reach **Luri Cave chorten** from Ghara. The altitude must be close to 4000m here. The path to the cave is steep and narrow, but recently renovated with two new proper bridges and even new ladders inside, so there's no excuse to miss it.

Mind your head on the low beams!

Trik La pass from Ghara

Luri Cave

The cave retreat of Luri is another famous and unmissable sight in Upper Mustang. Locally the place translates as the White Chorten on the Naga Hill. A Guru Rinpoche images of considerable age is featured inside.

Fortunately the access path has been much improved. Once up the ladder, the first area hosts twelve images of Buddha. The second small chamber keeps Guru Rinpoche in the dark with what seem to be two donor lamas beside him. A drum also fills the chamber. The third chamber is what all the fuss is about. It's a wonder of Lo. A shiny and quite large chorten sits squarely in this small but better-lit chamber. Above the chorten hosting the eight noted 13th-century paintings of the Mahasiddhas is a beautifully decorated black ceiling. One image is that of the seated Nagarjuna, a bright red colour. Other images on the domed ceiling are easy to see, like Dombi Heruka riding a tiger.

Other Classic Mustang Routes

A grey image on a white background is Savaripa, while another seated with crossed arms is Ghandapa. Around the walls are found images of Vajradhara (white with crossed arms) and Sakyamuni Buddha with some disciples.

On the bumpa dome of the chorten are the famous paintings of a white Chenresig, a dark blue Vajrapani, Shadakshari Lokeshvara and another unidentified image on the north side. Around the base, look for the squat bluish Vaishravana (Kubera, a guardian), Palden Lhamo on a horse, a Garuda and a wrathful blue Vajrapani. Luri Cave Gompa has some amazing frescoes painted by Newari artists from the Kathmandu Valley in the 12th century.

Outside the three chambers are the kitchen and a living area.

Luri Cave complex and inside

The famed chorten inside the cave

Located nearby is **Luri Gompa**, in a dramatic setting overlooking the river, but more impressively below some even stranger looking fins, turrets and jumbled-up outcrops of gigantic proportion, perhaps 150–200m high. It's less than 10mins down the hill from the cave.

Luri Gompa

A wheel of life, the wise man, the four guardians and a prayer wheel watch guests entering the monastery. Once inside, on the left are paintings of the protectors. These two are Mahakala and the guardian to the gates of heaven or hell, Yamantaka. The left wall hosts some wise arhats and Mahasiddhas (selected historic Buddhist sages and masters). Unusually the main altar wall has an array of small icons around a mysterious door that is not to be opened. Books are stored here on the left. On the right wall one prominent image is that of Samantabhadra in yab-yum and the lesser-known icon Chakrasambhava, also in yab-yum. This icon is linked in embrace to Vajravarahi (Dorje Phagmo in Tibetan). Along with Guru Rinpoche, the right wall is covered in paintings of protectors surrounded by rings of fire. Also on the inside right wall next to the entrance are the protectors Vajrapani and Hayagriva (Tamdrin).

The trail back to Yara follows a zigzagging pathway down into the riverbed. Some striking outcrops dominate the walk, looking like a mix of the troglodyte turrets of Göreme in Turkey and Bryce Canyon in the western American state of Utah. The path is stony and indistinct, but descends to a junction where a sign points the way to Damodar and Luri.

> **Tashi Kabum Cave**
> The cave is also called Tashi Geling Chorten Cave and is normally accessed by a short scramble. Apparently one of the main features here is the chaotic collection of clay Tsa Tsa tablets. Otherwise all eyes are drawn upwards to the amazing dome artistry, where the 8 auspicious symbols of Buddhism are fabulously displayed. The paintings are subtle and appealing, done in the Indo-Newari Kashmiri period styles so famous across the Buddhist world of the 11th century. The four-armed white-faced Chenresig referred to as Shadakshari Lokeshvara is a major icon here. Good luck on your visit. For more information dating from 1992, read an article by Gary McCue written in June 2001 for www.asianart.com

Further on are the sometimes-inaccessible **Tashi Kabum Caves**. Even if the caves are inaccessible, the astonishing setting is over-powering. Sentinels of the gods, reaching to the sky, watch passing trekkers far below. The canyon becomes very narrow and dark, perhaps a little eerie in the late afternoon light. From a new irrigation channel the path begins the shortish climb back up to home from home for the night, **Yara**.

Dirt roads are creeping ever further in to rarely charted country south and east of Luri, probably eventually to help pilgrims get to the remote and sacred lake at Damodar below the snow peaks surrounding Bhrikuti Peak.

Tsarang – Tange (3–4hrs)
Tsarang – Dhechyang Khola – Tange

Before any roads appeared in the vicinity, it was quite a tough trekking day to reach Tange, since the deep canyon of the Dhechyang Khola prevents the path from staying high. It is, however, a day of fabulous, unexpected scenery. Today a new dirt road may be offering non-trekkers a glimpse of this once wild and desolate corner of Upper Mustang. We have not enticed anyone to take their precious jeep this far and that may remain the case. However, should the road and route become better engineered, we add this enticing offer in this guide for the future. The road, such as it is thus far, is apparently already built in outline to Dhey. Like Samdzong, Dhey is almost deserted these days; maybe the coming of a passable dirt road will regenerate the settlement.

The route is initially the same as that going to Yara, but on crossing the Kali Gandaki the new option heads southeast. It would be possible to head directly east to explore the Dechyang Valley for a few minutes and maybe take tea at **Riverside Hotel** (est. 3300m). This is up to 3hrs from Yara. The owner Mr Tsering L. Gurung says the place will usually close around late November/early December. It opens in March/April; tel 9846590621.

The road climbs steadily in loops and zigzags to navigate the gullies and troughs of the hillside. You may catch a glimpse of the peaks to the south – Dhaulagiri, Yakawa Kang, Khatung Kang, Annapurna I, Tilicho and the Nilgiris. The route is variously steep or less steep. Once it begins to ease off, the trekkers' pass is at hand. It's had no name, but we called it the **Slo-Go La** (est. 4000m) for obvious reasons.

There is a junction of dirt roads near the pass. One supposedly goes more east to the **Sertang La**, the other to Tange.

Dhey or Dhye – soon to be lost?
Dhey is the last major settlement east of the Mustang Khola in the area towards Tibet, but the future of this remote village is not assured. There are plans to resettle the people of Dhey (Dhye) higher up the narrow Dhechyang canyon to a place near the Riverside Hotel. Apparently 26 families live in Dhey. The easiest approach to Dhey is along the sheer-sided canyon, although like any river route it's fraught with challenges: rockfall, landslides and wet feet. In high water season, people have to take the high path to their village from high above Riverside (initially using the same path as for Tange). The new road, if it remains usable, might save the village and add to the destinations on offer further east.

Bharal – Blue sheep can be spotted in remoter areas

Map: Yara – Tange

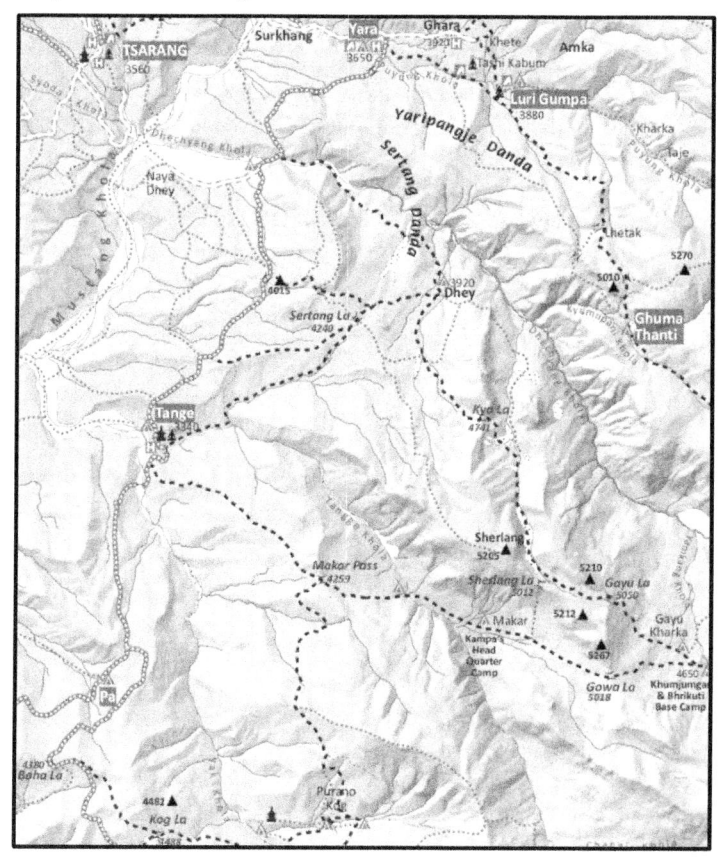

The drop-off from the trekkers' pass was quite steep with gullies, so the road must have to negotiate some difficult terrain. It keeps to the east of the trekking trail as it descends to Tange. There should be views looking east towards the **Khumjungar peaks**. On the trekkers' trail a strange area of mud buttresses is crossed and further down were more mud outcrops to a plateau area. The road also needs to negotiate these amazing features. The final descent must cut through a band of notable turrets that sit above Tange village. **Tange** (3240m) is a great village to explore, with stunning outcrops high above, especially at sunset.

Dominating Tange are a series of picturesque chortens, one of which is said to be the largest in Upper Mustang. There are a few lodgings to choose from. The Shambala has en suite mud-floored facilities, while others are the hidden-away Pa Hotel, the Hotel Laxman and the River View Guest House.

> **Tange monastery and chortens**
> Tange has a small red gompa near the cute clump of eight chortens. It belongs to the Ngorchen-Sakya school, like most of the Upper Mustang monasteries. There is no main idol in the sparse chamber, but it does have some butter tormas and a collection of dusty books. The lay lama was in full song reading his texts, and there is a kitchen section. Two ancient but script-less prayer wheels are laying idle in a corner. Just south of the gompa is the impressive line of chortens. One kani-style chorten has some paintings inside its ceiling.

Tange chortens

Side trips from Tange

If you get this far by road, Tange is a good place to take a break. There are three choices to keep exploring and all are wild and remote; whether trekking or when possible driving.

Tange Tashi Kabum

The easiest option is looking for the secretive Tashi Kabum, said to be in the vicinity. We assume it is located in the caves just up the Tange Khola valley towards the east. There are caves, but none appear to be accessible, and the village people are not keen to say where this shrine is to be found.

A vague trail climbs up towards the caves to a spot just above some small turret outcrops but soon peters out. There are no caves around to the north, where the line of sentinels heads before being buried in the plateau hillside. Our valiant porter tried to access one of the easier caves, but after fighting off loose slopes and the odd missile from above, he had to give up. There is no road to this hidden chamber.

Sertang La Pass (est. 1–2hrs)

This is the pass that leads over to Dhey, from where one might anticipate a good view down to the besieged, waterless village. A dirt road is also making its way up around here for purposes unknown.

The trail leaves Tange near the Shambala Hotel and keeps low above the bridge and east along the Tange Khola. Later on the trail can be seen climbing steadily but relentlessly up through some very dark-coloured soils mixed with yellow sandier material. It seems to climb forever to the notch on the skyline, assumed to be the **Sertang La** (4240m).

We gave up on this option, which did not really inspire with any predictable panoramic view until the elusive topside. We do need to leave some undiscovered destinations for future intrepid explorers!

Makar Pass (est. 1–2hrs)

Why would anyone want to explore the Makar Pass area from Tange? – the only answer to date is: "because it's there" – to quote a famous phrase of the old Everest mountaineers.

The trail begins across the main Tange Khola bridge just east of the Shambala Hotel. It's a constant climb up, but not that bad for the most part. The new dirt road heads up more to the east, but it ends fairly abruptly higher up so the purpose of this project remains unknown.

It takes about an hour to reach the **first col** (est. 3600m), where a stone pile and prayer flags mark the top. The views over Tange and the lower river area are well worth the effort, with dark, brooding peaks south of Mansail on show to the west. Sadly there are no views of the much sought-after Bhrikuti Peak cluster to the southeast.

There is a view over the Yak Khola that drains from the Teri La pass miles out of sight. Further on, the climb continues at much the same gradient through sweet juniper and berberis thorn bushes. Another 30mins brings the slightly frustrated trekker to another **false col** (est. 3800m), with at least a view towards what appears to be the **Makar Pass** (4259m).

By now we had run out of time and steam, and retreated (in just over 1hr) to the comforts of our mud-floored en suite paradise. So the Makar Pass remains elusive to us at least, but maybe not to you.

We do understand that the valley beyond the pass has some sparse woodlands and was used by the Khampa rebels in the 1950–60s when fighting the Chinese in Tibet. And so the mystery is left unsolved for now – what can be seen from the Makar Pass? Let us know if you reach there!

High above Tange

As mentioned, it's likely that a dirt road will eventually lead to the sacred site at **Damodar Lake** (4890m) from this area. To the south of the lake are the tangled peaks of the Damodar Himal, with Khumjungar and Bhrikuti Peak the main summits.

> **Damodar Lakes**
> There are several glacial lakes here – the Brahmakunda, Rudrakunda, Anantakunda and the largest, Damodar Kund (or Kunda). Many pilgrims come here for the August full moon. There is a small Hindu temple here containing a statue of Vishnu. Followers of the Hindu god Krishna believe a pilgrimage to the Damodar Lakes and a bath will absolve them of all their sins. Above the lake is a chorten and numerous prayer flags. Buddhist pilgrims pay homage to Avalokiteshvara/Chenresig here. The lake is mentioned in various Hindu texts dating from 400–1000AD. Another text calls the Kali Gandaki (Black Gandaki) the Krishnagandaki River, the river formed of seven torrents. The river is said to be the sweat running off the cheeks of Vishnu. Muktinath is where the mouth of the god is found and Kagbeni is the location of his neck.

Other Classic Mustang Routes

Bhrikuti Peak and Khumjungar from the road near the Bhena La

Typical Tsa-tsa relics

Typical dining area in Lo Manthang

The Sungda chorten – have a peaceful and safe trip

MONASTERY CAVE CIRCUIT TREK

Samdzong, Chodzong and Mardzong (4 days plus)

These two attractions are normally only visited by anthropologists spending extended periods in Upper Mustang. For trekkers, it is very expensive to plan to take in these historic destinations. So far, any people remaining in Samdzong have been reticent about foreigners staying overnight and most have relocated to the new village. This **ground-breaking** adventure has thus far rarely been on offer.

Fully supported camping trips with guides, cooks and porterage, including all services like tents and food, might cost more than US$100 per day per person for a small group of two trekkers. Costs would reduce accordingly for more trekkers, especially in the off season, with some hard bargaining. The itinerary below should only be taken as a rough guide for planning ideas. Timings are estimated, often local speeds are far too optimistic for most trekkers. Going anticlockwise might reduce the effects of altitude if in doubt.

Lo Manthang – Samdzong (5–7hrs)
Lo Manthang – Samdzong La – Samdzong

Ideally start by heading across the Samdzong La to Samdzong as described earlier. Camping is apparently allowed now in the vicinity of the village, but check about any rather high 'fees' levied. The village has a dramatic setting, but the lack of life here is a little eerie.

The trail begins near Dhuk, climbing on a relatively gentle slope to the pass, with ever wider panoramic views across the area around Lo Manthang and the border region. The descent to the valley is wild and exciting through gullies, turrets and weird outcrops. As mentioned before, water would need to be carried to this camp by jeep or extra ponies that can then return to Chosar. One camping option is on the plateau just above the saltwater river here. To reach Samdzong village is quite a long detour. Allow 2hrs for this, one way.

Samdzong – Chodzong (6–8hrs)
Samdzong – Chodzong La – Chodzong

Previously it was reported that camping close to Chodzong was not allowed. However, we were informed that it should now be possible, and there is a shelter just below the monastery entry gully. Konchok Ling can just be picked out from the trail as it climbs above the Samdzong Valley towards the **Chodzong La** (4450m).

Leaving Samdzong, the route retraces the inbound trek to the trail from the Samdzong La.

Climbing now, the route is ill-defined at times and a guide or ponyman who knows the way is vital. It's a steady climb around gullies and outcrops to a broad saddle. The descent is spectacular and not so steep at first. Once down to the trail above the Chhuchhu Khola on the bluff, it's down the steps from the chorten viewpoint to the valley floor and on to Chodzong.

The trail on the bluff approaching Chodzong

Approaching Chodzong Valley (photo: Sanjib)

Chodzong – Chaka Canyon (3–4hrs)
Chodzong – Chaka Canyon

This is effectively added in to make the going easier, so some of it may be spent exploring whatever is open or accessible of the caves at Chodzong. The trail to the Chaka Canyon camp has to cross the high bluff, where the river is almost swallowed up by the deep canyon of the Chhuchhu Khola.

As described earlier, this is quite a hard trek down once the bluff top has been reached. Take care down through the maze of outcrops and especially on the super white slopes where the trail is very narrow, dusty and loose in places. The exposure is best not contemplated, although most will be fine.

From the saltwater waterfall it's all about wading across the river or trying to avoid that by skirting around the river. The scenery is sublime but it's rather cold in the shadows for most of the day.

Chaka Canyon (3700m) is an inviting spot at least, just for its remote setting.

Chaka Canyon – Lo Manthang (5–6hrs)
Chaka Canyon – Mardzong – Lo Manthang

The route is do-able, but there will be many river crossings. It's not a route for the high-water monsoon nor the immediate post-monsoon seasons. Probably it is best done in November. This is where having extra ponies would be a great blessing, despite the costs. The icy water is quite an issue at any time, especially as the canyon gets little sunlight even at midday. Riding takes 2–3hrs!

Pony trekking in the Chhuchhu Gumba Canyon

Monastery Cave Circuit Trek

According to the maps, there is the option of retreating up the **Chodzong La** and taking a cross-country route down the ridge southwest to the **Mardzong Caves**, but it looks to be a long difficult rollercoaster of a hike. **We do not know how easy or feasible this route on the map actually is!** Paolo Grobel managed this pioneering journey some years ago, but erosion and changes might have made this a risky route.

Take a look at Google Earth for hints. Good luck, it's bound to be a big adventure!

Higher up the Chhuchhu Gumba canyon

Strange outcrops of salty deposits

The Chhuchhu Gumba Canyon

Narrow ravine in the Chhuchhu Gumba Canyon

Organ pipe features from the Siyarko ridges above Tetang

Looking into the abyss high above the Narsing Khola

LOWER MUSTANG

Lower Mustang holds a great deal of cultural interest and, being that bit lower, is a joyfully easier area to explore than its northern counterpart. There are excellent lodges across the region, in Muktinath, Jomsom, Marpha and Tukuche. Other settlements hold different charms, like Thini, Chairo, Syang, Jharkot, Lubra and Chimang. These later villages are often bypassed by visitors eager to get to the hotspots and hot showers of Tatopani or Pokhara.

For the local people, therein lies the main sadness that the road has imparted to the region, although of course most also welcome the convenience of the new transportation links. The village of Tiri, north of Kagbeni, is home to the Sumdu Choide monastery; an Upper Mustang permit is not required to visit this village.

Kagbeni – Muktinath (30mins)
Kagbeni – Khingar – Jharkot – Muktinath

There are in theory two routes between Kagbeni and Muktinath, but the northern route is probably not passable for wheeled vehicles all of the way. There does seem to be a route between Kagbeni and Jhong on this northerly option – see below. The main sealed road climbs from Kagbeni passing the Dragon Hotel on the left. Higher up also on the left is the so-called Selfie Park, where some odd posing plinths and ponies are provided for the guests. The road climbs on through Khingar and comes to Jharkot.

Siân and Sanjib in Jharkot

Lower Mustang

> ### Jharkot
> The full drama and setting of Jharkot is a refreshing sight after the trials of the high country. The Sakya-pa gompa contains an image of the Sakyamuni earthly Buddha that dates to the 15th century. The kani chorten of the village displays some imagery that includes Guru Rinpoche and Maitreya. There is no information about the age of the current structure, other than its being a Sakyapa-era shrine. The gompa is rarely open and has been enlarged.

Wheel of Life in Jharkot

Ideally explore Jharkot from the west side, where the ancient houses of the village illustrate the typical Tibetan styles of Upper Mustang. It's a short walk up to regain the road for Muktinath.

Alternative: Kagbeni – Muktinath via Jhong (1hr)
Kagbeni – Jhong – Muktinath

The road from Kagbeni to Jhong, such as it is, departs from across the river north of Kagbeni and loops up to the right on to a long broad plateau area. Be sure to ask if this road is actually open. No permit is required – cyclists have used it for years already.

The dirt road skirts an area of saline ponds, where white salt crystals form strange patterns around the edges. The countryside is very arid after this, but it's an easy route, steadily up. This is a wild and desolate zone, with tantalising views of the Mustang (Thak) Khola Valley to the north. There is a fabulous view of the Thorong La ahead. The jagged ridges of the Muktinath Himal are on view to the southeast. If the route is still viable, the next village is the scenically located **Putak** village with a prayer wheel and mani wall.

> **Jhong**
> The fort at Jhong is called Rabgyel Tse Fort, meaning 'Peak of Supreme Victory'. Jhong or Dzong was once the capital of the whole region. It was founded by Pondrung Throgyal, who also ruled most of Upper Mustang. Lo Kenchen Sonam Lhundrup established the monastery in the 15th century. The Sakya-pa monastery, called Dzong Chode Shedrup Chopephel Ling, has an image of the founding red-hatted lama. Until the 18th century the gompa was home to monks from all around the region. Today the monastery acts as a school (and retreat) for preserving ancient knowledge and promoting Buddhist traditions. Inside the main chamber are a Black Buddha and his three accomplices. Other images include Chenresig and a Medicine Buddha. Outside are the typical four Lokapalas (guardians) and a Wheel of Life. Jhong Gompa has a great view of the Thorong La and the intriguing-looking Purang. This village is missed on this route but offers a route back to Muktinath that would make a fine circular day trip in itself.

Jhong village (3600m) has a café and basic lodge. It's from here that a road route might prove unusable, so be sure to check before embarking on this side trip.

The old trail/dirt road heads up to the village of **Chhonkar** with some shady trees. The Tantric monastery here is at least 200 years old but expect it to be closed (the key was probably lost years ago). The village houses are brightly painted. Muktinath is around the hillside.

Muktinath

Muktinath (3760m) has always been a pilgrimage site for centuries, During the days when the only way to get to it was on foot, it was a small, almost sleepy, destination on the Annapurna Circuit Trek. Today it's a rapidly growing settlement catering for the influx of Indian and Nepalese domestic tourists and pilgrims. Most arrive by jeep or bus from Jomsom to the large parking area on the west side of town. There is a large new Guru Rinpoche statue sitting high above the main street. A long main street leads past all the shops and hotels to the shrine some way above the settlement.

Arriving in the modern-looking suburb of **Ranipauwa** (3700m) is quite a shock, with shops full of goods, souvenir vendors and concrete hotels. Not to mention the checkpost, which in theory might want to look at the ACAP permit, probably not any TIMS permit and rarely that horribly expensive Upper Mustang permit. The restricted area permit is only checked at the roadside checkpoint in Chuksang. When we exited Upper Mustang at Muktinath, the authorities were completely uninterested in stamping our restricted area permits and only wanted to see our ACAP fee receipts. The same thing happened at the checkpost in Jomsom. For us this was a significant annoyance, as we walked long hours to cover everywhere we wanted to see in our thirteen days. We could still be in Upper Mustang now! Draw your own conclusions, but be aware that things may change.

As for all those lodges and hotels, take your choice. We were invited to stay at the Grand Shambala, a pleasant and well-designed new place with tasty food, en suite rooms and great hot showers. Having a hot shower on tap at 3700m was an unexpected and greatly appreciated pleasure!

See www.hotelgrandshambala.com
e-mail: hotelgrandshambala@gmail.com
tel: 9851187371 / 9813834630

Menu in Muktinath: (Hotel Grand Shambala)
Nepali dishes from Rs550; international dishes from Rs650
Standard room: double Rs3000, single Rs2200 inc breakfast
Deluxe room: double Rs6000, single Rs4500 inc breakfast
Super-Deluxe suites: double Rs7000, single Rs5500 inc breakfast
Deluxe and super-deluxe rooms have heating, electric kettle in the room for tea/coffee, toiletries and bathroom items.

The pilgrimage places of Muktinath
The walled-in pilgrimage sites of Muktinath are uphill to the left. Muktinath has pilgrimage shrines sacred to both Hindus and Buddhists. Many Hindu pilgrims come from India; some walk all the way. Scantily dressed sadhus (holy men) are a common sight. The goddesses Lakshmi and Saraswati flank the Hindu temple, devoted to Vishnu. There are 108 cow-headed waterspouts around the main shrine. Buddhist devotees come to witness the eternal sacred flame, hidden near the Dhola Mebar Monastery (its Hindu name is Jwala Mai). This temple of fire burns from a natural gas jet near a spring. The various attributes of the whole complex represent the elements of earth, fire and water, hence the significance of this holy spot. The monastery of Sarwa (Marme Lhakhang) houses images of Chenresig (Avalokiteshvara), Sakyamuni and Guru Rinpoche. A Bon deity, Sengye Droma (lion), is also found here. He is linked to Narsingha, the Hindu avatar of Vishnu. For more details see www.muktinath.org

Lower Mustang

Mustang Trail Race
For those who enjoy trail running, what could be more of a challenge and a pleasure than a race through this fantastic scenery and culture?

This is beyond the scope of this guidebook. For more information please see:

www.mustangtrailrace.com

Muktinath high street and Yakawa Kang peak above the Thorong La pass

Map of Lower Mustang

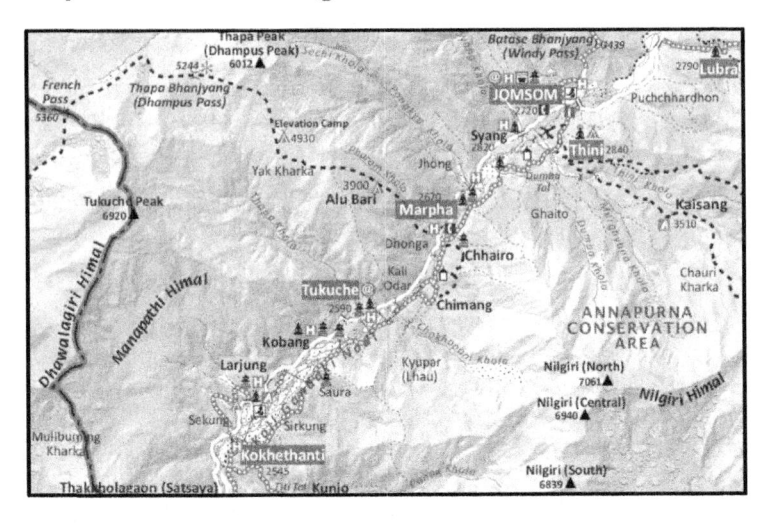

Sample menu in Kagbeni

Black coffee cup Rs150	Coffee pot Rs750
Beer Rs600–750	Cold drinks Rs350
Cornflakes Rs400	Chapatti w/jam Rs300–350
Porridge Rs450	Tibetan Bread Rs400–450
Soups Rs500–600	Dal Bhat Set Rs650–900
Noodles Rs550–650	Fried rice Rs550–600
Stir-fried veg Rs500	Chicken curry Rs600–750
Spaghetti Rs550–750	Steaks & sizzlers Rs850–1250
Sandwiches & burgers Rs550–700	Pizzas Rs600–900
Momos Rs500–650	Potato dishes Rs450–600
Rooms Rs1500–Rs2500	Desserts Rs450–650

Muktinath – Kagbeni – Jomsom (1–2hrs)
Muktinath – Kagbeni – Jomsom

The drive down from Muktinath is pretty quick and soon enough Kagbeni is reached. The Kali Gandaki canyon will blow your mind as much as the wind will bowl you over! Battling along the deepest gorge in the world can be quite a chore when exploring on foot.

Alternative: Muktinath – Jomsom via Lubra (5–6hrs)
Muktinath – Lubra – Jomsom

Those needing to stretch the legs after a lot of jeep driving around Upper Mustang might consider this great trekking option between Muktinath and Jomsom. This is a day to savour and discover one of the best major Bon settlements in Nepal. The fabulous cultural attractions – the monasteries in Lubra – are enough excitement for one day, but the scenery is also a winner. The Dakar Lodge in Lubra has great apple pancakes as well as enough sustenance, and clean bathrooms, to stay for a week.

The trail leaves Ranipauwa by the jeep station and heads up left around the hillside. There are good red/white markers and the path soon climbs high above Jharkot. Viewed from above, Jharkot has grown enormously over the last few years.

There are a couple of junctions ahead, all well marked for Lubra (turn right at both). The terrain to the southeast is said to host snow leopards; there are some ideas about developing trips into these wild and high places.

Ask at the Grand Shambala for more details on this proposal. The **'snow leopard'** trails go left from somewhere around the two junctions. The path finally has to get steeper and, as always, it is just before the top. The **col with no name** (est. 3900m) is reached in a little over 1hr or more. The hillock to the right offers a view of Dhaulagiri, although it will be seen better 10mins ahead at the **true col with no name** (est. 3910m).

Marked by a big collection of fluttering flags (or wind-threaded in the afternoon), the view of Dhaulagiri is tremendous. It's the best view yet of this turbulent monarch of the Himalaya. Tukuche Peak and those tantalising sentinels of Dolpo to the west are also not to be ignored. The magical Lubra valley is seen far, far below – oh no, not another knee-cruncher to come! The path heads down on the north, but soon reverts to the southern slopes. All too soon the big descent begins. It really is a big down, and it really is a knee-cruncher, especially in the late stages of a long trek.

Pine trees can be seen across the valley on the lower bastions of the guarding ridges of Tilicho; these mark the geographical change in the landscape from the southern fringes of the Tibetan Plateau to the main Himalayan chain.

A long way down the route reaches a walled enclosure, where fruit trees are struggling to survive. The last drop to the riverbed of the Panda Khola is a tricky affair guaranteed to keep you on your toes, if not on your knees, already crunched. After crossing a very long suspension bridge, the route drops to the actual riverbed.

After 5mins along the stony route the path climbs up to the left and is a little narrow. In the shade of trees, a real novelty, the path meets a bathing area and then contours uppish into the delightful village of **Lubra** (2900m). Head straight for the cosy Dakar Lodge with 4 rooms and a blue-tiled toilet. Blue is a favoured colour of the Bon.

Lubra village

Lubra should be called Lubrak, according to the local language: *Lu* as in spirits and *brak* as in crag. The 'crag' is the significant outcrop seen high above the village. It could take up to 4hrs if walking to get here from Muktinath for those taking lots of pictures.

A new dirt road now connects Lubra village with the main Jomsom–Kagbeni road, so it's easy enough to get to Jomsom so long as a wheeled vehicle is available.

Trashi Gyaltsen

As founder of Lubra, Trashi Gyaltsen is also known by the honorary title of Drogngon Lubrakpa, the 'protector of living beings' (in Lubra). He is also referred to as Yangton Lama. His sons later migrated to Dolpo and set up Samling monastery north of Shey Gompa, near Bhijer. For a long period, Lubra had to pay tribute to Thini as the main power centre of the region. Geling and Marpha also paid tribute to Thini. Thini monastery still has some Bon icons in its arsenal of deities.

A legend tells how Trashi Gyaltsen defeated a demon goblin called Kyerang Tragne, who had taken the form of two snakes. Having been defeated, Kyerang Tragne became the guardian of Lubra and took up residence on the strange outcrop that dominates the upper village.

> ## Lubra Bon Monastery
> The lady with the key lives within Tibetan spitting distance of the monastery. There has been a Bon settlement at Lubra since the 12th century, when it was established by Trashi Gyaltsen. Called the Yungdrung Phuntshokling gompa, it is a simple affair from the outside, although quite a large structure. The gompa was founded by Karu Drupwang Tendzin Richen, who came from Western Tibet.
>
> Similar to the Buddhist monasteries, this Bon example also has four guardians painted on the entry walls. On the left wall is an image said to be of Drenpa Namkha, the great Bon master, and another of unknown name. Religious books are placed in the left corner. Along the main altar are some of the nine notable clay icons: Nampar Gyelwa, Tonpa Shenrap (the Buddha figure of the Bon), the whitish Kunzang Gyalwa Dupa, a very blue and intertwined Drupa Namkha in the yab-yum pose and the Lubrakpa icon Trashi Gyaltsen. There are two wild-eyed icons on the right side.
>
> Along the right wall are more faint paintings and then a familiar image, the four harmonious friends Bon-style. A deer and the wise sage are the last images on this right wall near the door. Above are the masks used for festivals; all but two are wrapped up and covered for the festive 'off season'. Apparently the officiating lama visits the isolated Bon families across Upper Mustang twice a year. In fact there is quite a large number of isolated Bon families in Mustang.

To visit the **upper monastery** from here too, ask the locals to show you the way steeply uphill to the gompa known as Gonphu Gompa.

From the lower monastery the trail goes down through the village to a large willow tree, said to be a descendant of the one planted by the founding figure of Lubra, Trashi Gyaltsen.

Cut across the riverbed and cross it on a good bridge to get a better view of the **Nyem Nyem** cave shrine on the sheer cliffs almost opposite the village. At a cursory glance, the caves appear quite inaccessible. Stay on the south side and continue down the valley. Be sure to glance behind for views up the Panda Khola to Yakawa Kang and Khatung Kang, on either side of the Thorong La.

The trail/dirt road follows the river down around a corner under an old suspension bridge and then passes the widened trail up near electric poles to the upper monastery called **Gonphu Gompa**. By now the dirt road has wandered over to the north side of the stony valley floor If the wind is blowing, it gets a bit dusty. The main Kagbeni–Jomsom road is joined – it's a bumpy 10–15min drive down.

Side trip: Lubra Upper Bon monastery (2–3hrs)

A sign on the south side of the Lubra side valley indicates that the path is south of the river, but it goes nowhere, below cliffs. The correct trail is before the river already crossed upvalley. That said, this river will need to be crossed at some point. The following notes are for trekkers, but a new stony track makes things quicker for those with wheels and inclination to explore more.

Continue up the stony valley floor, keeping to the dry, cracked mud areas that are easier to walk on. Do not climb out of the riverbed on to the left (north) bank, where an old, disused trail runs beneath the pylons.

The river eventually meanders across to the north side of the stony valley and it's here you'll find a couple of crossing points (varying with the seasons). It is about 20mins to the hillside on the south bank, where the trail can be seen climbing to upper Lubra. The ascent is steep and there is a junction in a few minutes. Once past a double pylon, the trail keeps mostly above the power lines, climbing steeply to a tree and fence. Around the fence and the walls are two buildings. Climb up towards some flags to find the Bon monastery, chortens and scripts on rocks. Beware of the big guard dog!

Upper Lubra Monastery
High above the village on a sunny shelf is the restored former retreat of Trashi Gyaltsen called Gonphu Gompa, meaning Temple of the High Cave. The retreat used by Trashi Gyaltsen for a nine-year period was rebuilt in 1996 with funding from the Danish Embassy in Kathmandu. Gonphu monastery has various wall paintings illustrating the life of the Bon. The main icons are the Red Apse, Dungmar, Shangshung Meri and Sipai Gyalmo. The multi-armed and multi-headed deity is Kunzang Gyalwa Dupa. Chiara Bellini and the Radhika Sabavala Marg Foundation in Mumbai have documented the monastery in 'Wonders of Lo, The Artistic Heritage of Mustang'.

From the Lubra turnoff the onward trail to Jomsom hugs the eastern side of the valley where transport, good, bad and ugly is on offer to **Jomsom** (2710m).

And so the delights of jolly Jomsom are reached, and suddenly it's all over.

Oh dear, no more grotty toilets, hard beds and freezing cold mornings. But no more dreamlike apparitions either...

If you haven't had enough by now, there is always the big hill of Ghorepani to climb further down the Kali Gandaki!

Jomsom – Kathmandu
Jomsom – Pokhara – Kathmandu

A lot of visitors take the flight to Pokhara due to time constraints and perhaps the need for some clean clothes, but linger if you can; the areas close to Jomsom hold more fascinating cultural highlights. See below in the Kali Gandaki Route section.

Chortens and cliff caves are a common feature across Mustang

Motorcyclists arriving at a lodge in Jomsom

Typical Mustang village (Ghyakar from above)

Nilgiri peaks from Tukuche

THE KALI GANDAKI ROUTE

It's a shame that the arrival of the road to Jomsom has caused such negative publicity and perception amongst trekkers about the Kali Gandaki trails. If time is no object, the sights on offer below Jomsom are well worth the effort. Quite a lot can be seen from the road in any case with short stops along the way. Other side trips need more time.

Side trip: Jomsom – Thini & Dumba (half-day)
Jomsom – Thini – Dumba Lake – Jomsom

This half-day trip to Thini, Dumba Lake and Ngatsapterenga monastery is full of interest. Although longer, this route could also be used to avoid the road from Jomsom to Marpha. Even here dirt roads have been carved out, so check locally if this loop can be done by jeep. Otherwise it's back to boots.

Cross the river on the long suspension bridge after the airfield and come to the signpost for Thini and Dumba Lake. Thini is signposted up and Dumba Lake is ahead, right. There are various tracks up to **Thini** (2820m), which has a lodge, school and monastery.

Whichever way you choose, it's a devilishly steep climb through a weird sandstone band.

Once on Thini 'high street', follow red/white markers to find the monastery above an open area. Tilicho Lake is also signposted here.

Thini Monastery
Thini monastery was once a Bon place of worship. It now belongs to the Buddhist Nyingma-pa sect. Significant icons are the Sakyamuni Buddha, Guru Rinpoche, Chumpi, Chenresig, Channa Dorje, Tsepame, Dorje Tsangpo, a fearsome three-faced Heruka, a Green Tara and a yab-yum image of Kundo Tsangpo. What a mouthful!

Two strange Bon idols predate the other images. The dark blue idol is Welse Ngampa: 'Fierce, piercing deity', representing power and ferocity. He has nine heads of white, red and blue. His middle heads are the tiger, lion and leopard. His top heads are the dragon, garuda and makara – the aquatic-looking monster. His eighteen arms destroy demons. This evocative image embraces his dark green consort, the lady of boundless space. Welse Ngampa stands on five animals: lion, elephant, horse, dragon and garuda.

The other Bon idol is the white Kunzang Gyalwa Dupa. His right hands holds a royal banner, a swastika and a wheel. In his left hands are the bow, arrow and noose. The sun and moon are held in his two hooked arms.

The path to Dumba is straight on below the monastery. Cross the Thini Khola and climb around the bluff to reach the brilliant turquoise green **Dumba Lake** (2830m). For a half-day outing, return to Jomsom, or continue around the lake to a kani on the next ridge.

Nearby is a 17th-century monastery, the Nyingma-pa **Ngatsapterenga** gompa.

At the kani go left for **Dumba village** (2900m). A track goes down around the cliffs with a crossing point to lower Syang and so back to Jomsom.

Ngatsapterenga Monastery
The name means 'five treasures' and there are different ways to spell the name of the shrine; it could also be Hutsaptemga. The treasures are clay statues carried here from Samye in Tibet and a foot imprint of Guru Rinpoche. It appears to date from the 17th century, constructed by a disciple of Dudul Dorje, who found the five treasures. The current structure was rebuilt after a fire in the mid-19th century and has been renovated frequently, even quite recently. An image of the eleven-headed Chenresig (Avalokiteshvara in Sanskrit) is one of the main paintings. Others are Amitabha and a bronze image of the Buddha to come, Maitreya.

Jomsom – Marpha (20 –30mins)
Jomsom – Syang – Marpha

South of Jomsom, above the route, is the village of **Syang**; the trail is uphill to the west. The butter festival held in October at the Nyingma-pa Tashi Lha Kang monastery is a colourful affair. Syang also has a nunnery – the Dhi Che Ling. The road out soon passes below Syang but there is a wide track up here as well. The road crosses an area of stony riverbed soon – this valley once hosted Tibetan Khampas resisting the takeover of Tibet in the 1950–60s. The road continues to **Marpha** (2670m). As mentioned, it's worth a 30–40min stroll through the old street of the village and maybe visit the monastery that dominates the settlement.

Side trip:

Jomsom – Marpha via Dumba (5–6hrs)
Jomsom – Dumba Lake – Chhairo – Marpha

Previously we commented: 'Don't come this way if you suffer the slightest vertigo.' But the route has been widened maybe even enough for a jeep trip; do ask locally, as it's unclear as yet how much work has been done here. We include the trekking notes for this option.

The Kali Gandaki Route

Probably the only people on the trail to Marpha taking this option are diehard trekkers and guidebook writers. Due to the exposed nature of some of the path, fully laden backpackers should note the dangers of being blown off the trail by those strong winds in the afternoon! Done as a longer day outing, the round trip from Jomsom all the way to Marpha and back may take 6–7hrs.

From Jomsom head to **Dumba** village directly (avoiding the steep climb to Thini). From Dumba, cross the wide, stony riverbed below the village. There is an obvious trail across the riverbed. Climb up the hill, passing a couple of markers.

The path zigzags and heads right, almost on the level. Watch for a faded red/white marker and continue around the corner with a first view way down to Marpha ahead.

The trail soon becomes very exposed and climbs over a bluff before dropping down with more scary drop-offs on the right side. The views are exhilarating but be warned: some of the path is very loose underfoot!

Eventually the trail cuts down to some fields. However, there is no crossing point for Jomsom here unless you can tiptoe across a water pipe. Head south for 20–25mins to a good bridge in **Chhairo** village.

Chhairo village has housed Tibetan refugees for many years. Near the small village monastery go through the trees beside the river and find the suspension bridge. **Marpha** (2670m) is over the bridge back up the valley with a choice of good lodges.

Day trippers can return from Marpha to Jomsom, taking 1–1½hrs or so along the road.

Marpha village and monastery

Marpha
This pretty village has traditional Thakali architecture, with quaint houses and paved streets. Dominating it is the imposing monastery of Samtenling. Images here include Guru Rinpoche and Chenresig as well as some strange animal headed deities. The Guru Pandita Anand meditation centre is above the monastery. Marpha is also famed for its orchards, providing the ingredients for the apple brandy sold locally and across Nepal. Much more recently it has become the 'in place' for domestic tourists to take Tik Tok selfies!

Marpha – Tukuche (3–4hrs)
Marpha – Chhairo – Chimang – Tukuche

With the motorable road hugging the west side of the Kali Gandaki south of Marpha, trekkers continuing on the Annapurna Circuit should follow the east bank trails to Tukuche. Don't expect to see many red/white markers on the east side route after Chhairo. This route tends to suffer much less from the winds than the road.

After Marpha continue along the main road. If you need sustenance, stop at Rita Lodge before leaving the road.

Continue downhill, cross the suspension bridge on the left to the east side of the Kali Gandaki. It is 10mins walk through trees to the centre of **Chhairo**, a village inhabited by Tibetan refugees. Follow the red/white marks from the village centre, south from the small monastery into the forest and then around to the right to another larger monastery being restored by the Heritage & Environment Conservation Foundation.

Chhairo Monastery
The Nyingma-pa monastery is over 400 years old and was founded by Nawang Tiling, a Tibetan monk. The gompa houses Chenresig, Sakyamuni and Guru Rinpoche, with a golden donor figure in front. There are many terracotta idols and some tablets. The other chamber has an imposing Guru Rinpoche with frescoes of arhats. In December a festival takes place to honour the powerful local deity called Gyalwa Puja. The masked dance festival of Dhekepchey, when astrological predictions are made, is also celebrated at the gompa. The Thakali family of Subba Bhatarchan has guardianship of it. So far the restoration has taken more than fifteen years.

Another extraordinary piece of background information about this monastery is the story of Karl Hendrick (1911–2007), who became known as Anagarika (homeless one) Sugata (walking happily).
See www.chhairogompa.org

If walking from the monastery, head south over a stream to the mani walls and then between the meadow walls to the settlement of **Lucky**. The village has a large chorten, where the route goes left for Tukuche. Continue to follow the signs to Chimang and Chokhopani until you reach a junction – left for **Chimang** and right for **Chokhopani**. (A visit to Chimang is recommended – this trail climbs steadily through meadows up to the village.)

Going right (to Chokhopani), the pleasant forest trail drops close to the Kali Gandaki. The path continues around to the large valley that drains the Nilgiris.

A sign indicates Chokhopani to the right, with Chimang now marked straight ahead up the valley. The village of **Chimang** (2750m) is perched precariously on the cliffs above. This is a second chance to visit the charming settlement.

Side trip: Chimang (1hr)

Chimang (2750m) is a typical, small Thakali village, with narrow paved streets, beautifully stone houses and wooden doorways. This is a trekking trail option, although road access is possible.

Follow the wide track uphill (15–20mins) to a path on the left. This wide track also continues up to Chimang, and is used during the apple harvest. The path zigzags up in a spectacular ascent beside a tumbling waterfall. At a junction go left (the right links to the jeep track). Shortly there is a traditional wooden ladder that must be climbed to reach some meadows. At a watermill go right to two more ladders. Ascend these to enter the village near a chorten and mani wall. There is a school at the top of the village. Nearby are signs indicating a path down to the right, along the wide track to Chokhopani / Tukuche. Return this way or take the zigzag path back down to rejoin the route to Tukuche. After some isolated buildings there is a sign to Chokhopani. Going right to the bridge for Tukuche is a more interesting choice. Once on the main road, it's only around 30mins to **Tukuche** (2590m).

Tukuche (2590m)
Tukuche grew to prominence from the salt and wool trade with Tibet. There are four monasteries and some exquisite, typical Thakali merchants' trading houses, now used as lodges. A museum details the time that the Japanese monk Ekai Kawaguchi spent here in 1899. The Qupar Nyingma-pa Gompa is around 400 years old. Entry is from the east side; donations are gratefully accepted. The main idol is the ancient classic, 1000-armed Chenresig with 11 heads. Side trips from Tukuche go to the vantage points of Yak Kharka, Buddha Lake and Shyokong Lake; guides are needed.

The Kali Gandaki Route

Tukuche – Kokhethanti (2–3hrs)
Tukuche – Kobang – Larjung – Kokhethanti

The area is full of cultural attractions and views of Dhaulagiri. This route really marks the end of the Lower Mustang region. From here on south the trails belong to the central hills of Nepal and Himalayan peaks of the Annapurna region – a very different sort of experience.

From Tukuche the road heads along to **Kobang** (2560m). The Makila Khang monastery is worth a look. The main idol is Guru Rinpoche, but the fading old painting outside of a chain and a tiger – the vehicle of Guru Rinpoche is the star. **Larjung** is not far ahead and high above is the little-visited settlement of **Naurikot** with a rare Bon monastery.

Side trip: Larjung – Naurikot (2hrs)

From central Larjung, across the dirt main road, a route climbs past chortens to two Nepali pagoda-style temples. After crossing a track and passing a small gompa on the right, there are more steps. Zigzag up into forest for a while to a chorten and then the Thakali village of Naurikot, on a sunny shelf.

Bon icon in Naurikot monastery

The Kali Gandaki Route

> **Naurikot Monastery**
> The 1000-year-old Bon monastery of Naurikot is simple but contains has some interesting images. Kunzang Gyalwa Dupa is on the left, Welse Ngampa is central, and Namse on the right. The Guru Sangbo cave linked to Guru Rinpoche is beyond the village. Don't expect it to be open very often, but the window glass is clear enough to get a glimpse inside.

Leaving Larjung, the road undulates around the hillside to a wide valley. Across the Kali Gandaki the next place is **Kokhethanti** (2560m) bypassed by the road. Already the forests have become much more luxuriant; the Hindu culture replacing the Buddhist chants south of Ghasa. The valley is rapidly becoming the deepest canyon in the world as the route heads to **Tatopani** and on via Beni to Pokhara.

Dhaulagiri and the Icefall from near Kalopani

Old house in Kusma

Road summary: Jomsom – Pokhara – Kathmandu

Jomsom – Pokhara (7–9hrs)

Driving from Jomsom, it takes around 20–30mins to **Marpha** depending on the time taken to get out of Jomsom and roadworks. **Tukuche** is only 5–10mins further down. It's slower going around **Kobang** and **Larjung** and the quiet forested stage to **Kalopani** reached about 30–40mins later. Continuing through **Lete**, the road descends around old **Ghasa**, where there is a 'proper' fuel station instead of the barrels used in Upper Mustang.

The road drops to the landslide area around **Rupse Chhara** waterfall – approx. 30mins from Ghasa. Delays may be expected on this stage. Around the hillside and down is **Dana**, but its old street is not in view. Motel de Dana café is on offer. The temperature is rapidly becoming warmer, as altitude is rapidly lost. It's just over 1 hour from Kalopani to Tatopani and the luxury of the Natural Springs Hotel if needed.

From the famed hot springs of **Tatopani** the road heads below cliffs that have had landslides in the past to the bridge that marks the side valley that leads to Ghorepani for trekkers. It too has a jeep road almost all the way to Ghorepani where the Poon Hill has long been famed for its views of Annapurna and Dhaulagiri at dawn. The old Hanuman temple was lost to the raging river and a new one has been reincarnated on the east bank still with a smaller image of the monkey god.

The road heads on down below cliffs through a narrow ravine. There are fleeting views north of Nilgiri and Fang. The Kali Gandaki is crossed 20mins from the Hanuman temple and then it's an easier trip down to **Galeshwar** with its Hindu shrines. Beni is around 1 hour from Tatopani if all is well with the road. The Yeti Hotel is a long established hotel for those who need a break, and now there is the Yak Hotel, before town.

The high road is currently the best route between **Beni** and Kusma, as the valley road is damaged and awaiting tarmac. Via Baglung it is around 1 hour to **Kusma** (Kushma) passing the noted 'The Cliff' bungy jumping spot. At 228m, it's the 2nd highest drop according to all the road signs if this is your 'cup of tea'. In town south of the Global Bank is a traditional three-hundred-year-old house that is being saved as a museum; that's worth a few minutes detour.

A good, sealed road leads to **Nayapul** in 30mins, where the Nayapool Kitchen is a pleasant break for drinks or food. Then the road climbs up for a while to **Khare** (Kande), which used to be a day and half tough trekking from Pokhara.

Naudanda is the next settlement up, around 30mins from Nayapul. There are great views of the Annapurna range from here on clear days. From here there are two choices – the main tarmac road that descends to the valley below Dhampus and on along a six-lane highway almost into Pokhara. The last bit is unfinished and has been for years.

The alternative is a narrow but scenic sealed road heading along the Naudanda ridge to **Sarangkot**. This takes 30mins. It's worth diverting at Sarangkot for the fabulous views of the whole Annapurna range from Annapurna South to Annapurna II including Machhapuchhre. The road descends to Pokhara and on to Lakeside, roughly an hour and a bit more or so from Nayapul.

Pokhara – Kathmandu (8hrs via Swayambhu route)

With endless roadworks all the way, the timings are pretty arbitrary as jams can occur frequently, especially as few drivers want to go give way or go backwards to unblock the road!

It might take 3–4hrs to reach Mugling (90km) via **Damauli**, **Dumre** and **Abu Khaireni**. Just before **Mugling** and the bridge is the peaceful Motel du Mugling, with a great garden and restaurant for a calming break. After Mugling the road soon reaches **Kurintar** and the cablecar for the **Manakamana temple** – always a busy spot. Just after this is the long running Riverside Springs with a new brewery on site for the Barasingha brand. By now a beer will be irresistible for most. Other watering holes are the E-Stop and Siddhartha restaurants nearby.

As a distraction from the grief of the road which is again a mess look for the Upset rapids on the left where countless rafters have taken a dip in the cool waters of the Trisuli River. The road continues above the canyon through **Fisling** and **Majhimtar** to **Malekhu** but it's anyone's guess how long it will take. The next point of note is **Galchi** where the junction for Dunche and the Langtang region is located. After this is a never-ending climb around the hills to **Naubise**.

Just before this is a new, narrow but generally sealed road over a pass north of the main pass which drops to Swayambhunath and town. It saves an hour on the main road, which climbs slowly to the pass and into **Thankot**.

The traffic is always bad from here into Kathmandu, with slow smoky trucks and unforgiving buses the main delaying factor. The volume of traffic is surprising.

Once away from Thankot, it's on to the tourist hotspots for a shower and welcome rest – thanks be to any gods for that!

The last word

Any trip in the highest mountains of the world will be laced with masses of eager anticipation and perhaps a little trepidation. The Himalaya were made for trekkers, hippies, pilgrims, philosophers, itinerants, climbers and adventurers. The reality far exceeds the dream. A trek in Nepal will rarely be a luxurious affair – with ghastly buses, brutal ascents, knee-grinding descents, midnight loo stops, hard beds, grungy dog patrols and relentless… exhausting… breathtaking… passes, but when all that privation is forgotten, the Himalaya become an incurable addiction.

> It's the beginning that's the worst, then the middle, then the end. But in the end, it's the end that's the worst.
> ***Samuel Beckett***

Have a safe and happy trek!

Things change – Boudhanath in 1975

APPENDICES

Appendix 1:
Trip summaries and suggested itineraries

Trek Stages Grading
The degree of difficulty is defined in the following grades. The grades are relative, but remember that there's hardly a flat area in Nepal. Easy (A) – still requires effort, with sections of steep ups and downs. Moderate (B) is harder, including higher altitude, and Strenuous (C) involves steep climbs and exposed paths with some at altitude. All treks listed require trekkers to be in good physical shape beforehand.

Note: Jeep or bus journeys are indicated as approximate. Elsewhere timings are split for jeep + trek time etc.

Typical river canyon near Dhi

Appendix 1

Road routes

Mustang Explorer

		Time
Day 1	Kathmandu – Pokhara	7–10hrs
Day 2	Pokhara – Kalopani	5–6hrs
Day 3	Kalopani – Kagbeni	2–3hrs
Day 4	Kagbeni or Khingar	
Day 5	Khingar – Tetang	1–2hrs
Day 6	Tetang – Tsarang	4–5hrs
Day 7	Tsarang – Lo Manthang	1hr
Day 8	Lo Manthang – Chosar day trip	4–5hrs
Day 9	Lo Manthang – Samdzong day trip	3–4hrs
Day 10	Lo Manthang – Chodzong pony trip	8–10hrs
Day 11	Lo Manthang – Rinchenling/Thinggar trip	3–4hrs+
Day 12	Lo Manthang – Drakmar/Ghami	1–2hrs
Day 13	Drakmar – Syangmochen/Geling	1–2hrs
Day 14	Syangmochen/Geling – Jomsom	2–3hrs
Day 15	Jomsom – Pokhara	30mins flight
Day 16	Pokhara – spare/recovery day	
Day 17	Pokhara – Kathmandu	7–10hrs

Alternatives:

Naturally there are far more alternatives travelling by road, these are some more obvious suggestions. Adding in some days trekking and rejoining the vehicle adds further choices – oh dear!

Day 5	Khingar – Geling	3–4hrs
Day 6	Geling – Tsarang	1–2hrs

Day 5	Khingar – Samar	2–3hrs
Day 6	Geling – Syangmochen via Chungsi trek	6–7hrs B/C
Day 7	Syangmochen – Lo Manthang	3–4hrs

Day 12	Lo Manthang – Yara	3–4hrs
Day 13	Yara sightseeing to Luri	
Day 13	Yara – Drakmar/Ghami	2–3hrs
Day 14	Drakmar – Syangmochen/Geling	1–2hrs
Day 15	Syangmochen/Geling – Jomsom	2–3hrs
Day 16	Jomsom – Pokhara	30mins flight
Day 17	Pokhara – spare/recovery day	
Day 18	Pokhara – Kathmandu	7–10hrs

Monastery Cave Circuit Trek (B/C)

Day 1	Lo Manthang – Samdzong Valley	5–7hrs
Day 2	Samdzong Valley – Chodzong	6–8hrs
Day 3	Chodzong – Mustang Khola Camp	3–4hrs
Day 4	Mustang Khola Camp – Lo Manthang	5–6hrs

Appendix 2: Bibliography

Allen, Charles **A Mountain in Tibet** 1982
Allen, Charles **The Search for Shangrila** Little Brown, London 1999
Anderson, Mary **Festivals of Nepal** George Allen & Unwin 1971
Batchelor, Stephen **The Tibet Guide** Wisdom, 1998
Beck Michael **Mustang: The Culture and Landscapes of Lo** Vajra, Kathmandu
Bell, Charles **The People of Tibet** Clarendon 1928, rep. BFI 1998
Bista, Dor Bahadur **People of Nepal** Ratna Pustak Bhandar 1987
Boustead, Robin **Nepal Trekking and the Great Himalaya Trail** Trailblazer 2011, 2015, 2020
Bowman, W E (Bill) **The Ascent of Rum Doodle** 1956 (www.rumdoodle.org.uk – a great skit on the big mountaineering expeditions of the past, written long before they became in vogue)
Chan, Victor **Tibet Handbook** Moon Publications 1994
Chorlton, Windsor and Wheeler, Nik. **Cloud-Dwellers of the Himalayas** Time-Life Books 1982
Crozier, Bill **Beyond the Snow Leopard** 2024
Dalai Lama **An Introduction to Buddhism and Tantric Meditation** Paljor Publications 1996
Dorje, Gyurme **Tibet** Footprint Handbooks 2004
Durkan, David **Glimpses of Everest** Swami Kailash 2023, 2024
Durkan, David **Penguins on Everest** Swami Kailash 2012 – 2023
Fleming **Birds of Nepal** reprints by Indian publishers
Francke, Rev. A. H. **A History of Western Tibet** 1907, rep. 1998
Gibbons, Bob & Pritchard-Jones, Siân **Kathmandu: Valley of the Green-Eyed Yellow Idol** Pilgrims 2004, 2020
Gibbons, Bob & Pritchard-Jones, Siân **Annapurna: A Trekkers' Guide** Cicerone 2013, 2017, 2022
Gibbons, Bob & Pritchard-Jones, Siân **Mount Kailash: A Trekkers' Guide** Cicerone 2007
Gordon, Antoinette **The Iconography of Tibetan Lamaism** Munshi Ram M Delhi 1978
Govinda, Lama Anagarika **The Way of the White Clouds** Rider and Company, London 1966
Hagen, Toni **Nepal: The Kingdom of the Himalayas** Kümmerley and Frey 1980
Handa, O. C. **Buddhist Monasteries of Himachal** Indus, 2004
Handa, O. C. **Buddhist Western Himalaya** Indus, New Delhi 2001
Hedin, Sven **A Conquest of Tibet** Book Faith India reprinted 1994
Kalsang, Ladrang **The Guardian Deities of Tibet** Winsome 2003
Lama, Sonam and Lama, Lopsang Chhiring **Manaslu and Tsum Valley** Map House
Landon, Perceval **Nepal Vols I and II** Pilgrims reprint
Lhalungpa, Lobsang P. **The Life of Milarepa** BFI 1997
Lonely Planet **Nepali Phrasebook** Frequently published

Appendix 2

Mierow, Dorothy and Shrestha, Tirtha Bahadur **Himalayan Flowers and Trees** Prakashan/Pilgrims
Noyce, Wilfred **Climbing the Fish's Tail** Heinemann 1958, reprinted by Book Faith/Pilgrims Publishing, 1998
O'Connor, Bill **Adventure Treks: Nepal** Crowood 1990
Pauler, Gerda **The Great Himalaya Trail** Baton Wick 2013
Pritchard-Jones, Siân & Gibbons, Bob **Himalayan Travel Guides: Manaslu, Dolpo, Ganesh Himal & Tamang Heritage Trail, Langtang, Everest, Rolwaling, Mustang, Kanchenjunga, Makalu, West Nepal, Dhaulagiri, Annapurna North, Jugal Himal, Nepal Himalaya, Bhutan** Map House and Amazon 2013–25
Pritchard-Jones, Siân and Gibbons, Bob **Kailash and Guge: Land of the Tantric Mountain** Pilgrims 2006, Expedition World 2022
Pritchard-Jones, Siân and Gibbons, Bob **Ladakh: Land of Magical Monasteries** Pilgrims 2006, Expedition World 2014
Pritchard-Jones, Siân and Gibbons, Bob **Ladakh: Land of Mystical Monasteries**, Expedition World 2018, 2023
Pritchard-Jones, Siân and Gibbons, Bob **Earthquake Diaries: Nepal 2015** Expedition World 2015, 2022
Pritchard-Jones, Siân and Gibbons, Bob **In Search of the Green-Eyed Yellow Idol** Expedition World 2015, 2019, 2022, 2023
Pye-Smith, Charlie **Travels in Nepal** Aurum Press 1988
Reynolds, Kev **Trekking in the Himalaya** Cicerone 2013
Reynolds, Kev **Abode of the Gods** Cicerone 2015
Roerich, Nicholas **Altai Himalaya** 1929, reprint BFI 1996
Snellgrove, David **Buddhist Himalaya** Oxford 1957
Snellgrove, David **Himalayan Pilgrimage** Oxford 1961
Tilman, H W. **Nepal Himalaya** CUP/Diadem 1983
Tucci, Giuseppe **Shrines of a Thousand Buddhas** 2008 reprint
Venables, Stephen **Higher than the Eagle Soars** Random 2007

Films
A wonderfully evocative film about the people of Dolpo in Nepal, **Himalaya** (first released as **Caravan** in Nepal) portrays the life of traditional village yak herders in the remote regions. Not about Nepal but good background is **Seven Years in Tibet**, about Heinrich Harrer's life as a fugitive from World War II and his life in Lhasa close to the Dalai Lama. A more recent release is **Himalaya Bhotia**, a French-made film about the people of northern Nepal, such as Tamang, Dolpa, Sherpa and others.

Music
Various Himalayan themes can be found on CD or online. A few are folk songs, others are amalgams of Tibetan chants, songs and 'Western Oriental'. These tunes resonate with calming and meditative music. Some are **Tibetiya, Sacred Buddha, Karmapa: Secrets of the Crystal Mountain, Journey to Tibet, Sacred Chants of Buddha**, soundtrack of the film **Himalaya, Nepali Folksongs**…

Appendix 3: Glossary

Religious and other terminology

Significant Buddhist deities

The **Dhyani Buddhas** face the four cardinal directions; they are often found on stupas and chaityas (small stone chortens). The Dhyani Buddhas were created from the wisdom of the Adi (first) Buddha, the primordial Buddha. **Vairocana** is the first Dhyani Buddha and resides in the stupa sanctum; Vairocana is the illuminator, to light the way. **Akshobhya** faces east; **Amitabha** faces west; **Amoghasiddhi** faces north, with a seven-headed serpent behind him; **Ratna Sambhava** faces south (these are the Sanskrit names).

The following are some other important deities; Sanskrit names are shown first.

Sakyamuni (Sakya Tukpa) The mortal Buddha, Gautama Siddhartha, born in Nepal.
Avalokiteshvara (Chenresig) Bodhisattva having renounced Nirvana, the end of the cycle of rebirth. He embodies compassion (*karuna*) and remains on earth to counter suffering. The Dalai Lama is considered to be his earthly representative.
Amitayus (Tsepame) Buddha of Boundless Life, an aspect of Amitabha; he is associated with longevity.
Vajrapani (Channa Dorje) Spiritual son of Akshobhya. He carries a *dorje* (*vajra*) and is a powerful, wrathful protector. He has monstrous Tantric powers and wears a snake around his neck.
Hayagriva (Tamdrin) Wrathful emanation of Chenresig, guards many shrines. Blood red with a small horse sticking out of his head, he wears a garland of skulls.
Manjushri (Jampelyang) God of wisdom, who carries a sword to cut through ignorance. Worshipping Manjushri gives intellect and intelligence.
Yamantaka (Dorje Jigje) 'Slayer of death', a wrathful emanation of Manjushri; a Gelug-pa deity with a buffalo head.
Tara (Drolma) Sacred to both Buddhists and Hindus, representing the maternal aspect, symbolising fertility, purity and compassion. With 21 versions, Tara appears in different colours: red, green, white and gold, and as Kali, dark blue, representing different aspects of her nature.
Maitreya Buddha (Jampa/Champa) The future Buddha.
Medicine Buddha Engaged for healing the sick, often a blue colour with four hands.

Mahakala Linked to Shiva with his trident. He tramples on corpses and is a wrathful Avalokiteshvara.
The Four Harmonious Friends
Found in many monasteries, depicting four animals, one on top of the other: the Elephant, Monkey, Rabbit and Bird. These represent harmony, peace and the removal of conflict.
The Four Guardians Seen at monastery entrances. Dhitarashtra is the white guardian of the east, holding a flute. Virupaksha guards the west; he is red with a stupa in one hand and a serpent in the other. Virudhakla is guardian of the south, holding a blue sword. Vaisravana guards the north, holding a yellow banner and a mongoose, usually seen vomiting jewels.
Padma Sambhava (Guru Rinpoche) The most famous icon of Buddhism, an Indian Tantric master who went to Tibet in the eighth century. He established the Nyingma-pa Red Hat sect. His consort Yeshe Tsogyal recorded his teachings to be revealed to future generations.
Milarepa Tibet's poet, magician and saint – a historical figure, associated with many legends. He meditated in caves as a hermit before achieving realisation.

Significant Bon deities

Bon has four main peaceful deities, the 'Four Transcendent Lords': Shenlha Wokar, Satrig Ersang, Sangpo Bumtri and Tonpa Shenrap Miwoche.
Others include: **Kuntu Zangpo** (similar to the primordial Adi Buddha of Buddhism); **Kunzang Gyalwa Gyatso** (very similar, and perhaps a precursor to the 1000-armed Avalokiteshvara); **Welse Ngampa** (a nine-headed protector representing 'piercing ferocity' and crushing the enemies of Bon); **Sipai Gyalmo** (a protectress called the 'Queen of the World').

Other definitions

Arhat Original disciples of Buddha who have managed to become free from the cycle of existence (samsara). Arhats are not often seen as icons, but when they are, their faces have moustaches and beards.
Bharal Species of blue sheep.
Bhatti Small rural dwelling.
Bodhisattva Disciple of Buddha who has delayed the attainment of Nirvana in order to teach.
Bon Pre-Buddhist religion of Tibet.
Chang Home-brewed barley wine/beer, sometimes made with other grain.
Chorten Similar to a small stupa (see below) but does not normally contain relics.

Appendix 3

Dakini Female deity who can fly.
Dorje/Vajra Thunderbolt: it destroys ignorance. A complex figure-of-eight-shaped metal object found at many temples and shrines.
Dzong Fortress, castle.
Gompa Tibetan word for a monastery or holy place.
Gonkhang Small, dark and somewhat forbidding chamber housing the protecting deities: Yamantaka, Mahakala and Palden Lhamo, among others.
Kani Entrance archway to settlements.
Kharka Herders' shelter and meadow.
Kora Circular pilgrimage trek around a sacred mountain or lake.
Lama Religious teacher and guide, male or female.
Lhakhang Temple chapel within a monastery.
Losar Tibetan New Year festival.
Mandala Circular pattern made of many colours, often a square or squares within a circle. Represents 'the divine abode of an enlightened being.
Mani stone Rock covered with engraved Buddhist mantras, sometimes painted.
Mani wall Long wall made of flat stones engraved with Buddhist mantras; may also contain prayer wheels. You should always keep these on your right.
Palden Lhamo Fearful Tibetan female goddess, always on horseback.
Paubha Religious painting on cloth, specific to the Kathmandu Valley. Predates the Tibetan thangka.
Prayer flag Seen in five colours, on which prayers are printed; these flutter in the wind, sending prayers direct to heaven. The colours represent the five elements: earth, fire, air, water, and ether.
Prayer wheel Engraved cylinder with Tibetan script and containing prayers. Generally fixed into a wall, or hand held and spun while walking; the spinning action activates the prayers.
Puja Ceremony offering prayers.
Rakshi Nepalese alcoholic drink, not always healthily prepared.
Rigsum Gonpo Three chortens seen above kanis and elsewhere, representing the three deities who offer protection to villages. The red chorten represents Manjushri, giving wisdom; the white chorten represents Avalokiteshvara, offering compassion; and the blue, black or grey chorten represents Vajrapani, to fight off evil. They ward off many spirits found in the three worlds: sky, earth and underworld.
Sadhu Self-proclaimed holy man/ascetic.
Sago Namgo Seen in the northern regions, these strange objects give protection against bad omens. They relate to the 'Mother Earth spirits' and translate as Earth Door and Sky Door. Made from ram skulls, wood or fabric.
Sky burial Form of burial where the body is cut up and fed to the vultures and large birds.

Appendix 3

Stupa Large monument, usually with a square base, a dome and a pointed spire on top. The spire represents the levels towards enlightenment. A stupa may often host the remains of a revered lama or teacher.

Tantra Oral teachings and Buddhist scriptures, describing the use of mantras, mandalas and deities in meditation and yoga. It is commonly associated with physical methods of striving for enlightenment but equally applicable to meditation methods using the energies of the mind.

Thangka/tangka Religious painting, usually on silk fabric. They are often seen in all monasteries, hanging on walls or pillars.

Tsampa Traditional Tibetan food: roasted barley mixed with butter tea, it is made into a sort of porridge.

Vajrayana Buddhism 'Diamond' branch of the religion found in Tibet and associated with Tantric ideas.

Yab-yum Depiction of two deities, male and female. The male represents compassion and the female wisdom. Deities depict the spiritual union and higher awareness.

Yidam A personal tutelary deity used in meditation practice.

Artwork at Rinchenling caves

Appendix 4:
Nepali language hints

> Language is an impotent substitute for experience.
> ***Abode of the Gods**, Kev Reynolds*

Useful words and phrases

Hello/Goodbye	*Namaste*
Goodnight	*Suva ratri*
How are you?	*Tapailai kasto chha?*
Very well	*Ramro chha*
Thank you	*Dhanyabad*
Yes (it is)	*Ho*
No (it isn't)	*Hoina*
Yes (have)	*Chha*
No (don't have)	*Chhaina*
OK	*Tik chha*
What is your name?	*Tapaiko naam ke ho?*
My name is Sanjib	*Mero naam Sanjib ho*
Please go slowly	*Bistaari jaane*
Where is a lodge?	*Lodge kahaa chha?*
What's the name of this village?	*Yo gaaunko naam ke ho?*
Which trail goes to Drakmar?	*Drakmar jaane baato kun ho?*
Where are you going?	*Tapaai kahaa jaane?*
I don't understand	*Maile buhjina*
I don't know	*Ta chhaina*
Please give me a cup of tea	*Chiyaa dinos*
How much is it?	*Kati paisa?*
Where is the toilet?	*Chaarpi kahaa chha?*
Where is there water?	*Pani kahaa chha?*
I want to rent a pony	*Malaai ghoda bhadama chaainchha*
I need a porter	*Ma kulli chaainchha*
I am sick	*Ma biraami chhu*
I have altitude sickness	*Lekh laagyo*

Other useful words

what	*ke*
where	*kun*
when	*kaile*
how much	*kati*
good	*ramro*
bad	*naramro*
cold	*jaaro/chiso*
hot	*garam/tato*
trail	*baato*
steeply up	*ukaalo*

Appendix 4

steeply down	*oraalo*
flat	*terso*
dangerous	*aptero*
river (small)	*khola*
stream	*kholsa*

Food

food	*khanaa*
spinach	*sag*
bread	*roti*
rice	*bhat*
noodle soup	*thukpa*
eggs	*phul*
meat	*maasu*
yoghurt	*dahi*
sugar	*chini*
salt	*nun*
water	*pani*
boiled water	*umaalekho pani*
black tea	*kalo chiyaa*
hot water	*tatopani*
cold water	*chiso pani*

Numbers

1	*ek*		11	*ekhaara*
2	*dui*		12	*baara*
3	*tin*		15	*pandhra*
4	*char*		20	*bis*
5	*paanch*		30	*tis*
6	*chha*		40	*chaalis*
7	*saat*		50	*pachaas*
8	*aath*		100	*ek say*
9	*nau*		500	*panch say*
10	*das*		1000	*ek hajaar*

For more phrases and detail, see the
Nepali Phrasebook by Pawan Shakya and Manjari Shakya
www.amazon.co.uk/Nepali-Phrasebook-Dictionary-Himalayan-Travel/dp/B0DNC5G6T2/
published by Map House,
available on Amazon
and from their shop in Thamel opposite KC's

Appendix 5:
Useful contacts (many more online)

Tour operators in Nepal
Advent Himalaya www.adventhimalayatreks.com
Alliance Treks www.rubyvalleytreks.com
Ama Dablam Adventures www.amadablamadventures.com
Asian Trekking www.asian-trekking.com
Beyond the Limits www.treksinnepal.com
Biking First www.bikingfirstadventure.com
Bochi Bochi www.bochi-bochitrek.com
Climbing Himalaya www.climbinghimalaya.com
Dream Himalaya www.dreamhimalaya.com.np
Explore Dolpo www.exploredolpotrekking.com
Firante Treks www.firante.com
Friends Adventure Team www.friendsadventure.com
Himalayan Companion www.himalayancompanion.com
Himalayan Deep Breath Trek www.hdbtrek.com
Himalayan Rock www.himalayanrock.com
Nepal Nature dot com www.nepalnaturetravels.com
Off the Wall www.offthewalltrekking.com
Responsible Treks www.responsibletreks.com
Sacred Himalaya www.sacredhimalaya.com
Sherpa Adventure Travel www.sherpaadventure.com
3 Sisters Adventure www.3sistersadventure.com
Snow Cat Travel www.snowcattravel.com
Trek Ethik Adventure www.trekethik.com
Trinetra Adventure www.trinetra-adventure.com
Trip Himalaya www.triphimalaya.com

Tour operators overseas
Aktivferien www.aktivferien.com
Earthbound Expeditions www.eeadventure.com
Exodus www.exodus.co.uk
Expedition World www.expeditionworld.com (authors' website)
Explore www.explore.co.uk
Intrepid Travel www.intrepidtravel.com
Kamzang Journeys www.kamzangjourneys.com
KE Adventure Travel www.keadventure.com
Mountain Kingdoms www.mountainkingdoms.com
Paulo Grobel www.paulogrobel.com
Take On Nepal (Batase Trails) www.takeonnepal.com.au
The Adventure Company www.adventurecompany.co.uk
The Mountain Company www.themountaincompany.com
Trekking Team Poland www.trampingi.pl
Wilderness Travels USA www.wildernesstravels.com
World Expeditions www.worldexpeditions.co.uk

Appendix 5

Online information
www.gov.uk/foreign-travel-advice – travel advice and tips
www.himalayanrescue.org – rescue information
www.info-nepal.com – general background
www.nepalimmigration.gov.np – immigration dept / visas and permits
www.kmtnc.org.np – conservation themes
www.mnteverest.net/trek.html – list of trekking companies
www.nepalmountaineering.org
www.taan.org.np – Trekking Agencies Association of Nepal
www.visitnepal.com – travel information
www.welcomenepal.com – tourist information
www.ekantipur.com – news
www.nepalnews.net – news
www.nepalnow.com – news
www.stanfords.co.uk – maps
www.themapshop.co.uk – maps
www.trekmag.com – French magazine

Important phone numbers
Fire Brigade 101
Police Control 100
Telephone Inquiries 197
Tribhuvan International Airport 4471933

Hospitals
B & B Hospital 5533206
Bir Hospital 4222862/63
Grande City 4163500
Ishan Hospital 4981962
Kanti Children's Hosp. 4427452

Nepal Medical College 4911008
Norvic Hospital 4258554
Patan Hospital 5522266
TU Teaching Hospital 4412505

Police
District Police Office, Kathmandu 4261945
District Police Office, Lalitpur 5521207
Emergency Police Service 4226999

Embassies
Australia Bansbari 4371678
UK Lainchour 4411590
China Baluwatar 4411740
France Lazimpat 4418034

India Lainchour 4414990
Japan Panipokhari 4426680
Thailand Bansbari 4371410
USA Maharajgunj 4411179

Please note that all phone numbers are likely to change.

Map of Nepal

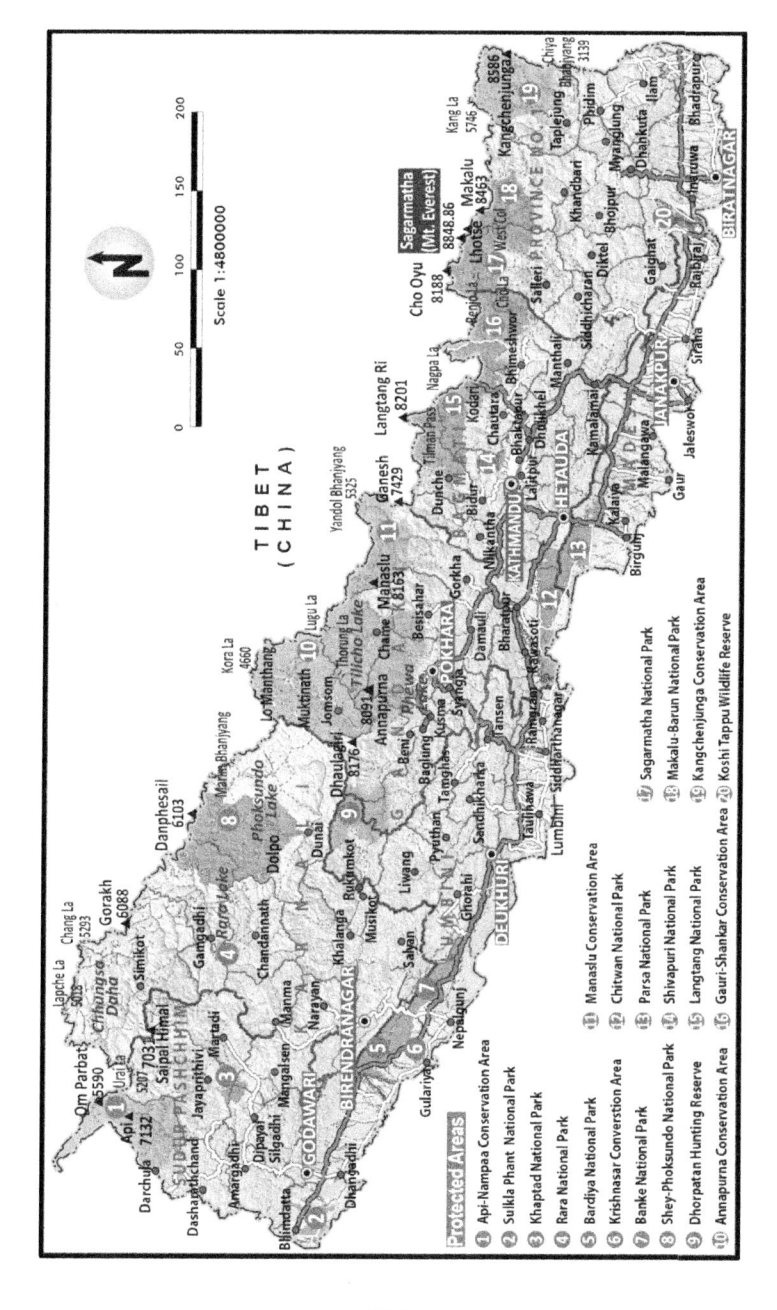

Protected Areas

① Api-Nampaa Conservation Area
② Sulkla Phant National Park
③ Khaptad National Park
④ Rara National Park
⑤ Bardiya National Park
⑥ Krishnasar Conversation Area
⑦ Banke National Park
⑧ Shey-Phoksundo National Park
⑨ Dhorpatan Hunting Reserve
⑩ Annapurna Conservation Area
⑪ Manaslu Conservation Area
⑫ Chitwan National Park
⑬ Parsa National Park
⑭ Shivapuri National Park
⑮ Langtang National Park
⑯ Gauri-Shankar Conservation Area
⑰ Sagarmatha National Park
⑱ Makalu-Barun National Park
⑲ Kangchenjunga Conservation Area
⑳ Koshi Tappu Wildlife Reserve

Maps

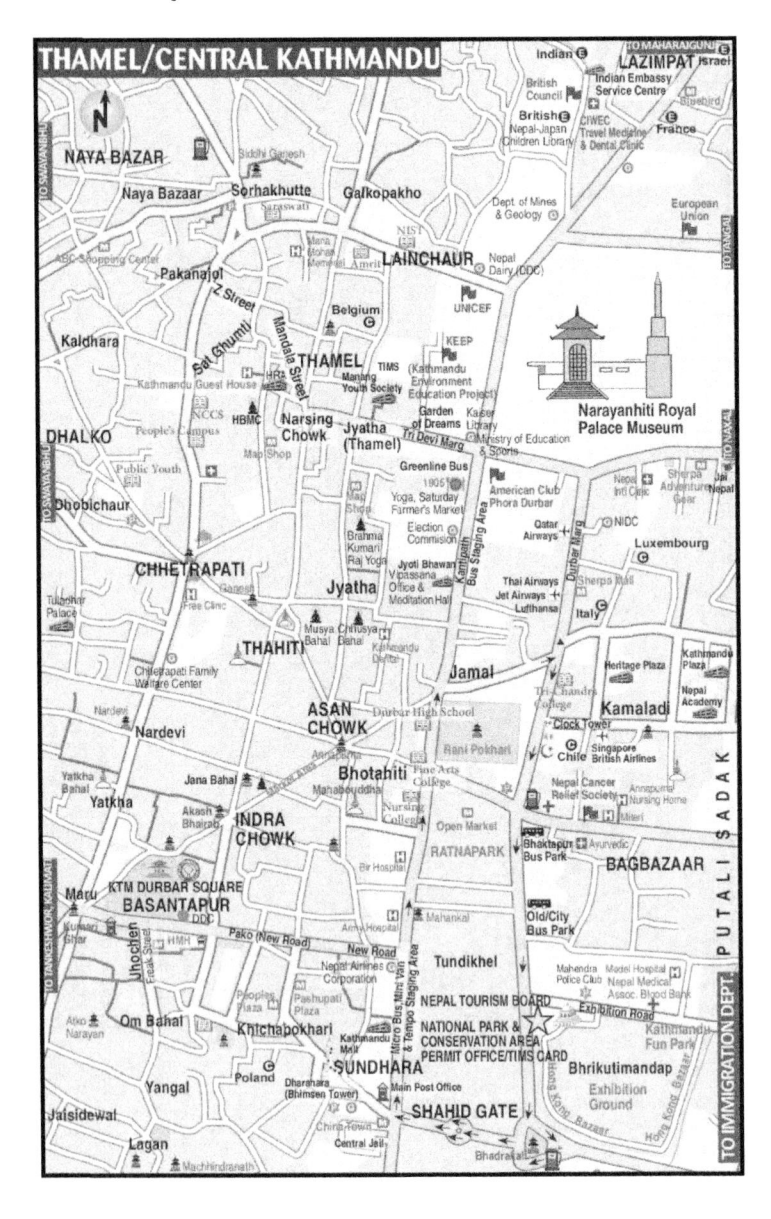

Map of Thamel/Central Kathmandu

Map of Central Kathmandu

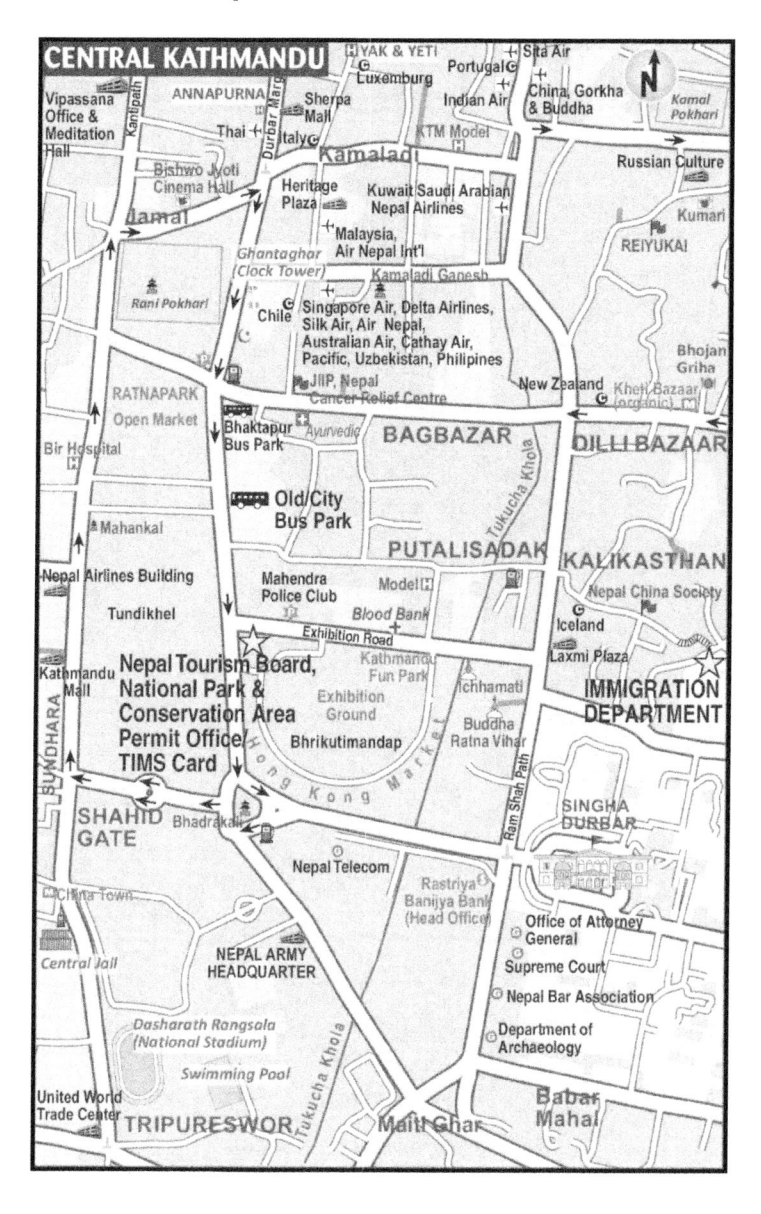

Maps

Map of Upper Mustang

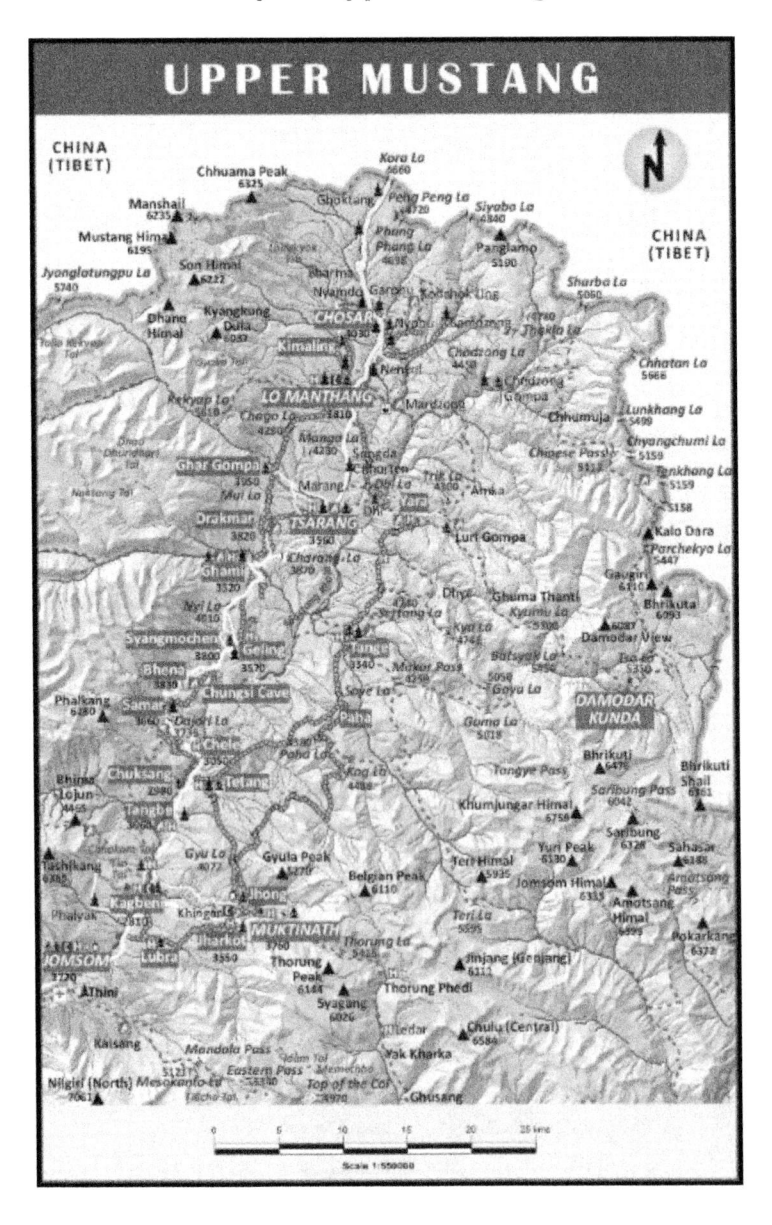

Farewell to the mountains – Brikuti & Khumjungar Himal

Sunset on Annapurna I from Kalopani

Boudhanath, a peaceful sanctuary in Kathmandu

The undisturbed Chodzong valley

About the authors

Authors in Old Samdzong

Siân Pritchard-Jones and Bob Gibbons met in 1983, on a trek from Kashmir to Ladakh. By then Bob had already driven an ancient Land Rover from England to Kathmandu (in 1974), and overland trucks across Asia, Africa and South America. He had also lived in Kathmandu for two years, employed as a trekking company manager. Before they met, Siân worked in computer programming and systems analysis.

Since they met they have been leading and organising treks in the Alps, Nepal and the Sahara, as well as driving a bus overland to Nepal. Journeys by a less ancient (only 31-year-old) Land Rover from England to South Africa provided the basis for several editions of the Bradt guide **Africa Overland**, including the sixth edition published in April 2014 and the seventh in September 2022.

In 2007 they wrote the Cicerone guide to **Mount Kailash** and Western Tibet, as well updating the **Grand Canyon** guide. Their **Annapurna** trekking guide was first published by Cicerone in January 2013, with the 2nd edition in 2017, revised edition in September 2022. In 2015 they were in Nepal during the earthquakes and published **Earthquake Diaries: Nepal 2015**. A Pictorial Guide to the **Horn of Africa** (Djibouti, Eritrea, Ethiopia and Somaliland), **Australia: Red Centre Treks** and **In Search of the Green-Eyed Yellow Idol**, a 40-year travelogue & autobiography, are published by Expedition World. See also **Saudi Arabia**, **Iraqi Kurdistan**, **Chad Sahara**, **Ladakh**, **Lebanon** and **Karakoram K2 treks**.

About the authors

For Map House they are writing a new series of trekking guidebooks: **Himalayan Travel Guides**. **Kanchi's Tale** is a new series of books covering various expeditions as seen through the eyes of a young Nepalese mountain dog – an educational doggie travelogue!

All books are also available on Amazon worldwide.

Another demon of Lo Manthang!　　　　**Rooftop views**

Chodzong Gompa outcrop

About the contributors

Tashi Gurung
Tashi is one of Lo Manthang's top thangka painters and has a deep interest in the art of Upper Mustang, as well as extensive knowledge of the city's monasteries. He is an excellent local guide for those keen to understand more of the culture. He also sells this guidebook, so he must be a great font of knowledge – ha ha!!!

Sanjib Gurung   www.climbinghimalaya.com
Our ever-patient, enthusiastic mountaineering guide from the Makalu region. Born in the small, isolated village of Mangsima, below the Tinjure Milke Danda ridge, he is one of ten siblings. His education was initially in Mangsima, but for further schooling he had to go to Khandbari. He studied management but his passion was mountaineering, trek guiding, mountain biking and photography. He is now President of the Mountain Guide Association of Nepal (MoGAN), involved with training programmes for Nepalese Mountain Guides, speaks excellent English and lives in Kathmandu near Balaju with his family. People like Sanjib are Nepal tourism's greatest assets: motivated, energetic and eager to promote his own country.

John Millen
John has been around the adventure travel scene for longer than he cares to tell. Working for Operation Raleigh, EWP, Exodus, Sherpa Expeditions and World Expeditions, he has led trips to many destinations across the world. His great passion was trekking in Ethiopia, until the troubles. He loves going to Nepal when chances arise, and is very experienced in the wilder parts of Europe, as well as the Coast to Coast walk across northern England. His hobbies include cycling, photography, playing guitar and spoon carving!

Rajendra Narsingh Suwal
See page 62.

Other books by the authors

Bradt (www.bradtguides.com)
Africa Overland --- 2005, 2009, 2014, 2022

Cicerone (www.cicerone.co.uk)
The Mount Kailash Trek --- 2007
Annapurna: A Trekker's Guide --- 2013, 2016, 2022

Amazon / Kindle (www.amazon.com)
In Search of the Green-Eyed Yellow Idol --- 2015, 2023 autobiography
Earthquake Diaries: Nepal 2015 --- 2015, 2022
Australia: Red Centre Treks --- 2016
Kanchi's Tale: Kanchi goes to Makalu Base Camp --- 2017
Kanchi goes to the Tibesti, Chad --- 2017
Chad: Tibesti, Ennedi & Borkou --- 2017, 2020
Karakoram: The Highway of History --- 2018, 2021
Karakoram & K2 Concordia (trekking guide) --- 2019, 2021
Ladakh: Land of Mystical Monasteries --- 2018, 2023
Lebanon: A Brief Guide --- 2019
Saudi Arabia: A Traveller's Guide --- 2020, 2023
Kathmandu: Valley of the Green-Eyed Yellow Idol --- 2021
Dad's War: A Schoolboy's Diaries --- 2021
Tough Medicine: A Doctor in Nepal (Dr Kailash Sah) --- 2021
Living Art of Kathmandu --- 2022
Iraqi Kurdistan: A Brief Guide --- 2022
Kailash and Guge: Lands of the Tantric Mountain --- 2022
Bhutan: An Introductory Guide --- 2022
Yemen: A Traveller's Guide --- 2023
Zanskar: Land of Monasteries & Mountains --- 2023
Oman by Road --- 2024

Pictorial Guides: Amazon / Kindle (www.amazon.com)
The Horn of Africa: A Pictorial Guide --- 2016, 2020
South America: A Pictorial Guide --- 2020
Africa Overland: A Pictorial Guide --- 2020
Asia Overland: A Pictorial Guide --- 2020
Saudi Arabia: A Pictorial Guide --- 2020
China: A Pictorial Guide --- 2021
Tibet: A Pictorial Guide --- 2020
Nepal Himalaya: A Pictorial Guide --- 2021
India: A Pictorial Guide --- 2021
Indian Himalaya, Karakoram & Bhutan: A Pictorial Guide --- 2021
Southeast Asia: A Pictorial Guide --- 2021
Far East Asia: A Pictorial Guide --- 2021
Central Asia, Russia & the Caucasus: A Pictorial Guide --- 2021
Central America and the Caribbean: A Pictorial Guide --- 2022
America's Wild West: A Pictorial Guide --- 2021
The Alps: A Pictorial Guide --- 2022

Iraq: A Pictorial Guide --- 2023
Yemen: A Pictorial Guide --- 2023
Australia, New Zealand & Pacific: A Pictorial Guide --- 2024

Pilgrims (www.pilgrimsonlineshop.com)
Kathmandu: Valley of the Green-Eyed Yellow Idol --- 2005
Ladakh: Land of Magical Monasteries --- 2006
Kailash & Guge: Land of the Tantric Mountain --- 2006

Map House (www.maphouse.org)
Books Himalaya (www.bookshimalaya.com)
& Amazon worldwide (www.amazon.com)
Manaslu & Tsum Valley --- 2013, 2016, 2019, 2020, 2023
Dolpo --- 2014, 2019, 2020, 2022
Ganesh Himal --- 2014, 2019, 2023
Langtang --- 2014, 2018, 2020, 2024
Everest --- 2014, 2018, 2021, 2022
Rolwaling --- 2015, 2019, 2023
Mustang --- 2016, 2019, 2020, 2022, 2025
Mustang by Road --- 2025
Kanchenjunga --- 2017, 2020, 2023
Makalu --- 2017, 2020, 2023
West Nepal --- 2017, 2021, 2023
Dhaulagiri --- 2018, 2023
Nepal Himalaya --- 2015, 2017, 2019, 2020, 2023, 2024
Annapurna North Base Camp --- 2023
Jugal Himal --- 2024

A rare sight of the Seto (White) Bhairab in Kathmandu Durbar Square

Printed in Great Britain
by Amazon